Grand Excursions on the Upper Mississippi River

GOLDEN ERA

Gayle Rein

A BUR OAK BOOK

Grand Excursions on the Upper Mississippi River

PLACES, LANDSCAPES, AND
REGIONAL IDENTITY AFTER
1854

EDITED BY CURTIS C. ROSEMAN
AND ELIZABETH M. ROSEMAN

UNIVERSITY OF IOWA PRESS

IOWA CITY

University of Iowa Press,
Iowa City 52242
Copyright © by the
University of Iowa Press
All rights reserved
Printed in the United States of America
Design by Richard Hendel
http://www.uiowa.edu/uiowapress

The publication of this book was
generously supported by the University
of Iowa Foundation.

"The Grand Excursion of 1854" originally
published in 1937 in *Steamboating on the
Upper Mississippi* by William J. Petersen.
Copyright 1968, State Historical Society
of Iowa. Reprinted by permission of the
publisher.

Printed on acid-free paper

Library of Congress
Cataloging-in-Publication Data
Grand excursions on the upper Mississippi
River: places, landscapes, and regional
identity after 1854 / edited by Curtis C.
Roseman and Elizabeth M. Roseman.
p.   cm.—(A burr oak book)
Includes bibliographical references and
index.
ISBN 0-87745-885-5 (pbk.)
1. Mississippi River—Description and travel.
2. Mississippi River Valley—Description and
travel.   3. Mississippi River Valley—
History—1803–1865.   4. Mississippi River
Valley—History, Local.   5. Landscape—
Mississippi River Valley—History.
6. Regionalism—Mississippi River Valley—
History.   I. Roseman, Curtis C.
II. Roseman, Elizabeth M. (Elizabeth
Mercer), 1948–.   III. Series
F353.G75 2004
977'.02—dc22   2003066341

03 04 05 06 07 P 5 4 3 2 1

To our remarkable sons,

Charles and Eric,

who have not (yet) lived on

the Upper Mississippi River

CONTENTS

PREFACE

In the mid 1990s Mark VanderSchaaf of St. Paul, Minnesota, envisioned a reenactment of the Grand Excursion in its 150th anniversary year, 2004. By the turn of the twenty-first century, a contagious fascination with the original excursion was spreading rapidly. The 1854 excursion, which celebrated in grand style the completion of the Chicago and Rock Island Railroad to the Mississippi River, had almost been lost to modern memory. That loss now has been rectified with a number of promotional and educational efforts, including this book, giving new weight to this important historical event. Upon first learning of the excursion, we decided to ask a group of creative people to contribute to a volume that would reflect on the original excursion and also address a set of broader topics that are rooted geographically and historically in the excursion.

This anthology is the result. It contains a set of essays, each having in common the examination of Upper Mississippi River activities and environments that stem from the purpose and experience of the 1854 Grand Excursion. Each essay can be thought of as an excursion in itself. The first five explore topics directly related to the original Grand Excursion. The remaining eight essays explore major landscape elements and activities along the Upper Mississippi as they have evolved over the 150 years since that 1854 event.

Stitching the volume together is a series of images of actual bridges on the Upper Mississippi River. Chosen to reflect a variety of themes imbedded in the book, these bridges serve as transitions — as "bridges" — from one essay to the next, from one excursion to the next.

In the first essay the editors and Dick Stahl describe the 1854 Grand Excursion and set the context within which it occurred. Drawing primarily on contemporary newspaper accounts, we detail the precise route and timing of the excursion. We also describe the natural and cultural features of the Upper Mississippi Valley through which the excursionists traveled. Drawing upon a register of guests, this chapter also features profiles of some of the prominent participants, including journalists, politicians, academics, artists, industrialists, and others.

In the second essay Roald D. Tweet presents an account of the building of the Chicago and Rock Island Railroad, a process that was relatively swift and efficient. Tweet shows how this railroad won the race to connect the East with the Mississippi River. Next is a reprint of "Steamboat Bill" Petersen's chapter on the Grand Excursion from his book *Steamboating on the Upper Mississippi River*, first published by the State Historical Society of Iowa in 1937, then reprinted in 1968. Petersen's is the most widely recognized work on the 1854 Grand Excursion. Other essays in this anthology extend, and in some cases revise, Petersen's interpretations of the excursion.

Following Petersen's are two additional essays that relate directly to the original excursion. Susan R. Brooker-Gross reviews eastern newspaper accounts of the excursion. Although not all reports were positive, the major themes of these accounts include the productivity of the land, the beauty of the landscape, the prosperity of the towns, and the marvels of rail transportation. Edwin L. Hill follows Brooker-Gross with a treatment of steamboating on the Upper Mississippi, both before and after the Grand Excursion. Steamboats were central to the life of river towns and commerce for most of the nineteenth century, until railroad competition and other factors severely limited their usefulness by the early twentieth century.

The remainder of the volume develops several themes on landscape and life along the Upper Mississippi River. The first of these is visual: Patrick Nunnally reviews the evolution of the concept of the picturesque and applies it to the interpretation of the Upper Mississippi's scenic physical landscape, especially by the nineteenth-century traveler. John A. Jakle's essay analyzes the genesis of nineteenth-century river towns, the principal characteristics of their buildings and other visible structures, and how they were viewed and stereotyped by travel writers and excursionists. Jeff Crump's discussion focuses on a powerful visual theme by exploring the evolution of the twentieth-century Burlington *Zephyr* streamlined diesel trains that plied three hundred miles of the Upper Mississippi. Not only were the trains themselves visually striking, but so too was the scenery through which they and their passengers sped.

Another theme encompasses the control and management of the river and its environs. John O. Anfinson reviews the evolution and implications of the control of the river for navigation purposes. Beginning before the Grand Excursion, the federal government undertook a major series of projects that included dredging and the construction of wing dams and a lock and dam system. Next, Gary C. Meyer writes about the remarkable extent to which the Upper Mississippi has been preserved and managed since the early nineteenth century by all levels of government, through wildlife refuges, preserves, parks, and recreation areas. Both of these essays also provide perspectives on environmental issues that persist today along the river.

The next two essays focus on two fundamental economic activities intimately associated with the river: logging and fishing. Perhaps no other enterprise had as much economic and environmental impact on the region in the nineteenth century as the lumber industry. Gayle Rein delineates the process through which logs from the pineries of northern Wisconsin and Minnesota were floated downstream in massive log rafts and tells the story of the people involved in it. In many river towns the logs were milled into lumber, which in turn was shipped outward in all directions. Malcolm L. Comeaux goes on to discuss commercial fishing on the river, which in a striking contrast to lumbering is a much smaller and less visible activity. Nonetheless, people have fished for a living continuously since the time of the Grand Excursion, and have used remarkably similar methods since that time.

The last of the literary excursions in this volume provides a twenty-first-century perspective on Upper Mississippi River towns. Norman Moline and Charles Mahaffey visited all seventy-eight incorporated places on the river between Rock Island and St. Paul to gather information on how towns and cities are embracing the river. Whereas some have always maintained something of a river orientation, especially the smallest towns, most have made a 360-degree turn. From an original river orientation, and then to development away from the river, many towns and cities have recently experienced a resurgence of river-oriented development. Mahaffey and Moline conclude by speculating on the extent to which this new interest in the river can provide for these communities a common bond. Will such a bond lead to the Upper Mississippi taking on a unified image that is nationally recognized?

ACKNOWLEDGMENTS

This book is the product of a truly cooperative effort. Throughout its writing, authors and editors shared information and advice. In perhaps the highlight of the process, we all gathered for a conference at Guttenberg, Iowa, on the banks of the Mississippi River, in May 2002. In that scenic and historic town we compared notes and discussed a wide range of ideas for the book and also had some fun.

We, the editors, have many people to thank for their contributions to this work. First and foremost, we appreciate the creativity and dedication of the authors who provided high-quality work and did so in a timely manner. Dick Stahl deserves special recognition for his research on the participants in the original Grand Excursion and for obtaining copies of its guest registers from the Yale University Archives. We also are grateful to Mark VanderSchaaf, who joined us in Guttenberg, for sharing with us his considerable knowledge of the Grand Excursion and other river topics and for reviewing an early draft of the book.

We are indebted to the Saint Paul Riverfront Corporation and its executive director, Patrick Seeb, for providing financial support for our authors conference. We appreciate the assistance of the staff at the Yale University Archives who gave us access to the Grand Excursion registers, and the Sheffield (Illinois) Historical Society and Mrs. Margaret B. Schmitt, Knight of Donnaborg (Denmark), its director, who provided materials and assistance.

We thank Cathryn Dowd, instructor of geography at Augustana College (which is located adjacent to the old Rock Island Railroad tracks as they enter Rock Island), who coordinated the design and construction of the maps in this volume. Her cartography class of the Winter 2003 term drew — and indeed contributed to the design of — those maps. For their contribution to this project we thank the following class members: Katie Derner, Laura Treasurer, Myk Skelton, Rachel Easley, Eric Anderson, Chris Pelczarski, Liz Lyon, Jodie Daley, Steph Gaspers, Stephanie Allewalt, Leann Barber, Patrick Long, Allison McAndrews, Patrick Wren, Trevor Wukasch, Genis Bullock, Dave Marincic, Luwanna Reed, Paul

Bailie, Amy Harris, Erik Myers, Eva Peterson, Michael Treve, Michael Urish, and Greg Walzer.

Others who provided assistance include Kathy Wine, director of River Action Inc., Daryl Watson, Bill Dailey, and Todd Orjala. A special thanks also goes to Timothy R. Mahoney for his inspiring review of the manuscript. Finally, we sincerely thank Holly Carver, director of the University of Iowa Press, along with Karen Copp, Prasenjit Gupta, Sara T. Sauers, Megan Scott, Lori Vermaas, Rhonda Wetjen, and Charlotte Wright for shepherding the book, and us, through the editorial process.

Now, let the excursions begin!

RAIL-ROAD EXCURSION.

•-•-•

Office Chicago & Rock Island Railroad Co.

CORN EXCHANGE BANK BUILDING,

13 William Street, New-York.

DEAR SIR:

The object of this excursion is to afford the Stockholders and Bondholders an opportunity of visiting and inspecting their Road.

The enclosed ticket of invitation will enable our friends to assemble at Chicago at their leisure, and by any of the several routes.

The party will leave Chicago on Monday morning the 5th day of June, and reach Rock Island in time to dine in the afternoon, and embark same night. Leaving Rock Island in the morning for the Falls of St. Anthony.

Returning to Rock Island the party will be conveyed back to Chicago, on Saturday, and with the same ticket, may take their choice of routes back to New-York.

As NO TRANSFER of tickets will be RECOGNISED by the several roads, it is particularly requested, that such tickets as are not intended to be used by the party invited, may be returned in an envelope by mail, directed to this office, before the 1st day of June, in order that the Committee may know how many to provide for.

The Excursion on the River may be made in four or five days, and the whole time from New-York and back, need not, necessarily, exceed ten or twelve days.

~~~~~~

COMMITTEE.

J. B. JERVIS,	THOS. C. DURANT,	ISAAC COOK,
A. C. FLAGG,	JOS. E. SHEFFIELD,	L. ANDREWS,
WM. WALCOTT,	HENRY FARNHAM,	EBEN. COOK,

NEW-YORK, May 1st, 1854.

Invitation to the Grand Excursion dated May 1, 1854. From MsC 159, Levi O. Leonard Rail Road Collection, Box #38, File: C. R. I. RR, 1854, Excursion May 1854. University of Iowa, University Libraries, Special Collections and University Archives.

Grand Excursions on the Upper Mississippi River

THE UPPER MISSISSIPPI
AND THE GRAND EXCURSION

Curtis C. Roseman, Dick Stahl,
and Elizabeth M. Roseman

In June of 1854 a festive affair, the Grand Excursion, carried hundreds of dignitaries on a combination rail and steamboat ride from Chicago to Rock Island, Illinois, then on to St. Paul in Minnesota Territory. Just five months earlier, the railroad had connected Chicago and the East to the Mississippi River at Rock Island. During the 1850s, steamboating was thriving on the river, and the Grand Excursion celebrated the newly created connection between the rail system and steamboats on the Mississippi. For this occasion, over six hundred people rode two long trains from Chicago to Rock Island; thence over one thousand traveled on five steamboats to St. Paul and back to Rock Island.

Among those invited to participate in this celebration were several hundred prominent people, many from the East, including former President Millard Fillmore, industry leaders, academics, writers, and artists. Invited, too, were dozens of newspaper editors and journalists, primarily from the East, whose daily dispatches kept readers abreast of the adventure. This wide press exposure contributed substantially to easterners' images of the exotic but developing West.

The focus of attention was the Upper Mississippi River, from Rock Island to St. Paul and St. Anthony (now Minneapolis). The remarkably speedy river trip — two-and-a-half days upriver and just thirty hours down — exposed the celebrants to a distinctively beautiful and bountiful section of the West. It also showed them a region that was undergoing rapid European settlement and development, Native American settlements having been largely eliminated or displaced.

This first essay sets the scene for the collection that follows. After describing the Upper Mississippi and its people at the time of the 1854 Grand Excursion, we draw upon the excursion *Register*, which was signed by guests in Chicago before embarking on the trip, to profile some of the prominent people who went on the journey. Finally, we utilize various contemporary accounts, especially newspaper reports, to describe in detail the route and timing of the excursion.

THE PLACE

Over the century and a half since the Grand Excursion, the beauty of the region's physical environment remains one of its signature features. The 1854 excursionists traveled a level rail route across the Illinois prairies to the Mississippi, then traversed the oft-treacherous Rock Island Rapids on the river and continued upriver through scenic blufflands. A brief look at the region's glacial history helps to explain the origin of these physical features of the landscape.

Over a period of hundreds of thousands of years, up until about ten thousand years ago, a succession of continental glaciers moved southward across the Upper Midwest. These large masses of ice and debris modified the landscape in various ways. They scraped and generally smoothed the land in some areas while depositing rocks and debris — glacial drift — elsewhere. They also modified drainage systems and, directly or indirectly, created enormous water runoff that helped to carve deep river valleys.[1]

Much of the river seen by the 1854 Grand Excursionists, however, was not directly touched by glaciers. Part of the Upper Mississippi flows through a four-state region aptly called the Driftless Area, which starts near Lake Pepin and reaches southward to near Clinton, Iowa, some thirty miles above Rock Island (fig. 1).[2] Nonetheless, the glaciers significantly altered the topography of the Driftless Area. Glacial runoff deeply eroded the valley of the Mississippi and its immediate tributaries in this region, creating bluffs that are higher than is typical of the Midwest, some of them reaching just over five hundred feet above the river. Because of their uniqueness, the bluffs are the signature feature of the physical environment in this region, and have inspired every imaginable descriptive superlative by European Americans for at least two centuries.

The glaciers also altered the course of the Mississippi. Before and during various stages of glaciation, the river had carved out various paths south of the Driftless Area. In the immediate preglacial period, the Mississippi took a sharp turn from present-day Clinton and flowed eastward to meet what is now the Illinois River near its modern big bend west of La Salle. It then proceeded southward on a path generally following the

FIGURE 1. *Physical features of the Grand Excursion region. The rail route of the 1854 excursion followed the Illinois River Valley, then an old channel of the Mississippi River. The steamboat segment traveled through the Driftless Area, a region largely untouched by glaciers.*

valley of the modern Illinois River. This eastward stretch of the preglacial Mississippi is called the Princeton Channel, named after the current Princeton, Illinois, which is located in that ancient river valley. It was not until approximately twenty thousand years ago that one of the glaciers coming from the northeast blocked the Princeton Channel. After forming several temporary channels, the river soon (in geologic time) settled into its present course south from Clinton to St. Louis.

The excursionists' trip across Illinois was largely on flat terrain. The Rock Island Railroad had been built westward on a level path, the "easiest" route as described by Roald Tweet in this volume. Most of its first one hundred miles out of Chicago ran parallel, and often very close, to the Illinois and Michigan Canal or the Illinois River. The remainder of the route was also quite level, part of it being in the ancient Princeton Channel west of the current Illinois River.

The excursionists' first experience on the Mississippi, however, was on a relatively treacherous stretch of the river, the Rock Island Rapids, or Upper Rapids. Located not far south of the Driftless Area, these rapids are on one of the youngest segments of the present-day river. Here the water falls relatively quickly through this narrow and rocky fifteen-mile gauntlet. Before major navigational improvements were made, as described by John Anfinson in this volume, the rapids were relatively shallow, and were hazardous for navigation via steamboat. However, while difficult for boat navigation, the narrow width meant that this was a good crossing place. The presence of the island of Rock Island, which is essentially a rock ledge in the middle of the river, made crossing even easier. Completed in 1856, the first railroad bridge to cross the Mississippi would use Rock Island as a steppingstone.

THE PEOPLE OF THE REGION

The story of the Grand Excursion involves three contrasting sets of people: the excursionists themselves who made a brief sojourn through the Upper Mississippi region; Native Americans who for centuries had lived there; and people of European origin who first explored and then later settled in the region. The excursionists were a privileged group of European-origin Americans, at least half of whom came from the East. By contrast, Native Americans in the Upper Mississippi region were considered to be of low status and were rapidly being displaced by westward expansion. Today Native American culture in the region is reflected in a number of place names, monuments, and museum displays, as well as some distinctive cultural activities, especially in the Twin Cities of Minnesota.

Native American Peoples

During the nineteenth century, the Native American population in the contiguous forty-eight U.S. states declined precipitously. By 1854 in the Upper Mississippi region, they had been pushed westward by a series of treaties and forcible actions.[3] However, scattered groups of Native Americans and a few of their villages did remain in the area touched by the Grand Excursion. On the east side of the river in Illinois and Wisconsin, major

Native American settlements had been gone for over twenty years. West of the river, scattered small settlements remained, especially in Minnesota Territory. Indeed, the last major Native American tribes living near St. Paul, the Mdewakanton Dakota, were removed from that area by the Minnesota Territorial government just weeks before the Grand Excursion.[4]

Another action against Native Americans is notable because it involved two locations on the path of the Grand Excursion.[5] A Sauk village, Saukenuk, had existed for at least a century at various locations near the Rock River, which enters the Mississippi a few miles south of Rock Island. Whereas virtually all Native Americans had been removed from Illinois by 1832, a group of Sauks led by Black Hawk resisted. In the spring of 1832, soldiers from the Illinois militia chased them for several days northward through northwestern Illinois, then into Wisconsin. In a tragic ending at Bad Axe, on the Mississippi between Prairie du Chien and La Crosse, large numbers of Black Hawk's group, including women and children, were massacred.

Native Americans did not participate in the Grand Excursion and their presence along the route was barely acknowledged by the privileged excursionists. In the extant literature on the excursion, most of the scattered references to Native Americans are brief and negative. For example, author Catherine Sedgwick, noting the relative absence of Native Americans visible to excursionists, recalled in 1854: "But a few years since, [that] was heard, only the yell of the savage, who had stealthily crept along the shore — tomahawk in hand, in quest of his foe."[6] That same year the *Albany Evening Journal* described a face-to-face encounter with Native Americans at the stop at Montoville (now Trempealeau), Wisconsin: "Here we were visited by three Indians, wild from the woods, their faces painted in all the hideousness usual among many of the tribes. Two of them were Sioux, the other a Winnebago. The only desire they seemed to have was for the firewater; and the contributions bestowed upon them will doubtless lead to riot, and then to abusing these denizens of the forest, goaded to madness by the liquor of the white man."[7]

Not all written accounts, however, offered such brief pejorative characterizations of Native Americans. Another *Albany Evening Journal* reporter, also writing in 1854, felt that Rock Island "reminded [him] of the celebrated warrior, 'Black Hawk.' His village, or station, was about three miles from the riverside, a country most delightful and no man can wonder that he fought as *we* would have done, to defend his fireside and his Indian home; but he was doomed, as are the rest of his race, to fall before the cupidity of the white man, and finally to be exterminated." He added that "well we may say, as a distinguished statesman said in relation to another matter, 'We may well tremble for our country, when we remember that God is just.' The old Fort Armstrong, on Rock Island, a small island in the river, is in tolerable preservation; but no longer necessary, as the poor Indian has been driven away from his home."[8]

In general, the written record of the Grand Excursion reflected the perspectives of European-origin elites whose focus was primarily on the present beauty and future promise of the area. The past and those who surrendered this land and its resources for European development were far from their minds. Today, however, some Native American place names remain along the route of the Grand Excursion. They include Tiskilwa (earlier called Indiantown) in Illinois on the railroad route; Camanche, Iowa; and Winona and Wabasha, Minnesota, on the river.

People of European Origin

Europeans had been in the Upper Mississippi region for two hundred years by the time of the 1854 Grand Excursion. Early explorers had plied the rivers, and trappers and traders had established settlements, most of which were transitory in nature. A number of place names along the route of the Grand Excursion remind us of their presence in the region, most especially the French. They include Joliet and La Salle on the rail route from Chicago to Rock Island, and Marquette, Prairie du Chien, La Crosse, La Crescent, Trempealeau, and others on the Upper Mississippi River.

Military forts were also present at the leading edge of U.S. expansion, including three along the path taken by the steamboats of the Grand Excursion. In 1816, forts were established at Rock Island (Fort Armstrong) and Prairie du Chien (Fort Crawford), and in 1819 above St. Paul (Fort Snelling, then called Fort St. Anthony). Although scattered European settlements could be found at that time, it was not until the 1830s that major towns emerged. In Illinois, which had become a state in 1818, Rock Island and Galena grew quickly to prominence. Rock Island fed off its location at the base of the rapids and by 1840 was surrounded by a cluster of growing communities (including Davenport and Moline), that eventually would become the Quad Cities. Galena emerged in the 1830s as one of the most prosperous towns in Illinois because of its location in a major lead mining area and its position as a major Mississippi River port. At its peak when the Grand Excursion visited in 1854, it gradually declined thereafter as the demand for lead diminished and the Galena River, which had connected it to the Mississippi, silted up, rendering it useless for steamboat navigation.

Davenport and Dubuque were well-established before Iowa became a state in 1846. So too were several communities along the river in Wisconsin, which became a state in 1848. By 1854, European settlements were emerging or growing at a rapid pace along the route of the Grand Excursion. Even though Minnesota Territory would not become a state until some four years later, St. Paul already had a population of about five thousand and St. Anthony about twenty-five hundred.

European immigrants were streaming into the region, settling on farms and in towns. Before the Chicago and Rock Island Railroad was completed, many immigrants took the Chicago and Galena Railroad to Freeport, Illinois, and then traveled by stagecoach to Galena where steamboats waited. The 1854 Rock Island Railroad route was the first of several rail connections to the Mississippi that would be used by immigrants over subsequent decades. Within two years, rail lines connected Chicago with Fulton and Dunlieth (later East Dubuque) in Illinois, and within four years, they connected Milwaukee to Prairie du Chien and La Crosse in Wisconsin. Therefore, when Minnesota became a state in 1858, several rail transportation options were available to immigrants wanting to settle there.

The rapid settlement of the Upper Mississippi and its surrounding region is reflected in the population growth of its major towns.[9] St. Louis, the focus of much of the water-based transportation in the early and mid nineteenth century, was the largest city in the region until the 1870s, having grown from about five thousand to over three hundred thousand people in four decades. Chicago grew a bit faster but a bit later, from just over four thousand in 1840 to over five hundred thousand in 1880. Chicago exceeded St. Louis in population in the 1870s and thereafter, partly because of its position as the focal point of railroads from the East to the Upper Mississippi and points west.

On the river itself, above Rock Island, towns were relatively small until 1860, when three of them actually appeared on the list of the country's one hundred largest cities. Davenport, Dubuque, and St. Paul each had populations between ten and thirteen thousand that year, numbers that swelled to about twenty thousand each by 1870. Throughout the mid-nineteenth century, Davenport and Dubuque alternated as the largest city in Iowa, a reflection of their important positions on the river, but by

1880 the centrally located Iowa capital city of Des Moines surpassed them. The two river cities also dropped out of the top one hundred cities after 1880, displaced by rapidly growing frontier towns in farther reaches of the West and in industrial centers in the Midwest and East. In Minnesota, the "other twin city," Minneapolis, a milling and service center for an area stretching far to the west, permanently eclipsed St. Paul's population in 1880 and never looked back.

PEOPLE ON THE GRAND EXCURSION

The Rock Island City Council sponsored a celebration on February 22, 1854, immediately after the completion of the rail line to the Mississippi River.[10] Invitees were locals and a few other people — including directors of the railroad — from Chicago and other towns along the new line from Chicago to Rock Island. Henry Farnam and Joseph Sheffield, builders of the railroad, seemed to want a larger promotional event, however. They decided to invite people to a grander celebration in June of that year, one that would bring national attention to their new railroad.

Holding an excursion to celebrate transportation improvements was not an original idea. Several smaller excursions had already been held in the region, including a railroad excursion of a few dozen people from Springfield to Jacksonville, Illinois, to celebrate the completion of the Northern Cross Railroad in 1844. In conjunction with the Chicago River and Harbor Convention of 1847 was an excursion on the Great Lakes, attended by about two hundred people, which extended as far north as Mackinac Island in Lake Superior. A steamboat/rail excursion took about four hundred St. Louisians to Springfield in 1852 and a rail trip was taken from Chicago to La Salle in 1853, both to celebrate openings of rail segments in the region. Additional excursions on the Upper Mississippi followed, as recounted by William J. Petersen in this volume, and some very large excursions occurred elsewhere in the United States. Among them were the Great Railway Celebration that involved two thousand people on three trains traveling from Cincinnati to St. Louis in 1857 and several others that celebrated the completion of various segments of transcontinental rail lines later in the nineteenth century.[11]

Up to 1854, however, Farnam and Sheffield's Rock Island Railroad Grand Excursion was the largest and most ambitious. To make their invitation list more national, the organizers did not have to go far from their roots. Farnam grew up in upstate New York (near the Erie Canal, upon which he worked as a young man) and Sheffield in Connecticut. Both had recently lived not far from New York City, in New Haven, Connecticut, where they had made strong connections with prominent people, both locally and elsewhere in that region. Indeed, three years prior to the excursion, when the Chicago and Rock Island Railroad was incorporated, they recruited some people from the New Haven area to serve as directors and investors, including its first president, John B. Jervis of New York.

The geography of their connections is revealed in a map that shows the origins of several hundred people listed on the *Register* that they had signed just before the excursion began on June 5, 1854 (fig. 2).[12] New York, the largest city in the country at the time, is well represented on the map. So, too, is New Haven, along with Albany and other upstate New York towns along the Erie Canal corridor, the major transportation route connecting New York City and New England to the West. Major cities south of New York were virtually absent from the guest list, including Baltimore and Philadelphia, the second and fourth largest cities in the country in 1850.

The Grand Excursion allowed guests to directly experience the West and also to examine the most westerly rail penetration to date. The invited guests — especially those from the East — were prominent in a variety of fields. Enthusiastic journalists described them as "all from the most intelligent classes"[13] and as comprising "about one half the distinque of the Union."[14]

The most prominent of the guests was Millard Fillmore, who ascended to the U.S. presidency and served for just over two-and-a-half years after Zachary Taylor became ill and died in July 1850.[15] Although not renowned as a great president, at that time or this, Fillmore was likely invited because he had been involved in the first land grants for railroad construction and generally favored river improvements. Fillmore was the subject of much attention on the trip. The president was accompanied by his son, Millard, and by his daughter, Mary Abigail, who piqued fellow excursionists' interests by riding a borrowed horse to the top of Trempealeau Mountain, an event described by William Petersen in this volume.

Other politicians included the former governors of Connecticut, New Hampshire, and Michigan — Roger Sherman Baldwin, Henry Hubbard, and John S. Barry, respectively; and Charles Johnson McCurdy, lieutenant governor of Connecticut, and his daughter. Illinois politicians included the mayor of Chicago, Isaac Milliken, and Ninian Wirt Edwards, son of

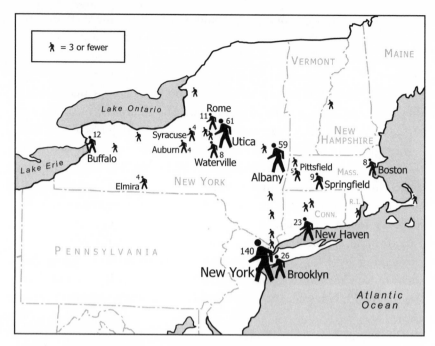

FIGURE 2. *Number of 1854 Grand Excursion participants from the East, by place of origin. From the* Register *of the Grand Excursion signed by guests in Chicago, Yale University Archives.*

the late Illinois territorial governor Ninian Edwards, who had married Elizabeth Todd, the elder sister of Mary Todd Lincoln. The judiciary was well represented by, among others, Joel Parker, a Dartmouth graduate, former chief justice of New Hampshire and Royall Professor of Law at Harvard; William Whiting Boardman, Speaker of the Connecticut House of Representatives; Thomas Jackson Oakley, judge of the Superior Court of New York; and John Catron, associate justice of the U.S. Supreme Court.

Railroad and other industry leaders also participated, according to the excursion *Register.* Invitees included Yale graduate Alexander Catlin Twining of the Hartford and New Haven Railroad Company and James Brewster, head of Brewster and Sons, a major manufacturer of carriages. Azariah Flagg, comptroller of New York City, was one of several officers of the Chicago and Rock Island Railroad who made the trip. John R. Munn, a businessman from Utica, New York, who came with his wife, wrote a rather extensive journal on the Grand Excursion that is now archived at the Chicago Historical Society.[16]

Clergy, academics, writers, and artists brought substantial creative diversity to the excursion. From New Haven came the Reverend Dr. Eleazar Thompson Fitch, Livingston Professor of Divinity at Yale, and Professor Leonard Bacon, pastor of the Center Congregational Church in that city. Also from Yale was Professor Benjamin Silliman, a chemist, natural historian, and geologist who had brought the largest collection of minerals at that time to the university, and Professor Chauncey Goodrich who, despite returning home after the Chicago-to-Rock Island train trip, penned a short poem on the Grand Excursion.[17] From Harvard came George Bancroft, who had recently completed five volumes of his ten-volume epic history of the United States.[18] His observations on the trip no doubt influenced later volumes in that series.

Perhaps the most prominent writer on the excursion was Catherine Sedgwick, widely known for her novels, including *Hope Leslie* and *The Lynwoods.* Her celebrity was more than matched by that of another guest, John Frederick Kensett, one of the most well-known artists of the Hudson River School. Experiencing the Mississippi for the first time on the excursion, Kensett went to complete a pencil sketch of Lake Pepin (1854) and to craft an oil painting of some bluffs, entitled *Upper Mississippi* (1855). Many visitors noticed parallels between the scenery on the Upper Mississippi and the Hudson Rivers before, during, and after the 1854 Grand Excursion. Thereby, Kensett's work joined the two great rivers in the world of art.[19]

Some guests were noted for their philanthropy. Moses Kimball of Boston, a legislator and financier, had bought the greater part of the old New England Museum (whose collections were dispersed), added his own collection, and opened the Boston Museum in 1841 with attractions in stuffed animals, Greek sculpture, and some original historical portraits by John Singleton Copley. Elbridge Gerry founded the New York Society for the Prevention of Cruelty to Children, the first of many Gerry Societies to be established in the United States.

The story of the Grand Excursion was recorded by numerous guest newspaper editors and writers, who presumably were expected to write glowing reports of the railroad and the western territory to which it was providing improved access. The journalists came from the same areas of the Northeast as the other guests. Baltimore and Philadelphia, not to mention the entire South, would not hear directly of the Grand Excursion, if at all, whereas New York City, most of New York State, and Connecticut and Massachusetts were flooded with accounts of this western adventure. Most reports were mailed back from Chicago, Rock Island, Galena, or St. Paul to be published within a few days. And indeed, most were glowing accounts, as documented by Susan Brooker-Gross in this volume.

Many of the excursion journalists were at the time or were to become widely known. Charles Anderson Dana of the *New York Daily Tribune* was widely known as a poet, and later published the *Household Book of Poetry*. William Cowper Prime of the *New York Journal of Commerce* wrote travel pieces and a biography of General McClellan, and Epes Sargent of the *Boston Evening Transcript* published children's books, plays, and poetry, including his book, *Songs of the Sea and Other Poems* (1849). The celebrity of William Schouler of the *Cincinnati Gazette* rose after he told President Lincoln that a Mrs. Bixby of Boston had lost five sons in the Civil War and the president responded with a letter (November 21, 1864) that became famous. Lincoln also aided the public renown of James F. Babcock of the *New Haven Daily Palladium* by appointing him a collector of the port of New Haven. Thurlow Weed of the *Albany Evening Journal* gained repute by helping to found the Republican Party.

What of the two creators of the Grand Excursion? Henry Farnam went on to design and superintend the construction of the first railroad bridge over the Mississippi River from Rock Island into Iowa, which was completed in April 1856. While he was serving as president of the Chicago and Rock Island Railroad from December 1854 to June 4, 1863, he promoted the plan for extending the railroad system across the continent to the Pacific Coast. After leaving the railroad, he took a few trips abroad and retired to his home in New Haven, where he made many contributions to Yale College and to his city. As early as 1863, he had given $30,000 to Yale for a new dormitory. Later he added another $30,000 to construct the first building of the new quadrangle, named Farnam Hall in his honor. He died in 1883 at the age of 79.

We found no evidence that Farnam's business partner, Joseph Sheffield, attended the Grand Excursion, although he sent out many of the invitations. Descended from a family of wealthy ship owners, he was also devoted to philanthropy. He gave Yale College money to purchase and renovate a hotel that became Sheffield Hall. With additional gifts of professorships in chemistry, metallurgy, and engineering, the Sheffield Scientific School was created at Yale in 1861. By 1873 he had financed additions to the building and added a North Sheffield Hall. Upon his death in 1882, his will bequeathed $500,000 more to the school.

Given the regional, and indeed national, significance of the 1854 Grand Excursion, it is surprising that historians have paid little attention to the event. Probably the most well-known piece on the excursion is the chapter written by William Petersen in his *Steamboating on the Upper Mississippi* (reprinted in this volume). Newspaper accounts from the time of the excursion carry the most extensive coverage. Less sustained reportage can be found in a number of other works from both the nineteenth and twentieth centuries. The essays in this book draw upon both kinds of sources.[20] Below is a summary of some key aspects of the Grand Excursion, with a special focus on the places visited and the timing of those visits.

Invitees from the East were asked to gather at Chicago for a June 5, 1854, departure to Rock Island. They were furnished with passage over a railroad of their choice to Chicago (and for the return trip east), and were afforded full accommodations for the six days of the rail and boat excursion.[21] More people showed up in Chicago than anticipated, largely because the guests brought along friends and relatives who had not been officially invited. "Chicago is about as full as it can be, and a little fuller," mused a *New York Daily Times* writer.[22] Our examination of the *Register* signed in Chicago suggests that fully one-third of the invitees at that point were female, including wives, daughters, and friends of male invitees, and many newspaper accounts — virtually all written by males — commented on the large contingent of women on the excursion.

The Train Excursion

On the morning of June 5, 1854, over six hundred invitees boarded two gaily-decorated trains and were given a festive sendoff from the Chicago depot. Several accounts emphasize the spectacle, highlighted by extensive decoration of the trains with flags and streamers, and even flowers and evergreens. The trains were to make the 181-mile trip to Rock Island in about eight hours. The first one hundred miles took them through several well-established towns on the Illinois and Michigan (I&M) Canal, which the railroad paralleled to La Salle, including Joliet, Morris, and Ottawa (see fig. 3 for a map of the route). At these and most other towns along the way, the trains were greeted by flag-waving crowds and bands and, in some places, the sound of cannon fire.

La Salle had become the head of navigation on the Illinois River, the place where the I&M Canal from Chicago connected Lake Michigan with

FIGURE 3. *Route of the 1854 Grand Excursion. On Monday, June 5, the excursion traveled by train from Chicago to Rock Island. Then, beginning about midnight that night, five boats traveling day and night took the excursion up the Mississippi to St. Paul. After arriving in St. Paul on Thursday morning, June 8, the excursionists visited St. Anthony and Fort Snelling later that same day.*

interior waterways of the Mississippi-Missouri system. It was also the place where the Rock Island Railroad crossed the new north-south route of the Illinois Central Railroad. The *New York Daily Times* was impressed with the spectacular five-thousand-foot Illinois Central bridge that was being built at La Salle across not only the river, but also the canal and the Rock Island railroad tracks.[23]

West of La Salle, the railroad continued along the Illinois River until the river abruptly turned southward. At this point, it left the river valley and headed west toward Rock Island.[24] West of the big bend in the Illinois River, the railroad and the excursionists passed through a series of prairie towns, most of them of very recent origin, and some of them built in anticipation of the railroad. The *New York Daily Times* was most impressed with the setting of the town of Sheffield, which it described as having been "dropped in [the prairie's] bosom."[25] Farnam and Sheffield had founded this town two years earlier on land they had purchased for its coal reserves. The coal mined there fueled trains on the Rock Island lines for decades after the Grand Excursion.

The naming of the town of Sheffield has been subject to some speculation. One newspaper account suggests that "there was a discussion as to whether it should be named 'Farnam' or 'Sheffield,' but in any event, it was a peaceable agreement as these two men were close friends."[26] Local lore in Sheffield, however, suggests that the two men simply flipped a coin, with Farnam coming out the loser.[27] If this account is true, the town would have had a fifty-fifty chance of being called "Farnam." As it turned out, the great railroad builder had to settle for streets in Davenport and Omaha as midwestern namesakes rather than a village on the Illinois prairie.

The trains stopped in several towns for water and fuel and to pick up new passengers, but evidence suggests that the excursionists did not get off the trains between Chicago and Rock Island, although one source reported that President Fillmore spoke at one of the stops.[28] The first train also stopped near Sheffield in the early afternoon to wait for the second, which had been slowed by a thunderstorm.[29] When they reached Sheffield, the passengers were served lunch on the train.[30] After lunch the trains passed through Geneseo, crossed the Rock River over a brand-new bridge at Colona, and steamed on to Moline. While approaching Moline, where the tracks emerged onto the floodplain of the Mississippi, most excursionists got their first glimpse of the mighty Mississippi.

The Boat Excursion

Late in the afternoon of Monday, June 5, at the town of Rock Island, excursionists were met by at least five steamboats to take them upriver to Minnesota Territory. Several reports indicate that either six or seven boats were waiting there to meet the group. However, virtually all upstream accounts of the excursion mention only five boats, the *Galena*, the *Golden Era*, the *Lady Franklin*, the *G. W. Sparhawk*, and the *War Eagle*. Ed Hill's essay in this book describes the origins and life courses of these boats.

After some confusion associated with steamboat accommodations, the boats were boarded and they crossed the river to Davenport, Iowa, amid a shower of fireworks shot from the old site of Fort Armstrong on Rock Island. The boats, all of which had been decorated, departed upriver from Davenport late Monday evening. As they moved upstream across the Rock Island Rapids — crossed easily because of seasonal high water levels — musical bands were performing on the boats. Soon, as general revelry ensued, the excursionists were greeted by a spectacular thunderstorm. The *Chicago Daily Tribune* exclaimed: "We can fancy but few more impressive scenes than that of a thunder storm, at midnight, on the bosom of the Mississippi."[31]

Estimates of the number of passengers vary, but most reports suggest that more than one thousand people were on the five boats, hundreds having joined the excursion at Rock Island. Perhaps one-third of the more than six hundred rail passengers had left the party at Rock Island. Some went down the river to St. Louis and others returned to Chicago. Added to the remainder for the boat trip to St. Paul were hundreds of locals and others who had gathered at Rock Island.

Boat registers and newspaper accounts suggest some patterns to the placement of people on the boats. President Fillmore and a number of his friends, including several from his hometown of Buffalo, occupied the *Golden Era*. A number of Albany people were on the *Galena* and most of the Springfield, Massachusetts, group was placed on the *Sparhawk*. The *Boston Daily Advertiser* put it this way: "There is no recognized principle governing the distribution of the party among the several boats, but the following scheme suggested by a young lady from Utica, N. Y., whose wit is not the least of her charms, will serve to give your readers an idea of the apportionment. The *Golden Era* has the official dignity; the *Galena* the intelligence; the *Lady Franklin* the fashion; the *Sparhawk* the Massachusetts men and women; and the *War Eagle* the piety of the party."[32]

The boats ran day and night to St. Paul, making several stops a day to "wood-up," although no such stops are mentioned in accounts of the first overnight between Davenport and Galena. At daybreak on Tuesday morning, June 6, the boats were near Bellevue, Iowa, below the mouth of the Fever (Galena) River. It was here that the excursionists got their first glimpse of the high bluffs that would accompany them for the next three hundred miles. The boats went up to Galena via the Fever River, arriving about 9 A.M. Galena's prominence, aided by some recent rains, prompted a *New York Daily Times* writer to compare it with Broadway. He complained:

"[Galena is] one of the muddiest places I ever beheld. Broadway, at its worst periods, is a perfect paradise in comparison."[33]

The four-hour stay at Galena — which included speeches and tours of nearby lead mines — was followed by a short trip to Dubuque for a late afternoon stop. At Dubuque the ceremonies were limited to a few speeches at the waterfront, a city tour having been canceled because of heavy rain. At these stops, and virtually every other one, President Fillmore was a featured speaker. This prompted one correspondent to conclude (prior to reaching St. Paul): "Ex-President Fillmore had declared in twenty-seven set speeches on the route, that he was not making a political tour."[34]

The boats steamed upriver Tuesday night past Cassville, McGregor, and Prairie du Chien (places where they may have stopped to wood-up). On Wednesday morning, they passed Bad Axe, the site of the massacre of Black Hawk's people in 1832. At midday on Wednesday, June 7, the party landed at La Crosse where some reports indicate that rain was falling. Then later in the afternoon, after the rain had stopped, most if not all of the boats landed at Trempealeau, which at the time was called Montoville. Most sources agree that the party spent some time onshore here, and that this was the place where Mary Abigail Fillmore made her fabled climb to the top of the bluff on horseback. The *Boston Daily Advertiser* reported that all agreed Miss Fillmore should be called "the Countess Montoville," after a tradition started by the first woman to climb Mount Blanc who was called "Countess Mont Blanc."[35]

Above Montoville, the boats passed Winona and arrived at Lake Pepin, just above the mouth of the Chippewa River, late Wednesday evening. Lake Pepin is the widest segment of the Upper Mississippi. Most reports agree that at least four of the boats were lashed together as they steamed onto the lake, giving excursionists the opportunity to participate in a multi-boat party. The steady rain that had accompanied them Tuesday night and most of Wednesday (between Dubuque and above La Crosse) was replaced by cool, clear weather. A shivering *New York Daily Times* correspondent concluded: "It is never warm in this region."[36]

Early on Thursday morning, June 8, the boats passed Prescott, Wisconsin, and the mouth of the St. Croix River into a relatively narrow segment of the Mississippi leading to St. Paul. The *War Eagle* led a grand procession toward the St. Paul riverfront, followed by the *Galena*, the *Sparhawk*, the *Golden Era*, and the *Lady Franklin*. A *Boston Daily Journal* correspondent who had arrived at St. Paul earlier, observed the approach:

[T]here they were, away down the river, five floating palaces, bringing hither a freight representing more of wealth and true dignity than any like squadron ever launched. Hark! The guns reverberate, and the sounds of distant paddle wheels break the silence of a lovely June morning. Now they round the bend, and one by one they heave in sight. The shrill whistles of the whole fleet, the pealing of the merry church bells, and enlivening strains of martial music, and the loud huzzahs of the assembling multitude, all conspire to give the scene a grandeur and beauty unequalled. . . . These splendid packets, now coming to town, were arranged and managed with great tact and skill, considering the rapidity of the current at this point, and after performing various revolutions, came up to the landing five abreast. The drums beat, the bells rung, the cannon roared, the whistle screamed.[37]

Although the excursionists spent only one day in St. Paul and its environs, it was a busy day. St. Paul was not prepared to host this large contingent, because people there had expected the boats' arrival a day later. Nonetheless, transportation was arranged for many of the excursionists to visit St. Anthony Falls, now the site of Minneapolis, some nine miles west of St. Paul. En route, they crossed "beautiful farming country, a great portion of which was under cultivation,"[38] and also passed the site of the University of Minnesota, which had been established three years earlier but was not yet offering instruction. Excursionists viewed the falls and some also visited the nearby village of St. Anthony.

Most of these denizens of the East and Midwest had reached the farthest point from their homes, and the most northerly and westerly point that they would ever see. Amid a flurry of speeches, a ceremony with deep symbolic meaning was conducted at the falls: the "mingling of the waters" of the Atlantic and Mississippi. The *Albany Evening Journal* observed that "the water . . . was taken from Sandy Hook on the 1st day of June, at 2 o'clock P.M., and here, at the very same hour, on the 8th of June, we are about to commit it to the bosom of the father of waters."[39]

After the ceremony, some excursionists traveled a few miles south of St. Anthony to visit fabled Minnehaha Falls, but most returned directly to St. Paul that afternoon. Then at 5 P.M., the boats took most of them upriver for a brief visit to Fort Snelling, which is about six miles west of St. Paul. Upon returning to St. Paul, a gala celebration was held at the new statehouse featuring a welcome by Territorial Governor Gorman and many other speeches. Then, late Thursday evening after a long day in the area, the excursionists returned to the boats for a midnight departure to Rock Island.

The trip downriver was swift, as the first boats, the *Lady Franklin* and *War Eagle*, arrived in Rock Island as early as 6 A.M. Saturday morning, June 10.[40] Some five hundred miles were covered in about thirty hours. Since written reports leave no record of any onshore gatherings along the way, it is likely that only brief stops were made to wood-up. All the boats had arrived at either Rock Island or Davenport by midmorning. Many of the excursionists participated in a Davenport ceremony, the last of many such gatherings en route, this one involving speeches by visiting and local dignitaries. Among the speeches was a toast to Henry Farnam's infant son along with the presentation of a golden cup to the son of the railroad builder.

After these ceremonies, excursionists scattered far and wide. Large numbers boarded Rock Island trains to return to Chicago and thence to their homes in the East. For many, however, the adventure was not over. Upwards of two hundred of them continued south to St. Louis on the *War Eagle* and the *Sparhawk*, and some went to St. Louis via the Illinois Central railroad connection at La Salle, arranged and paid for by Mr. Bliss, president of that railroad.[41] From Chicago a number of excursionists scattered to a wide range of places, from Cincinnati to Wisconsin, before returning home.

The 1854 Grand Excursion was over, but our twenty-first-century excursions — the essays in this volume — are just beginning.

FIGURE 4. *"First suspension bridge, Minneapolis." On their trip from Rock Island to St. Paul, the Grand Excursionists saw evidence of construction on two bridges over the Mississippi River. On Rock Island they saw the piers for the first railroad bridge, which was completed two years later. At St. Anthony (Minneapolis), they viewed the first Mississippi River bridge, of any kind, under construction. It was completed some six months later. The correspondent from the* Springfield Daily Republican *(15 June 1854) reported that "[a] wagon load of a dozen [excursionists], crossed the river above the falls by a ferry, which is to be substituted by a wire suspension bridge, now erecting." Subsequently, three other bridges have been located on the same Hennepin Avenue site, the last completed in 1990. Photo of the daguerreotype, ca. 1857, from the Minnesota Historical Society.*

Building a Mighty Fine Line
The Chicago and Rock Island Railroad *Roald D. Tweet*

On the morning of October 1, 1851, in a vacant Chicago lot just west of Clark Street and south of Jackson, a "help-wanted" sign arose: "Good railroad work for the winter. Apply to Sheffield and Farnam, contractors, Chicago and Rock Island Railroad at 12th Street."

The response was good. Chicago was swelling with a flood of Irish immigrants fleeing the potato famine of 1847–1851, and they were eager to work. Those hired were sent to the Chicago and Rock Island's first railroad camp at Prairie Avenue and 22nd Street (now Cermak Road), then the southern city limits of Chicago. Teams of mules and oxen with slip scrapers were gathering dirt from borrow pits on each side of the slightly elevated railroad tracks.

Under the supervision of Henry Farnam, the general contractor, and his assistant, Samuel B. Reed, in charge of the construction gang, the railroad embankment would head due south toward Englewood, five miles away, before curving westward to Joliet, and then toward its final destination, the Mississippi River at Rock Island, 181 miles away. At Englewood, the Chicago and Rock Island tracks would connect with the Michigan Southern and Northern Indiana Railroad just coming around the tip of Lake Michigan from the east. On May 22, 1852, this Indiana line became the first railroad to use the Chicago and Rock Island tracks for access to Chicago.

Meanwhile, back at the 22nd Street construction site, the beginnings of the new railroad attracted little fanfare or attention; no ceremony, no reporters, no mayors or other dignitaries. By the fall of 1851, railroads were no longer headline news. A dozen railroads had come and mostly gone on the Illinois prairie. As early as 1834, Illinois Governor Joseph Duncan convinced the Illinois legislature to approve construction of a state-owned-and-operated railroad, the Northern Cross Line, which ran from Quincy on the Mississippi across the state to Danville on the Illinois-Indiana border. Only the fifty miles from Meredosia to Springfield was ever built, but the first train to operate in Illinois began on this stretch in May of 1842.[1]

Several other early railroads struggled to survive as well. Chartered in 1836, the Galena and Chicago Union Railroad and the Illinois Central Railroad both had run into financial troubles in the late 1830s but were still alive. On December 15, 1848, the Galena and Chicago Union began service on a small stretch between Chicago and the Fox River. The Illinois Central was resuscitated by a new 1850 charter. Its main line between Cairo, at the junction of the Ohio and Mississippi Rivers, to the terminus of the Illinois and Michigan Canal at Peru, was in the planning stage. Just to the east of the Chicago and Rock Island project, skirting the shore of Lake Michigan, the Illinois Central was surveying a fourteen-mile stretch from Chicago to Calumet, intending to connect with railroads from the East Coast. A short railroad was operating between Aurora and West Chicago by 1851, and two others had already begun construction at the Mississippi River at Alton and East St. Louis.

In addition to these railroad projects already under way, a dozen or so other railroads were vying to be the first to reach and cross the Mississippi River. According to the *Rock Island Advertiser* of November 23, 1853, Mississippi crossings were planned at an average of every sixteen miles between Dubuque and Keokuk. In addition to Rock Island/Davenport, these included Dubuque, Savanna, Fulton, Muscatine, New Boston, Burlington, Fort Madison, and Keokuk.

It is no wonder, then, that this latecomer, the Chicago and Rock Island Railroad, attracted so little attention. In contrast to the other Illinois railroad projects with grander visions than they were able to carry out, the original Rock Island road had begun in 1847 as a modest, regional venture of some eighty miles, designed merely to connect two waterways, the Mississippi and Illinois Rivers. Even then, the project remained on hold until 1851, when a new charter extended the tracks all the way to Chicago. What no one could have guessed on October 1, 1851, was that most of the difficulties lay behind. Just over two years later, on February 22, 1854, the Chicago and Rock Island Railroad would become the first to connect Chicago and the Mississippi River and, via the Michigan Southern and Northern Indiana Line, to provide a continuous link between the Mississippi and the Atlantic Ocean.

Most accounts trace the beginnings of the Chicago and Rock Island back to a meeting in June of 1845 at the home of Colonel George Davenport on the island of Rock Island (now Arsenal Island). Davenport had come to Rock Island in 1816 as sutler (supplier) to the troops at nearby Fort Armstrong, but had quickly branched out into fur trading with the Native Americans in the region and then into real estate. He had helped found the cities of Rock Island and Davenport across the river from each other. Present at the meeting were Judge James Grant and Ebenezer Cook, Davenport lawyers; A. C. Fulton, a Davenport storekeeper and entrepreneur; Lemuel Andrews and P. A. Whittaker, Rock Island businessmen; Charles Atkinson, one of the founders of brand-new Moline, just east of Rock Island; N. D. Elwood of Joliet; and Richard P. Morgan, a railroad and canal engineer from Peoria, Illinois. The men discussed a copy of the *Chicago Daily Journal* for June 4, 1845, that Judge Grant had brought, filled with notices of all the railroads rushing east toward Chicago. Was it time for Rock Island, Davenport, and Moline to get into the railroad business?

There were two reasons for doing so. One was practical and modest, the other visionary. On the practical side, the three towns at the foot of the Rock Island Rapids in the Mississippi were looking for a more direct way to ship their goods to eastern markets. As it was, all produce and manufactures had to go by steamboat down the Mississippi past St. Louis and her tolls, continue all the way to New Orleans, and then finish the journey by ship around to the East Coast. Even to reach Chicago, steamboats had to go down the Mississippi nearly to St. Louis, and then all the way back up the Illinois River to the head of navigation at La Salle.

In 1845 the State of Illinois had begun construction of the Illinois and Michigan Canal. It started from the head of navigation on the Illinois River at La Salle and ran ninety-six miles through seventeen locks to the south branch of the Chicago River, a project that would permit steamboats to go all the way to Lake Michigan, five miles away. For Judge Grant and most of the others, a small, eighty-mile railroad from Rock Island to the Illinois and Michigan Canal at La Salle would conveniently connect the two waterways and permit direct access to Chicago, and thus diminish their dependence on St. Louis. A railroad would serve, not compete with, the older waterways.

At least one person at the meeting expressed a larger vision. Morgan, the engineer, had worked on railroads and canals in New York State and believed that a railroad would eventually span the United States from the Atlantic to the Pacific. Such a railroad would have to cross the Mississippi. Of all the places to do so, the narrow part of the river between Rock Island and Davenport, with a limestone island to use as a steppingstone, would be the logical place. A railroad here could be more than a spur to La Salle, it could become transcontinental.

Morgan had support for this idea from an engineer he had worked with in New York, William C. Redfield. In 1823, as an amateur scientist, Redfield had explored the Upper Mississippi Valley looking for the best route for a transcontinental railroad. Coincidentally, 1823 was the same year that a small vessel, the *Virginia*, became the first steamboat to venture above Keokuk, Iowa. The *Virginia* reached Fort Armstrong, crossed the Rock Island Rapids, and made it to Fort Snelling just below St. Anthony's Falls twice that summer. In 1823, there were no railroads in the United States, nor was there a Chicago or a Rock Island. Yet the route mapped out by Redfield, published in 1829 in "A Sketch of the Geographical Route of a Great Railway between the Atlantic State and the Great Valley of the Mississippi," turned out to be virtually identical to the path actually followed by the Chicago and Rock Island Railroad.[2] William Redfield, incidentally, lived just long enough to return to Illinois twenty-five years later to ride the Chicago and Rock Island as a guest on the Grand Excursion in June of 1854.

Plans for a Rock Island railroad were halted less than a month later. On July 4, 1845, as his family celebrated in Rock Island, George Davenport was murdered in his home. It was not until early in 1847 that Judge Grant and his partners were ready to petition the Illinois legislature for a charter, and then only for the more modest Rock Island-to-La Salle route. The fate of the Illinois Internal Improvement Act of 1836 was still fresh in everyone's mind. In that act, the Illinois legislature had appropriated just over ten million dollars for a vast system of canals, roads, and railroads across Illinois, by which every Illinois town was to have some access to water or land transportation. The act called for 1,341 miles of railroad alone. It was money the state did not have. Many small investors, from bankers to farmers, subscribed more than five million dollars in stock. In the countrywide Panic of 1837 the following year, the state nearly went bankrupt and investors lost all their money. In the end, the only railroad completed was the fifty-mile stretch from Meredosia to Springfield.

On February 27, 1847, by a special act of the legislature, the General Assembly of Illinois granted a charter to establish the Rock Island and La Salle Railroad Company, giving it the right to "survey, locate, and construct, and during its continuance to maintain and continue a railroad with single or double track and with such appendages as may be deemed necessary for the convenient use of the same, from the Town of Rock Island, on the Mississippi River, in the County of Rock Island, to the Illinois River at the termination of the Illinois and Michigan Canal." Capitol stock for the corporation was fixed at $300,000.[3] The following January, stockholders met in Rock Island to elect directors and officers. Judge Grant was elected president, Napoleon B. Buford, secretary, and A. K. Philo, treasurer. Elected to the board of directors were Lemuel Andrews, Charles Atkinson, Ebenezer Cook, John Stevens, James M. Allen, William Bailey, L. D. Brewster, Churchill Coffing, and M. B. Osborne. Richard Morgan was selected as chief engineer. Because the money was to be raised locally — from farmers, merchants, and others whom the railroad would benefit — rather than from capitalists, sales of stock dragged on for three years. Four groups of commissioners, one for each county through which the tracks were to run, reported pledges as extremely slow.

In the end, it may have been the California Gold Rush in 1849 that reawakened interest in western railroads, and that finally brought Judge Grant and his partners closer to their goal.[4] At a meeting of commissioners on November 12, 1850, it was discovered that the stock was just $500 short of the necessary $300,000. Several commissioners made up that amount on the spot. November 27 was then set as the date for the stockholders to meet in Rock Island to organize the corporation and officially elect officers and ten board members.

On November 27, Judge Grant was elected the first president of the Rock Island and La Salle Railroad. William Bailey of Rock Island was elected treasurer, and Napoleon B. Buford, also of Rock Island, was elected secretary. Nearly all of the remaining board was comprised of those who had been elected in 1848.

From this November meeting on, developments moved more rapidly than the board could have imagined. Morgan had already begun surveying the route from La Salle to Rock Island, and would be nearly finished by the following April. From Geneseo westward, Morgan surveyed two possible routes to Rock Island, one along the south bank of the Rock River to Camden (now Milan) and then north into Rock Island to the waterfront, skirting the bluffs lining the north bank of the Rock River. The other crossed the Rock River near Colona, then passed by the eastern side of the bluffs through an opening known as Pleasant Valley (now East Moline), and then along the Mississippi River through Moline to Rock Island. The route finally chosen through Moline proved to be less expensive. In addition, even before the new charter the following February, Morgan had surveyed a route from La Salle to Aurora, "just in case" the railroad would continue on to Chicago.[5]

Earlier in the fall of 1850, Davenport's Judge Grant had heard that one of the most respected railroad contractors in the United States, Henry

Farnam of New Haven, Connecticut, was coming to Chicago to visit William Ogden, Chicago's first mayor and at the time president of the Galena and Chicago Union Railroad. Ogden was trying to convince Farnam to take over the job of completing his railroad, which had been stalled by difficult construction through the hilly country west of Freeport. Henry Farnam's credentials were impeccable. A self-taught engineer who had begun as a surveyor on the Erie Canal, Farnam had quickly moved to more responsible positions. From 1825 until 1850, he had served as the chief engineer for Connecticut's Farmington Canal. In 1845, he had convinced the canal's major stockholder, Joseph Sheffield, to build a railroad along the canal, and eventually abandon the canal.[6]

The relationship between Farnam and Sheffield grew. They became partners in several other major railroad projects, most notably an extension of the New Haven and Hartford Railroad along the Long Island Sound all the way into New York.[7] In this partnership, Sheffield secured the financing while Farnam handled the actual construction.

Accounts differ as to how Henry Farnam ended up as the general contractor on the Rock Island and La Salle rather than the Galena Line. According to F. J. Nevins, a former employee of the Rock Island Railroad who wrote a history of the line, Grant, along with Charles Atkinson, P. A. Whittaker, N. D. Elwood, and Isaac Cook, visited Farnam at the Ogden home and talked him into utilizing their route. Farnam, however, never mentioned the meeting in his memoirs. Instead, according to Farnam, he made a trip down to see the Illinois and Michigan Canal and was so impressed with the possibilities that he returned to Connecticut to get Joseph Sheffield and brought him back to Illinois. This time the two men went all the way to Rock Island and were convinced that of all the possible rail routes to the Mississippi and beyond, this route was the best. They saw what William Redfield had seen in 1823: a level route along the Illinois River until it turned south, where it followed a slight grade up the Bureau Valley over to Rock Island, the easiest place to construct a railroad bridge over the Mississippi.

Farnam and Sheffield, however, were not interested in a local railroad connecting two waterways. Their mindset was to compete with waterways rather than cooperate. They saw the Rock Island Railroad as one of the links in a transcontinental route connecting to the Michigan Southern and Northern Indiana at one end, crossing the Mississippi, and continuing across Iowa on the other.

At the November 27, 1850, meeting, Henry Farnam told the board that he and his partner would contract to build the entire railroad, provided that the board secure a revised charter from the Illinois legislature extending the railroad into Chicago, roughly following the Illinois and Michigan Canal. With the board's efforts, the bill to amend the original charter easily passed the Illinois senate in early January 1851. It had many railroad supporters here, even though house members were skeptical. Many house members were afraid that the railroad would take income away from the state-owned-and-operated canal. Had it not been for some careful maneuvers orchestrated by Representative James Allen of Geneseo (a member of the Chicago and Rock Island board), with help from the Speaker of the House and legislators such as Ninian Edwards, Jr., son of a former Illinois governor, the new charter might have been postponed for months.[8] As it turned out, the amended charter passed on January 27, 1851, and was authorized on February 7. The name of the corporation was officially changed to the Chicago and Rock Island Railroad, and the capital stock was increased from $300,000 to "any sum deemed necessary to construct the road — up to $3,000,000."[9]

On April 8, 1851, the board met to accept the new charter and new name.[10] Because the railroad would now compete with rather than complement the state-owned canal, the act revising the charter contained an onerous stipulation. The railroad was required to pay to the canal a toll on all commodities, except cattle, equal to canal rates for everything shipped between Chicago and a point twenty miles west of La Salle. The tolls were to be paid only in seasons when the canal operated. In return, the railroad was to receive free right-of-way across state-owned lands along the canal, and they were to be excused from taxes equal to the amount of the tolls.

As it turned out, the railroad did not pay a dime in tolls. The act specified that the canal company had until the first Monday in June 1851 to agree to these arrangements. If not, the railroad would be excused from all tolls. Instead, the canal company sought an injunction against the railroad. When the Illinois Supreme Court ruled against such an order by the end of June, the railroad was home free.

The Illinois and Michigan Canal had every reason to be worried about the railroad competition. Within three months of the opening of the railroad along the canal right-of-way, all passenger traffic on the canal ceased, leaving the canal little but bulk shipping, much of that consisting of iron rails and wooden ties for railroad construction.[11]

Another victory for the railroad occurred on May 26, 1851, when it received permission to extend its tracks north to Polk Street. Plans were revised to include a roundhouse there and a brick enginehouse for five engines. Eventually, the railroad would also build a six-hundred-foot wharf on the south branch of the Chicago River for its own supplies of rails and ties as well as for commercial use.

Farnam had already been hard at work surveying the remaining route from La Salle to Chicago, and estimating the costs of labor and materials in order to prepare a bid for the board of directors. In addition, the route from La Salle to Rock Island surveyed by Richard Morgan had to be redone. Fortunately, as it turned out, the spring of 1851 brought the highest water on record in western Illinois, and much of the route was underwater. The route was straightened and moved to higher ground.

By September, Sheffield and Farnam were ready to submit their bid. They did so on September 6, 1851. They proposed building the railroad from Chicago to Rock Island — 181 miles — for $3,987,668. The price included everything except the rights-of-way, station grounds, station buildings, fencing, and incidentals. Work was to begin on October 1, 1851. The board of directors accepted that bid on September 16, and on October 1, the first spade of dirt was turned at 22nd Street in Chicago.[12]

The railroad that now headed toward Rock Island was competing with waterways, not complementing them. The railroad had also shifted its goal from a small regional road to becoming the major link connecting the Atlantic and the Mississippi. It had become nationally significant. Even more important, the railroad was no longer to be funded by the small-time users along the route. Through Joseph Sheffield and his connections, the necessary millions would come instead from eastern investors. The railroad was to be funded, the *Rock Island Republican* announced, by "a company of New Haven capitalists."[13]

The change in funding also meant a change in control of the railroad. At the board of directors meeting at the Tremont Hotel in Chicago on December 22, 1851, Judge Grant, eager to return to Iowa politics, where he had just been elected Speaker of the House, declined election as president.[14] Instead, John Jervis of New York was elected president. Jervis had been chief engineer of the Mohawk and Hudson Railroad built to bypass the Erie Canal. He had also designed the first suspension system that was successful in keeping engine wheels from pounding rails to pieces.[15] Judge Grant remained as vice president. Isaac Cook of Chicago was elected treasurer and N. D. Elwood of Joliet as secretary. Several local men remained on the board, but outsiders replaced many on this expanded board, including George Bliss of Springfield, Massachusetts,

Elisha Litchfield of Detroit, and Azariah Flagg and John Stryker of New York. Henry Farnam was also elected to the board.

Starting in October 1851, work progressed rapidly on the railroad. Farnam appointed William Jervis of New York, who had been the engineer in charge of the Michigan Southern Railroad, as the project's chief engineer. The schooner *C. Y. Richmond* already lay moored in the Chicago River near Clark Street with the first of seventeen thousand tons of iron rails Farnam had ordered from the Ebberville Company of London. They had been brought over bit by bit as ballast in ships sailing to New York. Ten thousand tons were to be delivered over the next year, enough to complete the tracks to Peru. Thousands of cedar railroad ties, six inches thick, seven inches wide, and eight feet long, were also arriving by boat down Lake Michigan from Evanston.

Which gauge to make the tracks? There was no standard among railroads in the United States. Between Chicago and New York, railroads used at least four different gauges. Farnam decided on four feet, eight and one-half inches, simply because that was the one used by George Stephenson and his London-to-Liverpool train in 1825, the famous *Rocket*. For a gauge marker, Farnam utilized a rough common board with a nail at either end. Eventually, the gauge Farnam used became standard on nearly all American railroads.

By the end of December, grading had been completed to Englewood. At 22nd Street the first Chicago and Rock Island depot went up, a whitewashed sixty-by-twenty-five-foot wooden structure. Contracts had also been let for the grading and masonry to Ottawa eighty-five miles away, and would soon be let to Indiantown (Tiskilwa) just beyond Peru. The bridge across the Rock River near Colona was also under contract.

At the end of January, the tracks had been laid and connected with the Michigan Southern and Northern Indiana at Englewood, and construction was progressing toward Joliet. Some eight hundred men were working on the road between Ottawa and Chicago. The roundhouse at Polk Street was completed by the end of July, and Farnam began estimating the need for equipment. He planned to bring engines and cars to Chicago by means of a recently patented variable truck system that could adapt to different gauges on the railroads. By October 1, 1852, the forty miles of track was completed to Joliet, and Board President Jervis could report that the roadbed the rest of the way to Peru was ninety-nine percent ready to lay track.

The first order of rail cars arrived via the Michigan Southern and Northern Indiana tracks. It included twelve first-class passenger cars, 150 covered freight cars, one hundred platform cars, five passenger cars, and forty boxcars. Farnam had planned to order eighteen engines, but did not actually place the first order with the Rogers, Ketchum, and Grosvenor Locomotive Works of Patterson, New Jersey, until October 21, 1852. Company records show that he ordered three 4–4-0 locomotives in October, three in November, and so on until 1854, for a total of twenty-nine.[16] Until those locomotives arrived, Farnam used three similar 4-4-0 locomotives on loan from the Rogers company, one of which was named the *Rocket*. It was by accident, then, that the "Rocket" name became associated with the Rock Island Lines.

Although Farnam had not intended to begin rail service to Joliet so soon, people along the track clamored to see the first train. Responding to such interest, train superintendent Addison R. Gilmore requested a trial run. On Sunday morning at 10 A.M., October 10, 1852, the *Rocket* stood ready at the 22nd Street station. James Lendabarker, the engineer, had the boiler stoked and a plentiful supply of pine knots in the tender and in front of the first coach. Henry Farnam assembled a handful of dignitaries, including Mr. Gilmore; William Jervis, chief engineer of the railroad; Joel A. Matteson of Joliet, the governor of Illinois; and a reporter from the *Chicago Daily Democrat*. Also on board at the personal invitation of Farnam was eight-year-old Mary Quaid, little sister of one of the construction gang, who thus became the first female passenger on the Chicago and Rock Island Railroad.[17]

The *Rocket*, pulling six yellow coaches, reached Joliet two hours later, and after a brief celebration returned to Chicago. Because Joliet still had no facilities for turning around, the train had to back up the whole way. That evening there was a "sumptuous dinner" at the Sherman House in Chicago, followed by a sightseeing tour of Chicago and a theater party.[18]

The railroad wasted little time in beginning regular service. The following day, October 11, the first Chicago and Rock Island advertisement appeared in the *Chicago Daily Journal*, announcing two daily trains between Chicago and Joliet, "on and after Monday, October 18, 1852."[19] The trains were scheduled to leave Chicago at 8 A.M. and 5 P.M. and Joliet at 6:30 A.M. and 7:30 P.M. This opening of regular service marked the official beginning of the Chicago and Rock Island Railroad. The Rock Island tracks extended west even more rapidly during the first half of 1853 (fig. 5). By January 5, the rails had reached Morris and crossed the Des Plaines River. They reached Ottawa on February 14, and approached mile ninety-nine at La Salle at the beginning of March. A local celebration was held after the tracks reached each station, followed shortly thereafter by regular rail service.

Meanwhile, there was also important activity at the Rock Island end of the line. On January 17, 1853, the Illinois legislature granted a charter to the Railroad Bridge Company to build a bridge across the river to Davenport. On January 26, the U.S. Senate, by a vote of sixty-eight to one, granted the bridge company the right to cross the Mississippi. On February 5, the Iowa legislature authorized the creation of the Mississippi and Missouri Railroad Company in order to build a railroad from Davenport to Council Bluffs. Several officials of the Rock Island road, including Henry Farnam, were also involved in this new railroad, which would merge with the Rock Island in 1867 to become the Chicago, Rock Island, and Pacific Railroad.

At La Salle, meanwhile, local businessmen who had invested in land on top of the bluffs attempted to raise an impromptu posse when they discovered that the tracks were to be laid down along the Illinois River. An injunction from the Illinois courts soon stopped the opposition.[20] Rail service to La Salle began on March 21, 1853.

When the railroad tracks reached Peru on April 16, construction halted for a few months for several reasons. First, Peru was a terminal on the line, as were Chicago and Rock Island. At terminals (as opposed to stations like Joliet, Ottawa, etc.) trains changed engines and engineers, requiring an enginehouse and other more extensive facilities. These had yet to be built. Second, the firm of Sheffield and Farnam was temporarily busy with a new venture. The Peoria and Bureau Valley Railroad had been chartered in February, and now the two contractors took on this additional project, which soon became a branch of the Chicago and Rock Island.

Peru was a natural place to stop. The town was the head of navigation on the Illinois River, making it an ideal place for the transfer of freight between steamboats and railroad going to or from St. Louis. Other transport companies used the town as a hub. The stage lines of Frink, Walker, and Company fanned out in all directions — from Peru to Rock Island; up to Galena, Dixon, and Dubuque; and throughout most of Illinois, Iowa, and Wisconsin.[21] In addition, that May the Illinois Central began operating its trains between Peru and Bloomington. But the major reason for the halt in further construction westward was simply that both passenger and freight service on the railroad so far exceeded expectations that there was little equipment to spare for construction. Planned passenger service was consequently forced to double and triple.

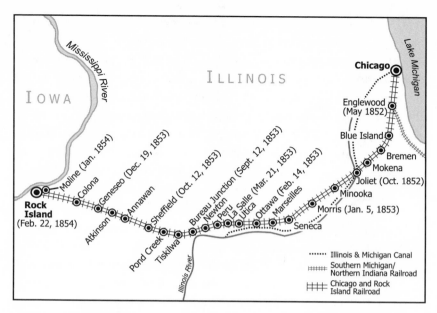

FIGURE 5. *Chicago and Rock Island Railroad construction completion dates from Chicago to the Mississippi River. Dates from F. J. Nevins, "Seventy Years of Service from Grant to Gorman."*

The halt in construction at Peru caused much consternation back in Rock Island. Neighboring cities in western Illinois fueled rumors that the original intention had been to stop at Peru rather than continue to Rock Island. Rock Islanders had long wondered why construction had begun in Chicago rather than Rock Island, or why, at least, construction had not been started at both ends. Farnam and Jervis were forced to make several trips to Rock Island to explain that getting supplies to that river town would have been difficult.

Farnam neglected to explain another reason for beginning at Chicago and extending service station by station. The contract with Sheffield and Farnam stipulated that the contractors were to receive all income from the railroad themselves, and be responsible for all debts, until the completed railroad was ready to turn over to the board of directors. The income, as it turned out, was beyond expectations.

By summer 1853, work on the railroad resumed. The rails reached Bureau Junction, fourteen miles from Peru, on September 12, where they met the tracks heading toward Peoria, forty-seven miles south. Meanwhile, west of Bureau Junction, the coming railroad changed more than the landscape. Fifteen miles from Bureau, Indiantown changed its plain name to the more colorful Tiskilwa. Further west, where a station was necessary to provide the frequent water and fuel supply needed by the locomotives, Joseph Sheffield and several investors, including Henry Farnam and Judge Grant, bought a large tract of land adjacent to the railroad right of way and established the town of Sheffield. The site included a coal mine, and for fifty years the Sheffield Mining and Transportation Company provided fuel for the Chicago and Rock Island.[22] The tracks reached Sheffield on October 12.

By December 19, the line extended to Geneseo, 159 miles from Chicago. With only twenty-two miles to go to Rock Island, President Jervis announced to the now expectant Rock Islanders that enough rails and ties were stockpiled in Chicago for the line to reach Rock Island by March 1, 1854. The tracks reached Moline in early January of 1854, and Henry Farnam suggested February 22, Washington's birthday, as a fitting date to mark the railroad's completion. On February 9, the Rock Island City Council responded by planning a grand celebration to mark the arrival of what would certainly be the first train to connect the Atlantic and the Mississippi. (The competing route via the Alton and Chicago Railroad from Alton to Bloomington, and the Illinois Central from Bloomington to the Rock Island lines at Peru, still required travel by stagecoach along a few uncompleted stretches.) The Rock Island City Council appropriated $1,000 for the celebration and set up committees to handle invitations, housing, meals, and programs. Davenport and Moline declined to share planning and expenses, making the celebration an entirely Rock Island affair.

By the middle of February, the tracks approached Rock Island, heading for the small frame depot at the northeast corner of 20th Street and Illinois (now 2nd Avenue). Invitations went out to officials and dignitaries from towns along the line, three hundred to Chicago and another three hundred to Joliet, Ottawa, La Salle, and all the others, and a select few to neighboring Moline and Davenport.

As the date approached, Rock Island distributed handbills all over town declaring: "Order of the Day/Railroad Festival."[23] They announced that the first train would arrive at 5 P.M. to the sounds of artillery and music, and detailed the evening's program. Although only invited local guests were allowed to attend the official dinner, the Rock Island House and its proprietor, Major Barrett, would offer everyone else a free dinner from 5:00 to 7:00 — an offer fifteen hundred local residents accepted on the evening of the 22nd.[24] To feed the six hundred invited guests, a temporary wooden building was erected near the station in less than three days.[25]

By 5:00 on February 22, hundreds of Rock Islanders, many of whom had never even seen a picture of a locomotive, assembled on the station grounds. There was a blast of artillery, and soon, as the *Rock Island Republican*, put it, "the iron horse appeared in sight, rolling along with a slow but mighty motion to the depot."[26] The gaily-decorated locomotive pulled six yellow passenger cars crammed full of joyful guests from Chicago waving flags and handkerchiefs. A second equally decorated locomotive followed, pulling five cars of guests picked up along the route from Chicago.

At the station, the guests were properly welcomed on behalf of the citizens of Rock Island by J. J. Beardsley, a prominent Rock Island lawyer and real estate developer. "On this day," he told the crowd, "the coast of the Atlantic Ocean has been bound to the shores of the Mississippi River with bands of iron."[27] The local guests then followed the out-of-towners to their assigned places for dinner. Following an exceptional "collation," Napoleon B. Buford, president of the day, arose to propose thirteen official toasts, many of them responded to by appropriate parties. He began by saluting the day as "February 22, Washington's Birthday." Next, he made a toast to "February 22, the espousal day of the Mississippi River and the Atlantic Ocean. May no vandal hands ever break the connection." Buford then raised a toast "to the Rock Island and La Salle Railroad — It never met death, but was translated."[28] When it came Henry Farnam's turn to be toasted, the audience clamored for him to respond. He did so briefly, reminding the guests that speech-making was not in his contract with the railroad. His response was a gracious one, identifying many of the others present who had made the railroad possible.

Several impromptu toasts followed the thirteen official ones. J. B. Danforth, editor of the *Rock Island Republican* (and a staunch Democrat) proposed a toast to the Irish workers who had actually laid the tracks.[29] D. N. Burnham, a member of the Chicago delegation, raised a toast to "the Temperance aspect of this elegant Festival [during which nothing stronger than coffee and tea had been served]. May your worthy example be followed 'all the country through.'"[30]

Following the dinner, the out-of-town guests paraded down Illinois Avenue from the station to the Rock Island House to view Rock Island and Davenport, in which nearly every house had been illuminated at the request of the city council. At the Rock Island House, the guests met the local residents at whose homes they were to stay, there not being nearly enough hotel rooms to house six hundred people. Some of the guests ended up at the Le Claire House in Davenport to participate in a ball throughout much of the night. The following morning, the guests boarded the trains for the seven-hour return trip to Chicago.

For Rock Islanders, this Washington's Birthday celebration was much grander than the Grand Excursion the following June, and it received far more publicity in the local press. The Grand Excursion of June 1854 was a national event, planned by Sheffield, Farnam, and the railroad, but February 22 was entirely a Rock Island affair.

On July 10, 1854, a month after the excursion, Joseph Sheffield and Henry Farnam officially turned over the completed Chicago and Rock Island Railroad to the corporation. Unforeseen expenses had brought the total cost to just under $4,500,000. The original contract called for eighteen locomotives, twelve passenger cars, 150 box cars, and 150 flat cars. But by July 10, the company owned twenty-eight locomotives (with ten more on order), twenty-eight passenger cars, 170 box cars, and 170 flat cars. The railroad had proved to be more successful than anyone involved could have imagined.

The completion of this project also marked a turning point in the working relationship between the two contractors. Joseph Sheffield retired back to New Haven to spend the remainder of his life pursuing philanthropic projects. Henry Farnam was already hard at work on the Rock Island Bridge and on the Mississippi and Missouri Railroad in Iowa. A year later, when the two men had settled their accounts with each other from the railroad project, Sheffield wrote to Farnam. "In closing these accounts of millions between us," he wrote, "it must be a pleasing reflection to you, as it is to me, that we have worked together with mutual confidence, faith and zeal, and that we amicably close them with the same kind feelings and high respect, and confidence, with which we commenced some dozen years ago."[31]

It was not only eastern capitalists and engineering know-how that let the Chicago and Rock Island Railroad proceed with so few of the problems that plagued and slowed most of the other Illinois railroad projects, but also this attitude of trust and respect between nearly all of the parties involved. That July, with Henry Farnam as its brand-new president, the Chicago and Rock Island Railroad was well on its way to becoming the Rock Island Lines, portrayed in a popular twentieth-century song as "a mighty fine line."

FIGURE 6. *Entitled "First Train over the Rock Island Lines Bridge over the Mississippi River, Rock Island, Illinois on Tuesday, April 22, 1856," this illustration actually depicts the second bridge, which was built in 1866 on the same piers used by the first bridge. Two subsequent bridges were built about six hundred yards downstream, the most recent in 1896. Information from Mary Charlotte Aubry Costello,* Climbing the Mississippi River Bridge by Bridge, Volume One, From Louisiana to Minnesota, *p. 116. Photo of a painting by W. H. Hinton, State Historical Society of Iowa, Iowa City.*

THE GRAND EXCURSION OF 1854

William J. Petersen

The first railroad to unite the Atlantic with the Mississippi River reached Rock Island on February 22, 1854. To celebrate this event leading citizens of the country were invited by the firm of Sheffield and Farnam, contractors for the construction of the Chicago and Rock Island Railroad, to participate in a joint railroad and steamboat excursion to the Falls of St. Anthony. The response was so hearty and the requests for passes were so numerous that the Minnesota Packet Company was obliged to increase the number of steamboats chartered from one to five.[359]

So lavish were the preparations that an eastern paper declared the affair "could not be rivaled by the mightiest among the potentates of Europe." The account continues: "Without bustle or noise, in a simple but grand manner, like everything resulting from the combined action of liberty and association — guests have been brought hither free of charge from different places, distant thousands of miles, invited by hosts to them unknown, simple contractors and directors of railroads and steamboats."[360]

John H. Kinzie was chairman of the reception committee in Chicago, where the Tremont House served as headquarters for the assembled guests. There, Millard Fillmore, a President by accident, met Samuel J. Tilden, who later failed by accident to achieve the presidency. Prominent western leaders such as Ninian Edwards (former Governor of Illinois) and Edward Bates of Missouri (later Attorney General in Lincoln's cabinet) exchanged views with notable Easterners such as John A. Dix, John A. Granger, J. C. Ten Eyck, and Elbridge Gerry. Francis P. Blair of Maryland greeted his son, Francis P. Blair, Jr., of St. Louis. New Haven and Yale University sent Professors Benjamin Silliman, A. C. Twining, Leonard Bacon, and Eleazar Thompson to match wits with Judge Joel Parker of Harvard and Professor Henry Hubbard of Dartmouth. George Bancroft, a Harvard graduate and already a national historian, accepted an invitation to make the "fashionable tour": he was repeatedly called upon to address the crowds which gathered to greet the Easterners. Catherine M. Sedgwick was one of the more notable women to make the trip.[361]

No profession was so ably and numerously represented as was the press. Almost every metropolitan paper of the East had sent a writer to accompany the excursion. Charles Hudson of the Boston *Atlas* and Thurlow Weed of the Albany *Evening Journal* were seasoned and nationally known editors. Samuel Bowles of the Springfield *Republican* and Charles A. Dana of the New York *Tribune* were at the threshold of long and famous careers. Hiram Fuller of the New York *Mirror*, Epes Sargent of the Boston *Transcript*, Charles Hale of the Boston *Advertiser*, and W. C. Prime of the New York *Journal of Commerce* were other eastern reporters. The West was represented by such editors as William Schouler of the Cincinnati *Gazette* and C. Cather Flint from the staff of the Chicago *Tribune*.[362]

Early on the morning of June fifth the excursionists assembled at the Rock Island station in Chicago. Shortly after eight o'clock two trains of nine coaches each, gaily decorated with flowers, flags, and streamers, and drawn by powerful locomotives, left the city. Speeches, military parades, and the discharge of cannon greeted the excursionists on every hand. A free lunch was distributed at Sheffield, Illinois. Notwithstanding frequent stops, the trains reached Rock Island at 4 P.M. There the *Golden Era* (Captain Hiram Bersie commanding), the *G. W. Spar-Hawk* (Captain Montraville Green commanding), the *Lady Franklin* (Captain Le Grand Morehouse commanding), the *Galena* (Captain D. B. Morehouse commanding), and the *War Eagle*, in command of Daniel Smith Harris, lay waiting to take the excursionists aboard.[363]

So large was the number of unexpected or uninvited guests that the five boats were quickly jammed, and it was necessary to charter two additional craft — the *Jenny Lind* and the *Black Hawk*. But accommodations still proved insufficient. According to Dana "state-rooms had been allotted at Chicago, where the names had been registered; but many of the tickets had been lost, and many persons had none at all. Besides there had been some errors — husbands and wives were appointed to different boats, and several young fellows were obliged to part from the fair ladies about whom they had hitherto revolved with the most laudable devotedness." The lack of berths caused fully one-third of the guests to renounce the steamboat trip and return to Chicago. Despite this fact at least twelve hundred remained aboard the boats, where they were served a "sumptuous feast" that was said to equal any afforded by the best hotels in the country.[364]

After listening to brief speeches at Rock Island and Davenport (including two addresses by Fillmore on internal improvements and the Great

West), the passengers were entertained with a brilliant display of fire-works from Fort Armstrong. Bells rang and whistles sounded as the boats, decorated with prairie flowers and evergreens, left Davenport at ten o'clock "and sailed with music on their decks, like birds by their own song, lighted by the moon, and saluted by the gay fireworks from the Old Fort." Captain Harris led off with the *War Eagle*, while the *Golden Era*, with the former President aboard, brought up the rear.[365]

Everyone was delighted with the bright moonlight and the refreshing river breeze which greeted the boats as they puffed upstream against the powerful current. Shortly after midnight a violent thunderstorm occurred. According to one passenger: "Impenetrable darkness en-shrouded us, and nothing could be seen of our fleet of seven steamers, save the lurid glare of their furnaces shining upon the agitated waves, and their red and blue lights suspended from their bows. A sudden flash of vivid lightning would illumine the entire scene for a moment, and then as suddenly would it be blotted from view. At such moments, so intense was the light, and so vivid the impression produced, that each separate leaf upon the trees on shore, each crevice in the bank, the form of each steamer, and even the countenances of those upon the guards, could be seen as plainly as if printed upon a canvas." After a few hours the storm subsided and the weary travelers were soon lulled to rest.[366]

The night was spent with varying degrees of comfort, for many of the young men were obliged to "rough it" on mattresses on the cabin floors. But none of them was heard to complain; Miss Sedgwick praised them for their good-natured and manly attitude. Another passenger, less opti-mistic, declared: "Through the whole trip many gentlemen who should by all means have had comfortable places have had no opportunity to sleep, except on mattresses on the cabin floor. As these could never be laid down before midnight, and must be removed before 5 o'clock in the morning, and were never very favorable to repose, their occupants have had but from two to four hours sleep at night, while sleeping by day was even more out of the question."[367]

Dawn found the boats a few miles below Bellevue, whence the *War Eagle* led the fleet booming up Fever River to Galena. A trip to the lead mines was followed by a picnic dinner in the woods. "Wines of Ohio and of France stood upon the board, sparkling Catawba the favorite, and glasses were drained to the health and prosperity of Galena and its citi-zens." Dana noted with regret "that total abstinence is not the rule of the Mississippi Valley, everybody feeling it to be a sort of duty to temper the limestone water of the country with a little brandy, or other equally ardent corrective."[368]

After leaving Galena the boats proceeded to Dubuque where, despite a heavy downpour, they were met by a throng of people. Fillmore, Silliman, Bancroft, Bates, Hudson, and others addressed the citizens of Dubuque. La Crosse was described by Dana as "a wooding-place on the eastern shore, with two or three frame houses." A dozen excursionists climbed a lofty cliff overlooking the embryonic settlement while the boats "were wooding up." According to Dana "Wide prairies, marked by Indian trails, or dotted with the plowed patches of here and there a chance settler, interrupted by oak forests, or by inland ranges of lower bluffs and knolls, made up the scene, with the river, its shores and islands, for the center of the whole."[369]

Frequent landings were made at the scattered settlements along the river, and wherever the boats stopped to "wood up," the excursionists invariably trooped ashore. "Our light boats," notes Miss Sedgwick, "skimmed the surface of the water like birds; and, with the ease and grace of birds, they dipped down to the shore, and took up their food, their fiery throats devouring it with marvelous rapidity." The process of "wooding up" always attracted the attention of passengers who were not inclined to go ashore and wander about. President Fillmore's daughter (while her steamboat was "wooding up" at Trempealeau) mounted a horse and scaled that "mighty rampart." Her appearance at the summit was greeted with a salvo of steamboat whistles and the prolonged cheers of those aboard.[370]

Amusements aboard the boats were as varied as human ingenuity could devise. Racing was prohibited; but the boats were often lashed together, and passengers enjoyed the opportunity of visiting with old friends and making new ones. Promenading on deck and allowing the ever-changing landscape on shore to "daguerreotype new pictures on the mind" formed the principal pastime for most of the travelers. When the boats were lashed together "dancing in one cabin would draw together the dancers or a *conversazione* in another, the listeners and talkers."

Slavery was probably the chief topic of conversation, for the Kansas-Nebraska bill had just been passed, and abolitionists were deeply aroused by the Boston slave case as a result of which a Negro named Burns had been sent back into slavery. The closing of stores in Boston, the hanging of effigies, the tolling of bells, the festooning of buildings in black, and the floating of the flag with the Union down were events that doubtless made the Boston newspapermen (Hale, Sargent, and Hudson) centers of attraction. The Austrian alliance, reciprocity or annexation with regard to Canada, and the influence of the discovery of gold in California and Australia in maintaining high prices elicited editorial comment in the New York *Tribune* of the day. Rioting of native Americans and Irishmen in Brooklyn, and the wreck of the *Powhatan* with a loss of over three hundred passengers were news items featured in the newspapers. The scientifically inclined probably found special interest in such inventions as a compact and almost frictionless steam engine, Ralston's portable sawmill, a new patent for making nails, and gas for country use — all of which were on display at the Crystal Palace Exhibition in New York. The distinguished Yale scientist, Professor Silliman, had a large audience one evening; but Dana was "attracted by gayer sounds from another boat" and was unable to report Silliman's speech to the readers of his paper.[371]

When Lake Pepin was reached at eleven o'clock on Wednesday night four boats were lashed together; and they then proceeded upstream shooting brilliant shafts of light that streamed and danced on the waters and shores of the lake. The remainder of the night was spent in "dancing, music, flirtations, *et cetera*."[372] Then as now there were romantic souls who found their greatest joy on the upper deck with only the moon to disturb a tryst.

A mock trial was held in the cabin of the *G. W. Spar-Hawk* one rainy and disagreeable evening. Schouler of the Cincinnati *Gazette* was tried for assault and battery on the person of Dr. Kennedy. The prisoner pleaded not guilty, and Moses Kimball of Boston was selected to defend him. Prime of the New York *Journal of Commerce* acted as prosecutor. Both Kimball and Prime appeared before the court heavily armed with dueling pistols and bowie knives. The closing speech of Kimball lasted three-quarters of an hour and was listened to with profound attention. Both attorneys attempted to bribe the jury. Happily the evidence showed that the plaintiff had been injured when a berth broke down while both he and the defendant were asleep. The case was promptly dismissed.[373]

The appearance of the fleet when it rounded the bend below St. Paul was described as "grand beyond precedent." The steamboats approached like an armed squadron taking its position in line of battle. "Two full bands of music were on board, both of which struck up lively airs as the boats neared the landing. This, with the rays of the bright June sun which broke forth in all his glory after three days' storm; the animation of the company on board the boats, and the enthusiasm of the assembled hundreds on shore and on the decks of the Admiral, then lying at the landing, produced a scene of excitement which St. Paul has never before witnessed, and perhaps will not again for many years."[374]

Although little more than six years old, St. Paul boasted six thousand inhabitants and made a fine appearance from the decks of the approaching vessels. According to Dana there were "brick dwellings and stone warehouses, a brick capitol with stout, white pillars, a county court-house, a jail, several churches, a market, school-houses, a billiard-room, a tenpin alley, dry goods' stores, groceries, confectioners and ice-creamers, a numerous array of those establishments to which the Maine law is especially hostile, and a glorious, boundless country behind."[375]

Shortly after the excursionists arrived they were bundled into every conceivable class and variety of vehicle and trundled away at various rates of speed to the Falls of St. Anthony. Three prominent New York editors were seen perched precariously upon a one-horse water cart. The editor of the Galena *Jeffersonian* declared that "The 'March to Finley' was nothing compared to our motley cavalcade. Here was a Governor bestride a sorry Rozinante of which even the Great Don would have been ashamed; here an U. S. Senator, acting the part of footman, stood bolt upright in the baggage boot of a coach, holding on by the iron rail surrounding the top, here the historian of which the country is justly proud, squatted on his haunches on the top of a crazy van, unmindful of everything but himself, his book, his hat and spectacles; there a hot house flower, nursed in some eastern conservatory, so delicate and fragile that a falling leaf might crush it, but a beautiful specimen of the feminine gender, withal, would be seated over the hind axle of a lumber wagon, supported on either side by opera glass exquisites, who only wondered 'why the h —— l the people in this country didn't send to New York for better carriages.'"[376]

After viewing the Falls of St. Anthony, the excursionists visited Lake Calhoun, Minnehaha Falls, and Fort Snelling. In the evening a reception was held in the Capitol, where Henry H. Sibley welcomed the visitors. Fillmore thanked the citizens of St. Paul for their cordial reception, and pointed out the significance of the city as a central point on one of the routes leading from the Atlantic to the Pacific. Bancroft responded on behalf of the railroad directors and bade Minnesota become "the North Star of the Union, shining forever in unquenchable luster." At eleven o'clock the tired tourists returned to the landing, where the boats lay illuminated and with steam hissing from their boilers. Shortly after midnight the fleet cast off from St. Paul, whose hills and lighted windows disappeared as the boats rounded Dayton's Bluff.[377]

While speeding downstream at the rate of ten miles an hour, the passengers found time passing all too fast. In addition to the usual dances, lectures, and musical entertainments in the cabins, meetings were called for the purpose of drawing up resolutions of thanks to the railroad directors and steamboat captains. Not only were many toasts drunk to the directors, captains, and boats, but generous contributions were made for the presentation of loving cups and gold plate to the officers. Fillmore presided over a meeting on the *Golden Era* where three hundred dollars were raised to purchase a silver pitcher for Captain Bersie.[378] According to the Chicago *Tribune* the pitcher bore the following inscriptions: "Presented to HIRAM BERSIE, Master of the Golden Era, by the passengers of the Steamer, on their Excursion to the Falls of St. Anthony, while guests of the Chicago & Rock Island Railroad Company, as a slight testimonial of their respect and their grateful appreciation of his urbanity, vigilance, and professional abilities, June, 1854."

A cup of solid gold, beautifully engraved, was awarded to Henry W. Farnam (then a well-behaved baby in his mother's arms) who many years later became professor of economics in Yale University. John A. Rockwell of Norwich, Connecticut, made the address of presentation, and Professor A. C. Twining responded for the six-months-old infant: "I, Henry W. Farnam, being young in years, and wholly unaccustomed to public speaking, feel incompetent to discharge in suitable terms the duty imposed upon me on this interesting occasion. When I came on board this boat, it was farthest from my expectation to make a speech. 'Man wants but little here below,' and babies still less. All my wants may be confined within this little cup which you propose to give me. Its contents are a baby's world — his universe. Heaven and earth and ocean plundered of their sweets may be compressed within the golden rim of this little measure. Some babies might cry for joy over my good fortune, but I am as unused to crying as to public speaking. I give you my best smile of thanks for your kindness, while I rely upon my interpreter for a further and more mature expression of the grateful emotion of my joyful little heart."[379]

Resolutions gave unstinted praise to the lesser officers and to the crew for their efforts to make the travelers comfortable and happy. Miss Sedgwick was delighted with the courtesy of Captain Morehouse and the "civil lads" aboard the *Lady Franklin* who performed their work as if it was "a dainty task, to be done daintily." Nor did Dana forget Captain Bersie and Clerk Dawley of the *Golden Era*, whose "many civilities and attentions" were gratefully acknowledged in the New York *Tribune*.[380] The other captains probably received similar recognition from the writers who graced the decks of their boats.

The responsibility for providing varied and well-prepared meals fell upon stewards who never before had been called upon to serve such an array of notable guests. Since the floors of the cabins were covered with sleepers, it was the stewards' duty to awaken them gently and diplomatically in order that the mattresses might be removed and the tables set for breakfast by seven o'clock. (No deck hand or roustabout could perform so delicate a task.) Breakfast over, the cooks were given the menu for dinner. Meats and vegetables were prepared in one kitchen, while pastry and desserts were made ready in another. When needed, fish, game, eggs, and vegetables were bought at the various towns along the way. At Trempealeau, two bushels of speckled trout were purchased; the fish proved a rare treat for the excursionists. Supplies of fresh meat (a dozen lambs or pigs) were picked up from time to time.

James F. Babcock of the New Haven *Palladium* described the meals aboard the *Golden Era*: "We have had oysters and lobsters daily, though two thousand miles from the sea. These, of course, were brought in sealed cans. Hens, turkeys, and ducks have given their last squeak every morning. Two cows on the lower deck furnish us with fresh milk twice a day. Beets are cooked, and every variety of stuff, and the dessert consists of all kinds of fruits, nuts, cakes, confection ices, and other things too numerous to mention. Such is our daily fare. Then there are meats for supper, with tea and coffee, with toast, dry and wet, cold bread, warm bread, Indian bread, biscuits, rolls, etc."[381]

The excursionists were never invited to visit the meat and vegetable kitchen, for the scenes enacted there might well have caused a loss in appetite: they were cordially urged to drop into the pastry and dessert kitchen at any time. The number and variety of puddings, pies, ice creams, custards, and jellies was astonishing. Miss Sedgwick declared: "Morning, noon and night a table was spread, that in most of its appointments and supplies would have done honor to our first class hotels, and its confections would not have disgraced a French artiste with all the appliances and means of a French cuisine. By what magic art such ices, jellies, cakes, and pyramids, veiled in showers of candied sugar, were compounded in that smallest of tophets, a steamer's kitchen, is a mystery yet to be solved."[382]

The notables who made the fashionable tour of 1854 were almost unanimous in their praise of the Upper Mississippi steamboats. Only one adverse (but by no means harsh) criticism was made by an anonymous writer in the New York *Tribune*. He observed: "As the Upper Mississippi must now become a route for fashionable Summer travel, it is only proper to say that those who resort here must not yet expect to find all the conveniences and comforts which abound on our North River steamers. Everything is very plain; the staterooms are imperfectly furnished, but the berths are roomy; the table is abundant, but butter-knives and sugar-tongs are not among its luxuries. But those who know how to overlook these little deficiencies cannot hope anywhere to behold nature in such multiform loveliness and grandeur as on the waters of the Mississippi, between Rock Island and St. Paul, nor in traveling to pass a week or fortnight of more genuine and constant enjoyment."[383]

But sugar tongs or no sugar tongs, the excursion of 1854 was by far the most brilliant event of its kind that the West had ever witnessed. Millard Fillmore declared it to be one for which "history had no parallel, and such as no prince could possibly undertake." Bancroft dwelt at length on the easy and agreeable manner in which more than a thousand people had been conducted a greater distance than from New York to Liverpool. The Chicago *Tribune* described the trip as "the most magnificent excursion, in every respect, which has ever taken place in America."[384]

On June 23, 1854, the New York *Tribune* urged travelers to follow "in the wake of the just completed Railroad Excursion, ascend the Upper Mississippi, the grandest river of the world, flowing for a thousand miles between shores of incomparable beauty — the boundaries of States destined to wealth, population and power almost without rivals in the Union." Miss Sedgwick observed that as a result of the completion of the railroad to the Mississippi, "the fashionable tour will be in the track of our happy 'excursion party, to the Falls of St. Anthony.' The foreign traveller must go there, and the song of the bridegroom, to many a 'Lizzie Lee' will be 'Ho! For the Falls of St. Anthony.'"[385]

In the years that followed, hundreds of excursions were made to this garden spot of the West. Solitary travelers, tired business men and their families, private parties, and various religious, political, and social organizations made pilgrimages to this Mecca of the Upper Mississippi. When the Milwaukee and La Crosse Railroad was completed to the Mississippi in 1858, a similar though less colorful party than that which constituted the excursion of 1854 was conveyed to the Falls aboard the *Northern Belle*, the *War Eagle*, and the *Northern Light*.

During the campaign of 1860 William H. Seward arrived at St. Paul with Charles Francis Adams and his son Charles Francis, Jr. Upon visiting the Falls, Adams complained that the beauty of former years was in danger of being spoiled because the sawmills had drawn off so much water. In the same year the "Governor's Greys," a unit of the Iowa National Guard from Dubuque, generously supplied with fiddles and champagne baskets, made the trip upstream on the *Milwaukee* and downstream on the *Northern Belle*. Four omnibuses and sixteen carriages were required to convey the "Greys" and their ladies to the Falls. Six years later (in 1866) the *Phil Sheridan* and the *Milwaukee* were but two of a score of boats which ran excursions to St. Paul and the Falls of St. Anthony. Probably no other single factor was so important in popularizing the fashionable tour with Easterners as was the grand excursion of the Rock Island Railroad in 1854.[386]

Editors' note: This was published in 1968 as chapter 32, pp. 271–286, in William J. Petersen, *Steamboating on the Upper Mississippi*, as a reprint of the original 1937 version. Reproduced here with the permission of the State Historical Society of Iowa, we have retained the original format and numbering in both the text and the endnotes, although a few punctuation inconsistencies have been standardized.

FOR

BURLINGTON, DAVENPORT,
ROCK ISLAND AND GALENA.

THE NEW AND SPLENDID, **FRIDAY PACKET**, PASSENGER STEAMER

GOLDEN ERA:

CAPTAIN HIRAM BERSIE,

WILL LEAVE FOR ABOVE AND INTERMEDIATE PORTS

On ~~Tuesday~~ the ~~21st~~ instant, at ~~~~ o'clock, ~~~~ M.

For Freight or Passage, having superior accommodations, apply on Board, or to

EEMLE & HAGEN. PRS. ST. LOUIS.

N. RANNEY,
AGENT.

FIGURE 7. *1852 advertisement for the* Golden Era, *captained by Hiram Bersie, who also commanded this boat on the 1854 Grand Excursion. Throughout the mid to late nineteenth and early twentieth centuries, day trips on steamboats were a popular form of entertainment and relaxation. Photo of the original poster from the Putnam Museum, Davenport, Iowa.*

THE EAST LOOKS AT THE WEST
Susan R. Brooker-Gross

Among the prominent people invited on the Grand Excursion were eastern newspaper writers, who documented the excursion for their readers
back home. Most were from near the northeastern home base of Farnam
and Sheffield, the Connecticut contractors of the Chicago and Rock
Island Railroad. By inviting news editors and publishers, the contractors
guaranteed a heightened visibility to northeastern business interests for
the new rail line. One hundred fifty years later, we have the journalists'
accounts of the trip preserved in the newspapers.

Promotional efforts for the entrepreneurs are reflected in the positive
tone of the press reports from the excursion. One summary reads: "You
could see a half dozen editorial pens in full swing, enlightening, I doubt
not, as many different quarters of the country in regard to the excursion,
and presenting very favorable reports of its pleasures and prosperity."[1]
Most of the invited represented commerce-friendly Whig papers of the
Northeast. The Northeast was the most populous part of the nation in
1854 and the seat of commerce, as well as the home of the excursion
hosts. Each newspaper writer was a typical mid-century news gatherer, a
correspondent, "a persona, although usually pseudonymous, who conveyed subjective impressions with an air of authority and confidentiality."[2]

Reading nineteenth-century newspaper accounts can be a joy. We are
too much creatures of the twentieth and twenty-first centuries to be trans-
ported to the past, but the papers give a flavor of the times. The reader
can be diverted into other interesting stories, whether the stories became
historically memorable or not.

Journalists of the nineteenth century have some of the news judgment
of today's journalists. "Man bites dog" is a more likely story than the
reverse, and biases arise from journalists' notions of what is newsworthy.
The mid nineteenth-century press was overtly partisan, and modern concepts of objectivity had yet to emerge.[3] Embellishment would not have
been unprofessional. What concerns us for the purpose of this chapter is

not the accuracy of the accounts, but rather the images of the excursion and of the Upper Mississippi that their writings painted for the readers back East.[4]

Overall, eastern newspaper accounts of the Grand Excursion were a result of writers sharing the same experience and of the conventions of journalism. Interviewing prominent people was not yet a journalistic device, but speeches were often reprinted in full. The labor of typesetting did not deter the correspondents from penning long letters that reflected the personal experience of the "journal-ist." Although telegraphic news by 1854 was common, accounts of the Grand Excursion did not qualify as "breaking news" over the wire. The reports instead were mailed to newspapers and printed in order of arrival, not necessarily in the order of the events.

The similarities in the news coverage included themes that also drew upon the conventions of travel writing. Travel books sought, in part, to entertain the reader, often calling upon the ornamental language of the picturesque, which emphasized the attractive qualities of the natural landscape. In newspaper accounts of the Grand Excursion, rural scenery was described as productive or beautiful or both. Prairies connoted potential agricultural wealth, while the river bluffs were referred to as picturesque and romantic. Urban scenes brought forth praise for sophistication, growth, and prosperity. In addition to landscape descriptions, the travel experience was given much ink, generally with gratitude showered on the railroad entrepreneurs for their excellent accommodations and entertainment. Like the travel books of the era, the writers engaged the readers as would a companion, providing details of the logistics of travel, as well as the sights or events at the destinations.[5] A third theme — linking West and East — garnered fewer words, but carried a powerful message, and underscored the business concerns of the Grand Excursion planners. Amid news stories reminding us that 1854 was a time of national uncertainty, the optimism — or hopeful skepticism — of these mostly Whig writers conveyed the equally powerful message of national integration, of tying West with East.

THE TRIP TO CHICAGO AND THE GRAND EXCURSION

Although the excursion proper began in Chicago, the eastern correspondents also recounted their experiences getting to that point. Contemplating that readers might undertake such trips themselves, the writers provided useful details, evaluating, for example, whether it was better to travel all the way by rail, or to take a steamboat across Lake Erie. One *Boston Advertiser* correspondent described his entire journey: on a Thursday, he started from Boston and went through Springfield to Albany; on Friday night he boarded a lake steamer at Buffalo; on Saturday he arrived in Detroit; and then he journeyed aboard the Michigan Central Rail Road, and arrived in Chicago on Sunday morning.[6]

After reaching Chicago, the writers sought accommodations for the night, not an easy task, since the city was overrun with travelers, a large number of whom seemed to have brought more family members than the planners had anticipated. Many of the more famous stayed in the Tremont Hotel, some in other hotels, while others lodged in private homes. Despite the confusion, the writers praised Chicago, including one from the *Albany Evening Journal:* "The young giant city of the West. [Chicago] . . . is now a full grown Lion, with all a Lion's vigor and strength. . . . It numbers 70,000 now, and has a business which furnishes occupation to all and prosperity to most. Perhaps I cannot better convey an idea of its business than to say that its Lumber trade equals that of Albany."[7]

Other newspapers presented the same themes in their descriptions of Chicago: the excitement and frustration of a crowded city and the idea that it was a growing city likely to rise to join the same class as the eastern cities from which the writers had come. "The prosperity of Chicago promises to prove as substantial as it has been rapid. The situation of the city on the Lake, its railroad radii, its steamboat facilities, and its rich prairies, ensure for it a continuous growth hardly less amazing than that of the last twenty years," wrote a *Boston Evening Transcript* correspondent.[8] The theme of a prosperous city full of promise was replayed in nearly all of the accounts of towns and cities along the excursion route.

The excursion itself was a spectacle, and this spectacle was newsworthy. The writers portrayed the event as much as an opportunity for the excursionists to have a great time as it was for the excursionists to see the destination. It was sometimes more notable that the townspeople at the destination see the excursionists. For example, on leaving Chicago one writer noted, "The morning was fine, and the gay assemblage were in excellent spirits. The locomotives were decked with flags and streamers, and the trains moved off amid the waving of hats and handkerchiefs."[9]

The first landscape that the excursionists saw once out of the city was the famed Illinois prairie. The prairie's vastness and fertility immensely impressed them, as did the possibilities of the land's development. "The

Trains dashed out of the City of Chicago into a broad and beautiful Prairie, the extent and fertility of which excited equal delight and amazement. . . . There is no limit to the Agricultural capabilities of this soil. The tens of thousands of Cattle now feeding upon the Prairies might be indefinitely increased, and these herds *will* be multiplied by thousands."[10] The *Hartford Daily Courant* commented: "Those who for the first time witnessed the beautiful level and rolling prairies of Illinois, were delighted with the view."[11] A similar perspective was given by the *New York Daily Times*: "Scarcely had we left Chicago before the peculiar features of Illinois scenery were presented to us in a series of level and rolling prairies, at first of inconsiderable extent. After passing the first station, Blue Island, a small village containing only some number 50 or 60 frame houses, the prairies began to increase in importance and became more beautiful and impressive."[12]

The very growth and prosperity of the towns along the rail route were credited to the railroad. "About each of these wilderness [railroad] stations, farming villages instantly spring up; so that the road makes the villages wherever it pleases, instead of the villages governing the line and the stations of the road."[13] Predictions of each town's prosperity were common; for example, the "Young men, whether Mechanics or Merchants, settling here [in La Salle], are sure to prosper," according to the *Albany Evening Journal.*[14]

The wealth potential of the prairies coexisted with romantic and picturesque descriptions of an old, settled landscape, although reporters knew that the landscape was, by their definition, newly or not-yet-settled. The *Cincinnati Gazette* reasoned that it was "impossible to convince yourself that this prairie country is new. It looks like an old and highly cultivated grazing land, and in part, like some of the old, magnificent English parks."[15]

Train travel through the countryside ended at the Mississippi River, which provided reporters with their first view of Davenport and Rock Island.

I have been quite amazed at the beauty, size and prospective importance of Davenport. It lies on the Mississippi, with a gradual ascent running from a quarter to half a mile or more back to bluffs, which command some of the finest river prospects that I have ever seen; and when I say this, I have a vivid remembrance of the Hudson and the

Ohio. This city must become not only a great business place, but from the salubrity and attractiveness of its situation, one of great resort for the wealthy and those seeking a pleasant residence. The river here has a rocky bottom; the low land is not overflowed, and there are no wet places to breed miasma. The air from the prairies west of the bluffs is as pure and refreshing as that of the middle of the Atlantic.

Opposite this place, near the Illinois side, is Rock Island, (Old Fort Armstrong) belonging to Government, and the city of Rock Island on the main shore, a place of great promise, and the terminus of the Chicago and Rock Island Railroad. This railroad will connect by a bridge, now in active process of construction, from the Illinois shore across Rock Island and the Mississippi, with the Mississippi and Missouri railroad to Iowa City and thence to Council Bluffs. This great enterprise of *bridging the Mississippi* must, when completed, add incalculably to the importance of this location.[16]

Several themes in this passage emerge repeatedly in the excursion coverage: growth and prosperity of towns and cities; commanding views from the bluffs of the river; comparisons of the landscape of the Upper Mississippi with scenes from the East; productivity of the rural lands; and the role that the railroad was playing in uniting the continent.

Boarding the steamers replayed the chaos of overcrowding that excursionists had experienced in Chicago. The *Boston Evening Transcript* reported that many left the excursion, anticipating that the number of people would be too large for the vessels assigned. Some eastern papers printed accounts of travel downriver to St. Louis, rather than upriver to St. Paul, and the *Chicago Daily Tribune* reported travelers foregoing the river trip to return by rail to Chicago. A number of passengers complained of not having proper accommodations aboard ship, some bitterly. But coverage again praised the hospitality of the excursion planners. "If any slight inconveniences were experienced by those who did not have the good fortune to secure state-rooms, all thoughts of complaint were soon forgotten in the delight and enthusiasms, which the beauties of the country and the quick succession of interesting incidents awoke in the minds of all."[17]

Once on the river, passengers viewing the bluffs recorded romantic and picturesque descriptions[18] such as this one: "High bluffs rose on the Wisconsin bank of the river, — steep, sloping green banks surmounted by perpendicular rocks, which were often so regularly smooth as to appear to be works of art rather than of nature."[19] Invariably, when the steamboats stopped, a climb provided the means to look down upon the river, its banks, and the spreading lands beyond. Reporters often coupled the adjectives "beautiful" and "magnificent" to describe panoramic views afforded by the bluffs' scaling. "From the bluffs of Davenport you have prospects of land and water, of green slopes and sweeps of shore with their delicate rims of sand, which form a succession of views that might long employ the pencil of the landscape painter."[20] Another, reporting from Fort Snelling at the junction of the Minnesota and Mississippi Rivers, declared that the high-angled view displayed a "scenery of singular beauty and agricultural richness."[21]

When presumably virgin landscapes were encountered, they were portrayed as resembling human structures lost in the mists of history. Rock formations resembled ancient castle ruins and the river was compared by many of the writers to Europe's storied Rhine River. The *Hartford Daily Courant* found that "interspersed like fortresses along the stream, majestic rocks rose on the brows of the hills, strongly resembling castles in ruins, moss and ivy grown,"[22] and the *Springfield* (Mass.) *Daily Republican* described "out-jutting rocks that often are so perfectly and symmetrically formed, as to seem to be the ruins of some old castle."[23]

As the river boats made their way up and down the Upper Mississippi, the journalists also took note of the towns, particularly at stops. They commented on the hospitality of the townspeople who provided for their inland excursions and generally cheered them on. Most of the towns were growing and prosperous urban centers. "The most prominent places on the Mississippi, between Dubuque and St. Paul, are Prairie du Chien, and La Crosse, to both of which points railroads are in contemplation from Milwaukie [*sic*]. Those towns are rapidly growing."[24] At "Prairie du Chien, associated in our minds as a frontier outpost to guard against the depredations of the Indians, we found a fine town, situated on a beautiful extended plain of land, with the evidences of a thrifty, flourishing town."[25]

An interest in the extraction of wealth was most evident at Galena. The detailed accounts of lead mining brought together the travel writer's tendency to be instructive with the practical economics of the region.[26] Galena "is surrounded by an agricultural region of great productiveness; but its pre-eminent importance is derived from its deposits of lead, which appear to be inexhaustible. The mineral affords 90 per cent of pure metal."[27] Note that this writer's description also reinforces the typical focus on the productivity of the region.

Despite the size and age difference between the towns and cities of the West and the easterners' hometowns, western towns were sometimes described as flourishing, thriving, and having the potential to rival eastern cities. "These cities, that is, Rock Island, Davenport and Moline, the three constitute the point of a great and most truly beautiful center, are improving rapidly under the effect of the completion of this road, and the whole presents a lively and business-like appearance."[28] The *New York Daily Times* added that "Dubuque, the oldest place in Iowa, was first settled by French Canadians, in the year 1786, for the purpose of trade. It seems to be a pleasant, prosperous city, and, indeed, very much civilized in comparison to many other Western towns."[29]

The other urban endpoint of the excursion was St. Paul, and its emerging sister city, the town at the Falls of St. Anthony, soon to become Minneapolis. Writers noted St. Paul's size and emerging urbanity as it came into view. "Being located just upon a turn of the river, the passengers on the steamboats coming up have a fine view of the front, and upon all of the visitors did it make a fine impression. It contains at present from 5,000 to 6,000 inhabitants, and is increasing every day."[30]

The *Springfield Daily Republican* correspondent estimated fewer inhabitants for St. Paul, but came to the same conclusion that it was a growing and thriving town. "St. Paul, the capital of Minnesota territory which spans the Mississippi river, is a surprisingly-developed town. It is five years old, has 5,000 inhabitants, a magnificent territorial capitol building, larger than any closed edifice in Springfield, four daily newspapers, and many other public and private buildings of solid and expensive structure and great taste of form. The evidences of rich material resource and advancement are most abundant."[31] St. Paul was also praised for its architecture and for being populated by easterners: "The State House is a large and handsome building, and only six years ago the ground on which it stands was covered with Indian wigwams. Many of the families in St. Paul went from the East, and we were told that there is as much intelligence and refinement there as in one of our New England towns of the same size."[32] The description of the smaller town of St. Anthony's Falls (Minneapolis) represents the common descriptions of many river towns: "The village of St. Anthony's Falls is said to contain about 2,500 inhabitants, and seems to be a very flourishing place. I noticed several houses which would have done credit to the oldest town."[33]

A special part of the destination was the river itself. The Upper Mississippi River that figured so prominently in the goals of the trip was mostly described by its banks rather than by its water. When the river water was described, its calmness, its width, and its imposing presence impressed the writers. "Certainly, of all our rivers, the Mississippi is the most imposing, the most picturesque, and the most beautiful."[34]

The excursion occurred during a period when the Mississippi's waters were relatively calm and thus easy to navigate. These conditions encouraged writers to assume that the river was suited to productive use and safe to navigate, and that they could take the waterway for granted as a conveyance. As the *Springfield Daily Republican* put it, "The Upper Mississippi is a clear, bright, quiet stream about one third of a mile wide, and pursues a tortuous course throughout its whole length, occasionally widening into a broad lake, and every where breaking into arms for the embrace of low islands."[35]

COVERING THE LOGISTICS OF THE JOURNEY

The excursionists' own experiences of the journey occupied much of the newspaper ink on the Grand Excursion — the trip's speed and the entertainment and comfort offered along the way. Writers expressed their wonder at the rail line's fast pace. The *Boston Evening Transcript* noted that the train seemed "to pass with almost lightning speed from city to city and village to village."[36] Entertainment came in the form of speeches and dances aboard the steamboats and at stops, and in their reception by the crowds — cheering, fireworks, and cannon firings. The journalists delighted in Fillmore's penchant for giving speeches at every stop and in the fun other excursionists made of Fillmore's behavior: "The Golden Era bore the ex-President Fillmore and his party who addressed the populace at the several stopping places, in such manner as to provoke the doubtless base suspicion that he has fresh hankerings after the flesh-pots of the White House. So, very soon, there were presidential aspirants on other boats, and at every wood-yard or village, these too were called out, and made speeches full of telling points and witty sarcasms."[37]

Comfort resided in two elements: technology that improved the ride, and the hospitality of both the host entrepreneurs and the townspeople greeting them. Two newspapers detailed the technology of a new train ventilation system by documenting the technology of water pumps that kept the dust of the rail journey away from passengers. The newspapers generally praised the trip's accommodations arranged by their hosts.

Even the *New York Daily Tribune*'s chagrin at not having sugar tongs had a positive conclusion. "Everything is very plain; the staterooms are imperfectly furnished, but the berths are roomy; the table is very abundant, but butter-knives and sugar-tongs are not among its luxuries. But those who know how to overlook these little deficiencies cannot hope anywhere to behold nature in such multiform loveliness and grandeur as on the waters of the Mississippi, between Rock Island and St. Paul, nor in traveling to pass a week or fortnight of more genuine and constant enjoyment."[38] Although a *New York Daily Times* writer was also pleased with the accommodations and reception in most places, he did find them objectionable at one stop. This noteworthy *Daily Times'* coverage stands apart as one correspondent's dyspeptic evaluation of the excursion's reception at St. Paul. (It also stands apart in its eloquence!)

At Galena, at Dubuque, at every place we touched during this, our more than Argonautic expedition, the people received us gladly. With firing of cannon they received us — but they fired no cannon at St. Paul's. With garlands of evergreen, and flaunting of banners, they received us — but there were not garlands or banners at St. Paul's. With vehicles, free of charge, to take us into the interior, they received us, giving us champagne into the bargain — but at St. Paul's there was no champagne, (which was a slight fault,) while the vehicles were charged at the following rates: a buggy, to carry two persons to the Falls of St. Anthony, eight miles distant, one hour and a half, mean time, $10; a stage, to convey eight persons, same distance, same mean time, $25. Those charges were a great sin, which will be chronicled against these Minnesota cormorants throughout the United States. Other charges were in proportion. A chewing friend of mine entered a store, chose a paper of tobacco — an ordinary paper, you might have bought it for two cents in New-York — and they kept the twenty-five cents that he threw down, assuring him that there was no change. A drinking friend, requiring some brandy, (to counteract the effects of the Mississippi water,) having a half-dollar in his pocket, placed it innocently on the bar-counter, and beheld it swallowed up by the till, or money-drawer, which yielded back not so much as a half-dime. The Hudson River is nowhere beside the Mississippi, and even the Long Island Yankees, who, after the money-changers that the Saviour whipped out of the Temple, are greediest after lucre, must retire before the people of St. Paul's, or they will be assuredly beaten in the contest. St. Paul's Minnesota, stands alone, unrivalled, unapproached, as the greediest place on all this Western Continent.[39]

The confusion of the reception at St. Paul was attributed by some to the arrival of the party a day before the excursion was expected. Other accounts — including another in the *Daily Times* — complimented the city on handling the early arrival as well as they did.

LINKING EAST AND WEST

The accounts linked the country from the eastern home of the writers to western destinations through rhetoric, politics, and economics. The rhetoric involved comparisons between the newness of the West and the familiarity of the East. The Falls of St. Anthony were compared to Niagara Falls, the Mississippi to the Hudson, and western towns to eastern cities. The *Hartford Daily Courant* noted that "the Falls of St. Anthony bear no comparison to those of Niagara; but they [the falls] have long been celebrated, and till within a few years, a person who had visited them was looked upon as one who had traveled almost to the end of the world. . . . The town of the Falls of St. Anthony . . . is finely located, has a water power equal to that of Lowell, and must eventually become a great manufacturing place."[40]

Politics and economics were also intertwined themes, particularly during these tense antebellum years, when "Union" was a term used freely by (north)eastern journalists. The very line of rails that the excursionists were traveling was one of the latitudinal lines that served both to connect east to west and to split north from south.[41] The railroad connection's orientation conveniently served antebellum political aims. Local booster elites across the northern "west" regarded the rail line as a way to tie their cities and regions to the emerging northern identity.[42] A *Boston Evening Transcript* writer shrewdly noted that "I would hint to those who are in favor of a movement for peopling Nebraska with a population from the North, that the most effectual mode of accelerating immigration to Nebraska is to furnish means for pushing on this railroad to Council Bluffs, which will not only forward their patriotic object, but will pay stockholders ten per cent."[43]

Finally, the excursion as a commercial promotion so profited the Connecticut Yankees behind the railroad that it inspired further hopes of the West's economic expansion. Citing a poem from the *Daily Jeffersonian* (Galena, Illinois), the *Hartford Daily Courant* conveyed the desire for economic and social union:

The East and West have now joined hands; their destiny is one;
And kind and social intercourse between us has begun.
Then like true-hearted Yankees, let's stand up side by side;
And on railroads and steamboats, we'll all take a ride.[44]

Of both political and economic import is the idea that the excursionists were witnessing merely the middle link in the drive to the Pacific. The *Hartford Daily Courant* dedicated space to the discussion, detailing the particular railroads that were likely to form the backbone of the westward drive. "The recent great excursion and Rock Island Railroad Celebration had its object in this connection. One thousand to twelve hundred citizens of the East — embracing capitalists, merchants, contractors, statesmen, geographers and journalists — many of them visiting the West for the first time, came to see — what? *The Proposed Railroad to the Pacific!* And their purses and their pens are henceforth to urge the work unceasingly, until the last rail is laid on the beach of the Pacific!" The *Courant* went on to cite the speech at Davenport by the president of the Chicago and Rock Island Railroad, General Dix, who pointed and claimed, "That is the road to California." [45]

The event most symbolic of all the themes embodied in the coverage of the Grand Excursion is the "mingling of waters," an event covered at length in the *Boston Daily Advertiser*. The narration points both to a bottle of Atlantic Ocean water brought westward by Hamilton Morton of New York and to the party from the *Sparhawk* steamer witnessing the bottle being thrown and smashed against the rocks at the Falls of St. Anthony, thus mingling Atlantic and Mississippi waters. In a speech by Colonel Johnson of the New York State Agricultural Society, reported by the *Advertiser*, Morton

> alluded to the fact that he had himself witnessed the first breaking of ground for the Erie Canal in New York. He was now able to witness the completion of the great work of uniting the seaboard with the Mississippi, which was then begun. He looked forward to the time when ocean should be joined to ocean. He hoped that the meeting of the company in this happy party, would tend to the perpetuation of the Union, which will make this nation the grandest on earth. The union of the salt water of the ocean with the fresh stream of the Mississippi

was a not inappropriate emblem of the harmonious junction of discordant elements which was necessary to the establishment and is essential to the preservation of the Union.[46]

This passage leaves no doubt that the integration of a grand nation underlay the enjoyment of the Upper Mississippi Valley's picturesque and romantic scenery with the entertaining speeches, dances, and fireworks passengers enjoyed along the excursion route. The newspaper accounts made it plain that the midsection of the continent was becoming a productive and prosperous part of the pathway that would unite East with this West, and with the West that lay as yet farther on.

THE FALLS OF SAINT ANTHONY IN 1881.

FIGURE 8. *In 1680 Father Lewis Hennepin was the first European to see these falls, located in present-day Minneapolis. Here in 1854 the Grand Excursionists celebrated the "mingling of the waters," introducing water from the Atlantic Ocean into the Mississippi River. While most of the excursionists had seen bigger falls, particularly Niagara Falls (182 feet high), they were impressed just the same. In 1892 Captain Willard Glazier wrote: "One is not here so completely overwhelmed as when viewing the incomparable Niagara, with its great height of waterfall, its deafening roar, and the lofty character of its scenery. Saint Anthony is more within the grasp of human comprehension, and is therefore looked upon with greater pleasure." He goes on to comment about the estimates of the height of the falls: Hennepin had estimated fifty or sixty feet; Lieutenant Zebulon Pike, "who is more accurate," sixteen and one-half feet; and Glazier's own measure, fifteen feet. Quotes and illustration from Captain Willard Glazier,* Down the Great River; Embracing an Account of the Discovery of the True Source of the Mississippi, *pp. 165–167.*

STEAMING UP THE RIVER
Edwin L. Hill

By the time of the 1854 Grand Excursion, the role of steamboats on the Upper Mississippi River was so clear and well established that the excursion's success necessitated cooperation between rail and steamboat interests. However, the event that the collaboration celebrated, the arrival of the railroad at the river, ironically marked the beginning of the railroad industry's domination over steamboats in this region. Both would prosper in these early boom years, but their fortunes soon diverged.

The first steamboat on western waters was the *New Orleans*, launched on the Ohio River in 1811. Other early boats included the *Western Engineer* in 1819 and the *Virginia* in 1823.[1] The latter was the first to make a round trip between St. Louis and Fort Anthony (later called Fort Snelling) near present-day Minneapolis in 1823. That trip was exploratory and did not directly influence investors or travelers. The Upper Mississippi was treacherous, unpredictable, and largely uncharted. Until the 1840s, steamboats made only one or two trips each year to the Twin Cities' landings, and the infrequency of such travel suggests that it was rarely profitable.

On the Mississippi River system as a whole, steamboat activity was recorded from about 1815, a few years after the launching of the *New Orleans*. At that early date, most of the boats were on the lower river, which had deeper water, larger populations, and more development, as well as better access to ocean ports. The first real surge in upper river activity occurred around 1825, after the voyage of the *Virginia*. Much of this activity involved the carrying of lead to St. Louis from the mines of northeast Iowa, northwest Illinois, and southwest Wisconsin. By the 1850s, the mines were essentially played out and the boats expanded their routes and schedules to meet the demands of a burgeoning immigrant movement and commercial trade.

The 1850s saw a tremendous increase in river shipping. At La Crosse, Wisconsin, for example, boat arrivals increased from 309 in the 1853 season to 1,569 four years later. During the first eighteen days of June 1856,

180 boats arrived, an average of ten per day.² While a fair amount of this increase was in freight, most boats also carried immigrants, as the upriver towns became gateways to settlement farther inland. Charting the movement of these new populations reveals some clear patterns. Immigrants streamed toward the Mississippi River, with Prairie du Chien in Wisconsin, and Rock Island and Galena in Illinois being favorite departure ports.³ These travelers went on to upriver towns and villages, and to larger cities, like the Twin Cities of St. Paul and Minneapolis. Farther south, many of the immigrants arriving at St. Louis opted to travel up the Missouri River. In general, steamboats carried adventurers, Yankee traders, and immigrants westward and northward, spilling them out along the way where they chose to settle or move farther into the hinterland. As towns and villages along the Mississippi grew, many retained the characteristics of the various immigrant groups that settled there. Even now, many of these towns display strong ethnic and cultural histories that date to the steamboat era. The agricultural products from the farms of these settlers, near the river or inland, were in turn shipped downriver on the steamboats.

THE PACKET STEAMBOATS

The most common and versatile boat type on the inland rivers for the period of the 1840s until after the Civil War was the packet. In its early English usage, "packet" referred to the carrying of mail, but these boats were all-purpose vessels that carried freight and passengers along with the mail. These workhorse boats could be either stern-wheelers or side-wheelers (or occasionally center-wheelers) and had at least two decks. Typically, the main deck was used for all manner of goods as well as livestock. Deck passengers, who paid the lowest fares, were quartered here. Such passengers enjoyed no amenities, slept where they could find space, and received little or no attention from the boat crew. Passengers on the upper or cabin decks paid a higher fare and received, at a minimum, basic sleeping quarters and meals. Stories about life on the cabin decks reflect a full range of superlatives and criticisms, with most of the superlatives appearing in company advertising.

Packets, which varied considerably in size and features, were the lifeblood of Upper Mississippi River trade in the mid nineteenth century. Trade was so varied and the demands of service so great that the packet steamer became the classic icon of the river. If we could take a snapshot of the levee of a typical river town during this period, the boats that were depicted would be almost exclusively packets. Many of these boats were built on the Ohio River, although boatyards could be found on numerous large and small rivers during the mid nineteenth century. Most of the Upper Mississippi River boats were, in fact, built on the Ohio River in Indiana and Ohio. Others were built in Wheeling, West Virginia, a major boatyard site, and some in Pennsylvania.

This was a uniquely American boat (although variations appeared in northern Europe and parts of Latin America), which possessed certain features that eased shallow water navigation. It was of shallow draft, usually built to displace no more than four feet on a large boat and sometimes as little as eighteen inches on a small one, with a flexible wood hull, low-pressure condensing steam engines, and a boiler or two. They had one or more cabin decks, a pilothouse, and paddle wheels on the sides or at the stern. The stern-wheeler was the most efficient design for propulsion since the driving paddles were directly behind the boat. The side-wheeler was more versatile and more easily maneuvered, as the wheels permitted the boat to turn more quickly and in a shorter space. One wheel could be reversed so that the boat could be turned almost "on a dime." Proportionately, the packets were about six or eight times as long as they were wide.

Other boat types, rafters and towboats, sometimes were used as ferries; but they were also used for pushing rafts of logs or lumber, and as snagboats or dredges for clearing obstructions from the river. Towboats, which emerged as a distinct type in the 1850s through the modification of packets, were usually stern-wheelers with a heavier deck and hull construction, towing knees at the bow for pushing the rafts, and few (if any) accommodations for passengers.

THE PACKETS OF THE GRAND EXCURSION

Packet steamboats were readily available for the events of the Grand Excursion in 1854. At least five boats were used for the trip from Rock Island to St. Paul. William J. Petersen (in this volume) concludes that seven packets made the trip, although there is disagreement about that number. He cites sources who counted seven boats at Rock Island, but virtually all eyewitness accounts upstream indicate that only five boats continued on the excursion. Nonetheless, seven boats will be discussed here: first, the five that all observers agree made the trip, the *Galena*, the *Golden Era*, the *G. W. Sparhawk*, the *Lady Franklin*, and the *War Eagle*; and second, the two others that Petersen claims also made the trip, the *Jenny Lind* and the *Black Hawk*. In terms of size and architecture, this collection of packets was quite representative of boats from the time.[4]

The *Galena*, a side-wheel packet, was built at Madison, Indiana, in 1854. It displaced 296 tons, had forty-six staterooms, and was captained by D. B. Morehouse during the Grand Excursion. A number of others captained the *Galena* during its four-year life. She burned and sank at Red Wing, Minnesota, on July 6, 1858.

Another side-wheeler, the *Golden Era*, was built in 1852 at Wheeling, West Virginia, with a displacement of 249 tons. Captain Hiram Bersie was in command during the Grand Excursion. It, too, had several other captains during its life span, including Stephen B. Hanks — famous for having created the first log raft in 1844 — who piloted it for a time in 1856. The *Golden Era* also served as a troop transport during the Civil War, making three trips to Vicksburg in 1863, and was dismantled (or abandoned) at New Orleans in 1868.

The *G. W. Sparhawk*, a 243-ton side-wheeler, was built in 1851 also at Wheeling. Although its first homeport was Cincinnati, Ohio, most of its operations were on the Upper Mississippi, where Montraville Green captained it during the Grand Excursion. The boat was either lost in the ice at St. Louis on February 26, 1856, or, according to another account, it sank just below Nininger, Minnesota, not far from St. Paul.

The *Lady Franklin* was a side-wheel packet built at Wheeling in 1850, with a rating of 206 tons. Captain Le Grand Morehouse was in charge for the Grand Excursion. This boat operated mostly on the Upper Mississippi under a number of owners and captains. In 1855, it carried five hundred immigrant passengers on a trip from Galena to St. Paul, with a $12 fare for cabins and a $6 fare for deck passage. It was snagged and sunk at Coon Slough, below St. Paul, on October 23, 1856.

The *War Eagle*, a side-wheel packet, was the longest-lived of the Grand Excursion boats (fig. 9). Built in Cincinnati in 1854, with a rating of 296 tons, it was a famous boat in its day. On June 22, 1861, it left St. Paul with five companies of the First Minnesota Infantry Volunteers destined for military service. It served briefly as a troop transport in 1862 during the Civil War, and operated for a time on the Tennessee River. Among the *War Eagle*'s many captains was Daniel Smith Harris, who was in charge during the Grand Excursion. The boat burned and sank with the loss of several lives at La Crosse on May 15, 1870.

FIGURE 9. *Steamboat* War Eagle *on the Upper Mississippi, 1860s. Built in 1854, this boat led the flotilla of the Grand Excursion and burned at La Crosse, Wisconsin, in 1870. Photo courtesy of Murphy Library, University of Wisconsin-La Crosse.*

The *Jenny Lind* was a smaller boat of 107 tons, and a stern-wheeler. It was built at Zanesville, Ohio, in 1848, and was first operated on the Muskingum River in Ohio. Afterwards, it was used on the Des Moines, Minnesota, and Upper Mississippi Rivers. The *Jenny Lind* went out of service in late 1854, apparently abandoned.

The *Black Hawk* was a small side-wheel packet, built at Rock Island, in 1852. It had a displacement of eighty-three tons. Its small size would have limited its usefulness as a passenger boat during the excursion. The *Black Hawk*'s last recorded appearance was at St. Paul in 1859.

Note that of the seven boats, only one, the *Black Hawk*, was built on the Mississippi River. Six of the seven were side-wheelers, and most ended their service through accidents or abandonment. One did not last the year; two others survived only two more years. Only two, the *Golden Era* and the *War Eagle*, survived into the 1860s. These are typical life spans, however, for boats from that period.

DAILY LIFE ON THE STEAMBOATS

As with other aspects of the American frontier experience, the steamboat era has been romanticized to a high gloss.[5] The boats represented a technological response to a need for transportation in a region made to order for them. They were an absolutely essential mode of transportation. Seldom have the qualities of period, place, and events come so perfectly together as with the inland river steamboat. But they were also dangerous, noisy, often carelessly constructed, and sometimes miserable for those on board. Life on these boats would not appeal to most contemporary travelers, and yet many of us would like to re-create the experience of spending an hour or a day on the *War Eagle* with Captain Daniel Smith Harris.

For first-class passengers on the cabin deck, life was comparatively civilized on the larger steamboats. Travel accommodations here were far more comfortable than that offered by horse-drawn stagecoaches, wagons, or the early railroads. They were civilized — that is, if one did not look into the galley, where food was prepared or at dishwashing or other aspects of sanitation and cleanliness. Dinners of chicken and pork came from creatures taken from pens and slaughtered on deck. One writer remarked that the passage of a chicken from life to dinner plate was so swift that he did not wonder if it was sufficiently cooked; he wondered if in fact it was really dead.[6] On a larger boat, the bakery might welcome visits by passengers. The galley would never invite such visits, for few passengers would keep their appetite.

Drinking water was, like all other water used on board, drawn up over the side in pails. The Mississippi has rarely been noted for its clear, sparkling water (although some early travelers did speak of its clarity), and we may presume that it took some fortitude to drink it from glassware at dinner. The same water, in fact, was used by the boat's boilers, which had to be cleaned often to remove sediment.

Furthermore, toilet facilities on the packet steamers often were simple outhouses perched over the rear of the boats. A larger boat might offer separate outhouses for men and women, but they still tended to be unsanitary after dozens or even hundreds of uses. Even a nearby washstand and towel, for example, proved to be of marginal value.

Passengers who paid deck fare, including virtually all immigrants, could expect far less in the way of attention. Life on the lower deck was not pleasant. Leftover food from the upper decks would be offered first to ordinary crew members and deck hands, then to the deck passengers. Many of the latter carried their own food and hoped it would survive the summer heat, vermin, and the grasp of other passengers. These people were crammed together in a small space with livestock, dogs, and whatever freight was being carried.

River travel sometimes had awful consequences. Immigrants and others risked experiencing deadly scourges of cholera, scarlet fever, diphtheria, and similar illnesses. The sandbars, villages, and miles of shoreline saw many a quick and often nameless burial. It is difficult to imagine that the sleep of deck passengers was peaceful or their days happy, although some accounts do record the wonders of upper river scenery, sunsets, and the diversions of homespun entertainment such as music, dancing, and simple games.

For the captain, pilot, and (on larger boats) higher-ranking officers, life was comparatively good. In fact, a skilled pilot could earn a salary undreamed of by most of his contemporaries. His responsibilities were immense and he usually earned more than the captain. In 1857, for example, a pilot might earn $400 to $500 per month, at a time when a common laborer earned less than a dollar per day. A large boat would have two pilots, working in shifts. If a boat took on more passengers than it could house in the cabins, the captain and officers might give up their own quarters and sleep on the deck, to increase the profits. First mates and other officers, if there were any, would earn perhaps $100 to $200 per month.[7] Deck hands received $50 per month. Ordinary crew members and deck hands slept where they could find space.

While the pilot had ultimate authority for the navigation of the boat, the captain was undisputed ruler of everything else. Because there were good captains and bad ones, crew members often sought better circumstances on other boats. These were a transient lot. The waterfronts of larger river towns saw a constant and brisk negotiation as crew members looked for new jobs. Few records of boat employment exist, and few passenger records were accurately maintained or preserved.

High attrition was a fact of life for Upper Mississippi River steamboats; boats and boat travel were indeed inherently unsafe. Along with the ordinary hazards of sandbars, snags, deadheads, rapids, and rocks, there were fires, boiler explosions, and collisions. In 1983, my analysis of the steamboat data files at Murphy Library, University of Wisconsin-La Crosse, showed that the average life span of a Mississippi River steamboat in the 1811-to-1820 period was five years. By the 1861–1870 period, its average duration had increased to seven-and-one-half years. Few boats survived beyond twenty-five years.

The steamboats used a ferocious amount of wood for their boilers. An average boat might require twenty or twenty-five cords per day and would stop to "wood-up" two or three times daily (fig. 10). The Northwestern

FIGURE 10. *"Wooding Up" on the Mississippi, originally published by Currier & Ives, 1863. Photo of lithograph courtesy of Murphy Library, University of Wisconsin-La Crosse.*

Union Packet Line of La Crosse owned twelve thousand acres of woodland from which approximately 150,000 cords, worth $350,000, were cut annually.[8] Small-operation woodcutters along the shore provided the most wood. Until coal became a primary fuel in the latter part of the steamboat era, the woodlands on either side of the Mississippi River were in many places denuded back to a distance of a mile or more. Over a period of decades, this woodcutting left the shorelines stripped of trees, resulting in both increased erosion and a changed habitat for flora and fauna.

STEAMBOATS AND THE RIVER ECONOMY

Steamboats were so intricately involved in the development of the Upper Mississippi that it is difficult to imagine its history without them. The boats were quite adaptable in their schedules, movement, and destinations, but they required a steady trade in the movement of people and goods. On the upper river, it was a seasonal trade. Winter ice shut down steamboat operations abruptly. The river trade was fiercely competitive and, for its successful operators, extremely profitable. Dependability, reflected by a reliable schedule, was desirable, but given the vagaries of weather, mechanical devices, and events, this was hard to achieve. Formal and impromptu races were held to establish at least a temporary advertising advantage for the faster boats. By the latter half of the nineteenth century the larger companies were more successful in satisfying the needs of customers than the so-called "wildcat" (small company) operations.

During the heyday of the boats, the towns and villages along the river grew, sometimes very rapidly and with considerable prosperity. A town's vitality was often measured by its steamboat activity. Steamboat arrivals, especially after a long, hard winter, were greeted with excitement and relief. After all, the boats brought newcomers and relatives, new fashions from the East, varieties of food, and long-awaited supplies of every kind. They also offered a way out for those who wanted to go farther north, west, or south, or to go home. The return of immigrants to their native countries was more common than is generally understood, and the degree of hardship and loneliness these people endured can hardly be overestimated. Upriver and down, steamboats carried many individuals whose lives and dreams had been hit hard.

For Minnesota and Wisconsin, the opening of the pineries for logging in the 1850s created an entirely new economy, which was quickly exploited by the steamboat companies. Lumber companies advertised for workers in foreign, especially Scandinavian, countries. These laborers brought their families upriver on the boats or, in some cases, from Canadian ports on the St. Lawrence River. Loggers stayed in the woods during the winter and spring, cutting logs for sawmills at many Upper Mississippi towns. Before the 1850s, finished sawn lumber and logs were sent downriver in immense rafts, floated by skilled raftsmen. Later, log rafts were pushed by steamboats, as detailed in Gayle Rein's essay in this volume.

The milling process created huge piles of sawdust that were left along waterfronts. Much of the sawdust eventually went into the river, along with fugitive logs from millponds and rafts that wrecked many a boat. An additional hazard was introduced in the mid 1850s when railroad companies began to build bridges over the Mississippi River. A bridge posed considerable difficulty to a steamboat pilot, especially where bends, tricky currents, and a row of pilings coincided.

The Grand Excursion of 1854 occurred at an auspicious time for Mississippi River steamboating. River towns were growing rapidly and steamboat companies were vying for a seemingly limitless trade. There was a fervor associated with steamboating that lasted for several more decades despite national recessions and the Civil War.

Steamboat companies, many of which underwent the same kinds of mergers and monopoly schemes we see today, consequently prospered.

By the 1860s, the up- and downriver trade was substantial, especially the carrying of agricultural products. In 1866, for example, the Northwestern Union Packet Line carried five million bushels of wheat downriver, 150,000 barrels of flour, and 200,000 pounds of hides, among other things. River ice was also shipped downriver, with St. Louis a major destination. Upriver, this line carried coal, iron, salt, and cement. Once the railroads crossed the river, however, virtually all grain was shipped by rail. There was no further need to transfer the grain to boats, which eliminated an expensive step and ended nineteenth-century grain shipping on the Upper Mississippi by 1879.[9]

In the 1850s — but especially after the Civil War — various river interests lobbied for and secured river improvements. The war had boosted the government's involvement in national transportation plans, resulting in improvements on the Upper Mississippi such as dredging to a four-foot channel in the 1860s, to four-and-a-half feet in the 1870s, and more wing dams in that latter decade. Wing dams force the current into a central channel, scouring the bottom and creating a more consistent depth, which eases boat travel. Such dams were enhanced, and their numbers increased, until well after the beginning of the twentieth century. Many wing dams are still present, and pose a formidable hazard for large and small boats that wander too far from the main channel.

THE DECLINE OF STEAMBOATING

The end of the Civil War in 1865 also represented the beginning of the end for steamboats. The war spurred expansion of the railroads, which enjoyed the growing support of the federal government for the movement of men and materiel. Federal land policies encouraged the building of tracks across the plains and through the Rocky Mountains. Furthermore, the railroads operated all year and ran on more convenient schedules. They dominated the east-west paths, whereas the Mississippi River boats operated on an essentially north-south path. The steamboat companies well understood the threat of the railroads and their conflicts were frequent and often bitter. Eventually, some of the railroads bought steamboat companies so that passengers would pay the same owners regardless of the conveyance. Although the railroads were not the only reason for the demise of the steamboats, they were a major factor.

During the second half of the nineteenth century, the frontier had moved farther west and Mississippi River towns settled into a comfortable routine, enjoying a growing industrial prosperity and often a diverse economy. Lumbering thrived until the 1890s, when the pine forests began to disappear rapidly. By the turn of the century, the great pineries of Wisconsin and Minnesota were nearly exhausted, so much so that most of the region's sawmills were closed by 1910. Many lumber companies moved south or west, and rafting all but disappeared. The milling and shipping of flour and other grain products, however, flourished, and machine factories became influential in river towns. The Mississippi supported other river-related industries such as pearl-button factories, fishing, ice production, and quarrying.

Yet the growth rate in boat activity had begun to taper off much earlier, around 1855, just after the Grand Excursion. Generally falling over time, activity peaked again in about 1865 and also in the 1870s, but fell sharply in the 1880s. The resurgence that occurred in the 1870s did not, however, represent activity by the classic steamboat. The packets were disappearing rapidly. Some entered a growing excursion trade, but most were converted into towboats, which became the dominant steamer of the period. Mostly stern-wheelers, these towboats actually pushed rather than "towed" barges, just like the powerful river towboats of today.

The conversion of a packet to a towboat required reinforcement of the wood hull and installation of "towing knees" (heavy, braced, upright posts for pushing) at the bow. By the 1880s, therefore, freight was most commonly carried on barges rather than on the boat itself. In addition to older converted boats, new steam towboats — most of them side-wheelers — were being constructed to meet the demand. Even as late as 1900, eighty-six side-wheelers, nearly half of the steam towboats still in service, were in the barge trade.[10] The earlier dominance of the stern-wheel towboat had dwindled considerably.

Freight traffic on inland rivers changed as the nation's economy changed and as railroads came into prominence. The tonnage of lumber dropped by 94 percent between 1889 and 1906. During the same period, grain (which had been a major revenue source for upper river boats), ice, and iron ore tonnage also decreased substantially. Tobacco shipments, however, increased by 311 percent; stone, sand, and gravel by 1,147 percent; and petroleum and other oils by over 10,000 percent.[11]

The nation was moving at a faster pace by now, using alternatives to the sometimes rickety but often graceful steamboats on the great river. Stern-wheel boat construction declined rapidly after 1880, while side-wheeler construction remained strong for at least another decade. The actual number of working steamboats on the upper river increased during the 1880s as new boats were added to those already in service, but declined thereafter. Records indicate 226 registered steamboats in 1889, 187 in 1895, and 197 in 1900. This compares to estimates of 100 to 150 boats in the 1860s and 1870s. As the new century approached, most of the new boats were smaller but more powerful than their predecessors. By 1906, propeller-driven towboats and steel barges were becoming common, but there were still many working steamboats on the river, as well as 166 steamers classed as "idle." Even at this late date, steamboats handled over 25 percent of all river freight tonnage.[12]

Although oil fields in Pennsylvania had been in production since midcentury or earlier, petroleum as a fuel source for Mississippi River boats did not come into popular use until the oil fields of Louisiana were developed after about 1905. With cheap petroleum fuel now available on the Mississippi, the internal combustion engine and the screw propeller-driven boats began to overtake the paddle wheelers in numbers. Through the early twentieth century, steel boat hulls replaced wood hulls, and the steel barge became the conveyance of choice for river freight transportation as it is today.

The U.S. Army Corps of Engineers created a six-foot channel for navigation in the early twentieth century. Then in the 1930s, the lock and dam system was installed on the upper river to create the present-day nine-foot channel, accommodating larger barges and greater loads for the shipment of commodities. This system changed the upper river forever; generally widening it while covering large tracts of agricultural land and modifying the waterfronts of many towns. Today, the Great River Road follows this course of towns, often separating town from water with a highway. Some of these towns are returning to their river heritage with parks and walkways on the waterfront, along with festivals and occasionally exhibitions of excursion paddle-wheeler replicas.

Tourism had been popular from the beginnings of upper river travel and by the mid nineteenth century was becoming a sturdy source of revenue for boat companies. Northern cities and resorts promoted the health benefits of a grand summer tour to Minnesota or Wisconsin. By the early 1900s, the river excursion trade again picked up speed in response to the growing interest in tourism and travel.

Well into the twentieth century, large excursion steamboats visited the upper river towns and cities, providing day trips for parties and organizations, dances, and a venue for the new jazz music that had worked its way upriver from New Orleans. Among the boats still functioning after 1900 were the *President*, the *G. W. Hill*, the *Capitol*, and the *J. S. Deluxe*. Not all of these steamboats have disappeared. Some, like the *Geo. M. Verity* at Keokuk, Iowa, have become museums, and a few still function as day excursion steamers. The *Idlewild* was built for the Upper Mississippi excursion trade in 1914 and made frequent stops at many towns. It was later renamed the *Avalon* and, since 1962, has settled into a magnificent dotage as the excursion boat, *Belle of Louisville,* at the levee at Louisville, Kentucky. It has a splendid whistle that will rattle the ribcage at close range. Another notable exception is the famous excursion steamer, *Delta Queen*. Assembled in California in 1926, this floating National Historic Landmark is still very much alive on the Ohio and Mississippi Rivers. The *Delta Queen* remains a visible reminder of the steamboat era on today's river.

Looking back at those decades of early immigration and development on the upper river, and at the emergence of the inland river steamboat as a means of transportation, one can almost imagine a master plan — a felicitous union of an invention with a time and place. At its foundation, however, was the simple, powerful fact of the Mississippi River. It centered the young nation, cleaving it as both barrier and promise, offering places to go and ways to get there. It drew upon a tributary system of over 15,000 miles. If we cannot forget the steamboats in our national memory, it is because they are unforgettable. The sound of a steamboat whistle stirs us even if we have never heard it before. A ghost sound, it rumbles in us and takes us back. It could take us nearly anywhere.

FIGURE 11. *Cass Street Bridge and the* Delta Queen, *La Crosse, Wisconsin. The Cass Street Bridge was built in 1939 and heralded as the "no delay" bridge. The* La Crosse Tribune *(2 January 1939) reported that "it was designed to meet the anticipated traffic demands to the year 2014." This bridge replaced the old Mt. Vernon Street Wagon Bridge, which had opened on July 4, 1891. A toll was charged until 1919. Information from Gene Purcell, "When a Bridge Tumbles Down." Photo by Curtis C. Roseman, 2000.*

THE PICTURESQUE MISSISSIPPI
Patrick Nunnally

In 1854, when the Grand Excursionists went upriver, the Mississippi was hardly unknown territory, nor was it wilderness. Native people had lived along the river for centuries and European American villages, farms, and trading posts had been established for a hundred years or more. The Upper Mississippi marked the leading edge of white settlement, anchored by the old French city of St. Louis. Lead mines had worked productively at Galena, Illinois, and Dubuque, Iowa, for some twenty years; Minnesota was still a territory and would not become a state for another four years. Still, what the excursion passengers saw and described was perhaps influenced more by what they had read about the river and about landscapes — what they *thought* they saw — than by the landscapes actually passing by. What they described was a picturesque landscape, containing very particular elements organized in a distinctive manner and emphasizing the attractive qualities of the natural landscape, particularly those featuring hills, woods, and rivers.

Catherine Sedgwick's piece in *Putnam's Monthly* offers a good window into the descriptive flights of fancy by the Grand Excursionists. She wrote of the bluffs: "They are planted, quite to their summits, with oaks mainly, and trees of other species, as Downing with his love of nature and his study of art, might have planted them: now in long serpentine walks, and now in copses, and then, so as to cover, with regular intervening clear spaces, the whole front of the declivity, producing the effect of a gigantic orchard."[1] For Sedgwick, the landscape of the Mississippi was a composition of particular forms laid out according to specific designs to achieve an intended look. The oak-savanna hillsides appeared to her as if they had been laid out according to the artistic theories popularized by Andrew Jackson Downing, a well-known landscape gardener of the era. For her, then, the unfamiliar landscape became recognizable. Consequentially, she could speculate on the landscape's future as a place of wealth and civilization.

Sedgwick's article raises critical issues of landscape aesthetics and the connections between how a landscape is perceived and how it is treated. This essay explores those issues by examining descriptions of the Mississippi written before and after the Grand Excursion. First, though, it is important to understand the idea of the picturesque that informed Sedgwick's view so heavily.

THE PICTURESQUE

Catherine Sedgwick's comparisons between the landscape of the Upper Mississippi and an orchard planted according to the dictates of art place her squarely in an aesthetic tradition that dates back to eighteenth-century England. Writers such as Edmund Burke, William Gilpin, and Uvedale Price reoriented discussions of art — and of landscapes — in two particular ways. First, they focused on the emotional effects that art had on viewers, rather than the moral, political, or religious lessons that could be derived from a work of art. Second, by using landscape paintings as the basis for their theory, they established extremely close ties between art and the physical landscape. Landscape — scenery in nature — was to be judged according to the same rules of composition, color, and light as were paintings. Indeed, paintings taught people how to see and appreciate the landscapes to which they were increasingly exposed. If a traveler saw a landscape that looked like a painting, it was appreciated and understood as "scenery." If it did not resemble a painting, for whatever reason, it was not "scenery," and was considered ugly, monotonous, or worse.

Burke's essays, published in 1760, coined new terms such as the "sublime" and "beautiful" for the appreciation of landscape art. For Burke, the sublime evoked emotions of awe and terror, while the beautiful summoned more pleasing emotions of peace and harmony. The English parson William Gilpin, who in 1782–1805 published several volumes that described his journeys throughout the scenic parts of Great Britain, coined the term "picturesque" as a mediating framework between Burke's sublime and beautiful. According to Gilpin, the picturesque stirred emotions and excitement, but not actual terror. Picturesque landscapes were rougher, less polished than beautiful landscapes, but they were comprehensible and manageable in scope and scale rather than awe-inspiring. Picturesque scenes were pleasing, rather than terrifying, but were exciting rather than peaceful. For Gilpin, landscapes were always regarded as scenes — as compositions that could be assessed in terms of their formal characteristics — and he intended that his writing educate travelers on how to recognize those scenes and thus gain more enjoyment from their travels. Gilpin's writing instructed his audience on how to regard the beauty of a landscape. For example, he wrote that river views have four "grand parts": "The area, which is the river itself; the two side-screens, which are the opposite banks, and lead the perspective; and the front screen, which points out the winding of the river."[2]

The third key figure who helped to develop the aesthetic of the picturesque was Uvedale Price, a landowner and author. He took the notion of the picturesque and used it as a standard against which to evaluate the construction of new landscapes. By this time, the early nineteenth century, England had been swept by a wave of large-scale landscape alterations. Large landowners began to realize that they could alter most aspects of their holdings to make them more pleasing. Villages were moved, streams diverted, trees planted, and artificial ruins constructed on dozens of estates that embodied the modern English landscape style of the early nineteenth century. For Price, the picturesque represented the highest aspiration of the English-designed landscape, and became the desired standard for constructed landscapes. Price's importance was that he extended Gilpin's views into principles for physically transforming landscapes. Gilpin's informed traveler, who transformed the landscape through imaginative application of the "picturesque eye," never actually made landscapes. Price made the aesthetic of the picturesque into a framework that could be acted upon, and the great English landscape gardens — artificial landscapes made to look natural — were the results.

The notions of the picturesque traversed the Atlantic in books and through travelers' accounts. Among those who read the tracts was Andrew Jackson Downing, a young nurseryman in the Hudson River Valley of New York. Downing was so captivated by the picturesque that he began a career in the 1840s as a landscape designer and writer. He argued that the picturesque was the ideal style for landscapes and houses in the new country estates then beginning to pop up outside New York and Philadelphia. Downing's works captured a wide audience and his influence has proved far richer than is suggested by the relatively small number of estates that he actually designed.

Downing's written works were didactic in nature, designed to teach his audience how to achieve the best picturesque effects. It was implicit, Downing argued, that because the landscape could be shaped by art, landscape design was an art form itself, a practice Downing referred to as "Landscape Gardening." "The Picturesque in Landscape Gardening," he

pointed out, "aims at the production of outlines of a certain spirited irreg-
ularity, surfaces comparatively abrupt and broken, and growth of a somewhat wild and bold character. The shape of the ground sought after, has its
occasional smoothness varied by sudden variations, and in parts runs into
dingles, rocky groups, and broken banks."[3] He then offered elaborate
instructions on how to achieve these effects. Downing's message was clear:
The picturesque, with its particular compositional elements, could be created through the wise application of landscape gardening principles.

Downing was a man of his times, for the 1840s and 1850s saw many
efforts to identify what was distinctly "American" about the culture that
was springing up in the new United States. Downing's collections of essays
went through numerous editions very rapidly, and scholars have suggested that every well-furnished country home had a copy of one of his
books. By the time of his death in a steamboat accident in 1852, Downing had truly become an "apostle of taste" to the growing American pro-
fessional classes.[4]

By the middle of the nineteenth century, then, travelers sought the
emotional effects of contact with wild, rugged (but not fearsome) landscapes. They sought the stimulation of varied, surprising landscapes without the threat of becoming overwhelmed by what they saw. They sought,
in other words, landscapes that could be tamed and put to improved
human use, yet that retained a sense of natural vitality that would stimulate viewers and remind them that they were in North America — a newer,
bigger, wilder place than Europe. Downing — and through Downing,
Gilpin and Price — influenced these travelers. Their work taught that
these landscapes were picturesque. Also, in places where a scene was not
naturally picturesque, they learned that the application of the principles
from art could make it so. This artful application helped to create Central Park in New York City along expressly picturesque lines in 1858, and
the picturesque became an important way to see and appreciate the
Upper Mississippi River for the next half-century or more.

THE PICTURESQUE ON THE MISSISSIPPI

The picturesque was neither the only sight or experience that travelers to the Upper Mississippi described, nor the only framework for their
descriptions of a sense of place. But as an affective framework which has
powerful connections to how a place should be treated this is indeed an
important lens through which to look at early descriptions of the river.

For through these texts, the reader saw the river itself. In the literally hundreds of travel narratives about the new United States written during the early and mid nineteenth century, the Mississippi River figures largely. Perhaps only Niagara Falls is more commonly discussed. "Romantic" and "picturesque" became practically interchangeable terms in these descriptions of the great river.

The picturesque became a basis for travelers' descriptions of the Upper Mississippi almost as soon as there was extensive travel in the region. In 1823, the *Virginia*, the first steamboat to reach Fort Snelling, located between present-day St. Paul and Minneapolis, carried among its passengers an expatriate Italian, Giacomo Beltrami. Beltrami's published journal of his trip established the picturesque nature of the Mississippi in travel writing. Beltrami compared the blufflands of the river to the Rhine when he noted that "from this spot (118 miles above Prairie du Chien) a chain of mountains, whose romantic character reminds one of the valley of the Rhine, between Bingen and Coblentz, leads to the *Mountain which dips into the water* [Trempealeau]."[5] The Upper Mississippi, most particularly the blufflands between what is now Dubuque and the widening of the river known as Lake Pepin, evoked comparisons to the Rhine and the Hudson for decades.

Beltrami also placed himself squarely in the picturesque aesthetic tradition when he compared nature to art. "It would be difficult anywhere to find a picture in which the pleasing and the romantic predominate with such delightful alternation, and such perfect harmony," he wrote. "One would think that it had been designed by art aided by the resources of nature, or by nature aided by the devices of art."[6] Not only does he regard the scenery of the upper river as a "picture," but one so skillfully composed that it is hard to tell what is artifice and what is nature.

Other writers deployed the picturesque in greater or lesser measure in their tour books and guides. As English professor M. H. Dunlop has observed, the picturesque served as a "familiarization" device, or organizing principle, to help visitors make sense of the new landscapes they were seeing.[7] For many travelers who wrote about their journeys in America during the middle part of the nineteenth century, much of the country was explicitly not picturesque. The endless miles of deep woods, vast prairies, and even the huge (to European eyes) Ohio and Lower Mississippi Rivers were bleak and "awful," not capable of inspiring emotions other than fear or dread. In that light, we should be cautious in our understanding of how truly picturesque the Upper Mississippi really was and instead examine other related issues, such as what specific elements attracted the notice of travelers and what observing stance they assumed.

George Featherstonehaugh, an English-born geologist who traveled the river in the mid 1830s, made many caustic observations about the manners and customs of the people he came into contact with along the river. As a geologist, he viewed topography relatively unemotionlly, but he did recognize a pictorial landscape when he saw one: "The river [Wisconsin] here was studded with charming little islands; on our right the hills came down close to the water, and we had a beautiful cloudless morning, smiling on the most placid of streams. The picture presented one of the finest subjects for a landscape painter, and I was tempted to stop a moment to enter a slight sketch of it in my portfolio."[8]

Artist Henry Lewis, writing in a journal of his 1848 trip, described Lake Pepin thusly:

> The view from the top of the mountain well repays the exertion of the climb. Four hundred feet below the astonished spectator the lake lies like an immense mirror, extending for miles, its surface scarcely troubled by tiny ripples. . . . City dwellers need go no farther than this if they seek romantic solitude; for in the whole expanse visible from this place, hardly one little house can be seen, and on the bosom of the mighty stream perhaps one small canoe. The song of the birds which flutter in the trees below, the humming of insects, and the soft murmur of the stream were the only sounds that broke the deep stillness around us.[9]

Here, the traveler's stance as spectator and the distant view seen from a high vantage point both recall the standards of picturesque travel writing as exemplified by Gilpin. The notation of stillness and solitude also are common in this genre. Of course, we have no way of knowing how representational their word pictures were — how likely was it that stillness instead of the whistle of the steamboat or the calls of raftsmen and keelboatmen would be what was actually heard? How likely was it that only one little house would be seen from any given point along the river at that time? Exact depiction, however, was not Lewis's goal. He aimed rather to create a feeling, an emotion engendered by contact with this landscape. Figure 12 offers a visual analogue, also by Lewis. Note the strongly vertical nature of the bluffs and the depiction of rocks in the foreground to

FIGURE 12. *"Maiden Rock, der Werona Felsen," by Henry Lewis, 1858. Picturesque landscapes were popular subjects for nineteenth-century writers and artists along the Upper Mississippi River. Photo of the drawing from the Minnesota Historical Society.*

break the expanse of water. Rather than evaluate this drawing for how it exactly represents the scene, we should understand the conventions and expectations of the painters and writers with whom Lewis worked.

The Swedish author Fredrika Bremer, writing in 1850, was explicitly picturesque in her description of the region. "A glorious morning, as warm as summer! . . . and bold, abrupt shadows, and heavenly lights played among the yet bolder, more craggy, and more picturesque hills. What an animated scene it was! . . . naked, ruin-like crags, of rich red brown, representing fortifications, towers, half-demolished walls, as of ancient, magnificent strongholds and castles. The castle ruins of the Rhine are small things in comparison with these gigantic remains of primeval ages."[10] For Gilpin, the ruins in the landscape were castles, churches, and monasteries dating back to England's medieval period, but the visualization of natural landforms as resembling ruins was common in European descriptions of the region. The assessment of landforms as "gigantic" and "primeval" also became common descriptive terms used by European viewers. Bremer, a well-read intellectual, faithfully re-depicted these scenic terms in her accounts of the Upper Mississippi.

A writer for the *New York Daily Tribune* along on the Grand Excursion of 1854 gave an extensive description of the river that is steeped in the conventions of the picturesque and merits being quoted at length.

> Certainly, of all our rivers, the Mississippi is the most imposing, the most picturesque, and the most beautiful. . . . Magnitude with the most delicate finish, grandeur of outline with exquisite beauty of detail, are the characteristics of its scenery. The broad and powerful stream is broken by frequent islands all covered with dense foliage . . . and bordered by lofty bluffs, far more beautiful than the Palisades of the Hudson, riding in every fantastic variety of form, with abrupt and craggy rocks in front, . . . that break the continuity of this river wall and give constant change and delight to the beholder. These hills all wear the aspect of old cultivation; and the groves of oak that dot their smooth surface, scattered along their sides or perched like orchards on their summits, have nothing wild and favor the illusion. The rocks that form the foundation of the bluffs . . . tower perpendicularly and broken, in the form of ancient walls, or castle battlements so that the very Rhine does not seem more historic in its appearance.[11]

In this account rocks resemble castles, the Rhine pales in comparison to the present scene, and the beholder is "delighted" by the constant variety in the scenery, particularly the "abrupt" and "craggy" rocks. The hills, though wild, do not appear so, but rather as orchards planted with the "aspect of old cultivation." Although the place being described does not have a long "history," as that term might be conventionally understood, this viewer's "picturesque eye" (to use Gilpin's expression) transformed it into a landscape steeped in history and meaning. The influence of the picturesque allowed the *Daily Tribune* writer to make sense of the new, even if that sense distorted the human and natural reality of the place.

The point is not to read these accounts strictly for the accuracy of their vision so much as for the emotive qualities they convey and the implications of those emotions. For example, nineteenth-century writers on the Upper Mississippi rarely mentioned the area's Native American inhabitants, who resided there at the time. Writers who did, such as Bremer, regarded them as objects of a half-fascinated, half-horrified wonder, savages who in her estimation were inevitably being replaced by the "better opportunities" of economic development brought by Americans and Europeans. Indeed, small straggling towns and settlements were typically seen only for their potential to grow into wonderful cities. Other implications were more subtle. The picturesque relied almost strictly on the visual senses — things that were not seen were not noticed, and consequently were not valued or esteemed. Observers rarely wrote about, for example, what plants and animals grew or lived in the region. Planners and resource managers can only guess, then, at what flora or fauna originally existed here and at what changes to the natural world have come about due to our presence. Conversely, travel writers tended to overemphasize certain sights over others, giving the impression that the whole Upper Mississippi was a series of beautiful bluff lands, with hardly any flat areas.

Authors who have described place in attractive terms have greatly impacted its land policy and planning. John Muir's essays on Yosemite spurred Congress to create a national park; the Sierra Club's coffee-table books have opened countless wild places to the scrutiny and interest of people who may never go there; and nature writings have often inspired passion and action to protect natural landscapes. Aesthetics and policy are inextricably interconnected in our environmental and natural resource history and policy. For better than a century, travel writing that incorporates a picturesque frame of reference has been important to environmental policy.

The picturesque, of course, was closely associated with the development of landscape architecture and was the dominant aesthetic of place-making in the nineteenth century until the modernist aesthetic superseded it in the mid twentieth century. As landscape architect Ethan Carr has demonstrated so clearly, the aesthetics of the picturesque governed the work of landscape architect Frederick Law Olmsted and others in creating landscape parks, like New York City's Central Park, in urban areas.[12] The first national parks likewise were shaped powerfully by the picturesque. So pervasive is the aesthetic that we no longer recognize the artifice in how national park "scenes" have been arranged for our viewing. What we think of as a park is a picturesque composition as surely as are early-nineteenth-century landscape paintings. But it is also the case that we seek the picturesque in landscapes not so explicitly designed.

THE PICTURESQUE TODAY

This pattern is emerging on the Upper Mississippi as well. Scrutiny of the literature of the river shows how dominant the aesthetic of the picturesque remains. Here's Jonathan Raban, an English travel writer who boated solo down the river in 1979: "The forest which rims it [the river] is a long, looping smudge of charcoal. You could make it by running your thumb along the top edge of the water, smearing in the black pines and bog oaks. . . . Somewhere in the picture there is the scissored silhouette of a fisherman from the town, afloat between the islands in his wooden pirogue, a perfectly solitary figure casting into what is left of the sun."[13] A solitary figure, at peace on the river, contrasts with all the sordidness, mean-spiritedness, and lowbrow culture Raban so relentlessly defines on shore. The scene, again, is pictorial, a visual composition that is pleasing in part because it resembles a painting.

For Raban, as for nineteenth-century travelers, the picturesque was a transforming aesthetic allowing him to make sense of a landscape he saw but did not understand. Raban came to the Mississippi hoping to find rejuvenation by coming into the landscape that had moved him as a boy reading *The Adventures of Huckleberry Finn*. Throughout his trip, he was disappointed in the people and places that did not match his preconceived notion of the place brought to him through literature. But the places that did fit, those that could be described pictorially through the conventions of the picturesque, brought him deep satisfaction. Ultimately, he always moved beyond these places and never really came to understand the landscapes that he simply regarded as "scenes."

Although Raban's experience and writing are particular, of course, review of the recent travel literature about the river reveals a striking pattern: we still see with Sedgwick's eyes. A century and a half after her trip upriver, we still have not found a good way to describe what we value in the landscape of the Upper Mississippi River in terms other than hers. Scenes that offer hills and water, with perhaps a small house or historic building tucked away into the vegetation, continue to be attractive to many writers of the Upper Mississippi. One could read dozens of travel narratives about the river that have been written since the mid twentieth century and not learn much about the region's cities, the river's role in transporting agricultural products, or the river's changing ecology.

What do cities, transportation, and ecology have to do with aesthetics? What place do these concepts have in a discussion of the picturesque? Simply this: Cities, transportation, and ecology are vital components of the river's future. Indeed, some have argued that the future of the river depends on how these three components of the landscape will be developed. Yet if the Upper Mississippi is only recognized as a picturesque landscape, then important parts of those components are overlooked, perhaps even ignored. Sedgwick's vision is not clear enough to understand the river's future.

FIGURE 13. *The text on the reverse of this postcard reads: "A breath-taking view is seen from Barn Bluff, known as Mount La Grange, when looking down on the high bridge, a free bridge between Red Wing and Wisconsin which provides one of the few means of free direct communication. This is an important tourist attraction in Red Wing." Here are two tourists seeking the "picturesque" from a prime overlook on the river. This bridge was replaced by the current bridge in 1960 and dedicated by President Eisenhower, after whom the new bridge was subsequently named. From a postcard by E. C. Kropp Co., Milwaukee, Wisconsin.*

TOWNS TO VISIT
SIGHTS (SITES) TO SEE
John A. Jakle

"What is to become of this great valley of the Mississippi, which already possesses the last physical achievements and results of civilization, railroads, telegraphs, aqueducts, and gaslights?" So asked Catherine M. Sedgwick in an article entitled "The Great Excursion to the Falls of St. Anthony" published in September 1854 in *Putnam's Monthly*.[1] That, of course, was the kind of question that excursion promoters hoped would be answered mainly in superlatives. Was not the Upper Mississippi Valley poised to become a prosperous new Eden as the energizing activities of frontier expansion fully overswept the area? Was not the region about to be fully "opened" to American society's persistent advance? Certainly, the coming of the railroad was prophetic in this regard. So also were the towns and cities already established on the basis of steamboat connectivity. In 1854, the region's urban infrastructure was very much oriented to the river. From Davenport and Rock Island north to Dubuque, Iowa, towns were numerous and well established, the largest very much citylike in size and in function, and certain to be reinforced through future railroad building. But, as *Putnam's* correspondent observed: "After leaving Dubuque, we saw no more towns of magnitude till we reached our terminus at St. Paul." Thus, beyond Dubuque, appraising the region was very much an exercise in prophecy. What were the most likely sites for town development? And what would those places be like?

Towns were civilizing places in frontier America. They connected isolated localities to a larger world beyond. It was through a town that a locality's agricultural products were sent to market and where, in return, manufactured and other commodities from afar were distributed. The economic, political, and social energies that combined to create a potentially progressive and powerful nation were concentrated in its towns. Urban places were networked, cities and towns of various sizes related hierarchically in an urban system. Big cities were more than just overgrown small towns. They replicated the general functions of lesser places while having, exclusively to themselves, various highly specialized functions. Enjoying the benefits of large scale, city merchants, at the top of the urban hierarchy, organized economic activities across great distances, assembling and distributing goods and administering services through lesser places. Small town merchants, for their part, were confined largely to developing local trade hinterlands. Urban activities were sheltered by, and thus symbolized by, physical infrastructure: the telling linkages of urban connection playing out in the number, scale, and elegance of retail stores, warehouses, and factories, and the look of stylish houses, churches, government buildings, hotels, and theaters, among other landmarks.

What was it that travelers taking the Grand Excursion noted regarding the Upper Mississippi's towns? What stood out as significant? And what was it that subsequent observers saw following the same route in later decades? Such are the questions I ask. I organize my essay as follows. First, I provide an overview of both the functional and the morphological growth of river towns along the Upper Mississippi. Second, I outline how travelers tended to typify or stereotype towns along the river, especially the smaller places of little consequence. Third, I consider what travelers remarked upon as unique, especially in the larger places, as they tried to get beyond mere stereotyping through their search for a sense of place. I rely on written narratives published by late-nineteenth-century travelers in books or in magazine articles. I also utilize a selection of engraved prints to reinforce their words. It is important to note that my comments relate not only to what existed to be observed, but also on what, once observed, was deemed important enough to report.

OVERVIEW

Small towns loomed large in the collective American imagination in the late nineteenth century. Although many Americans idealized the family farm as the place where American democracy located its roots — especially in images of landowning, independent farmers tilling the soil — life on the farm was very much organized around urban institutions. Small-town life provided an emotional anchor midway between the farm, the idealized base of opportunity and success for the masses, and the city, where more and more Americans were actually working on factory, office, or sales floors. Although the American frontier tended to be conceptualized as fundamentally pastoral, small towns were actually on the vanguard of frontier expansion.

Part of the frontline networking strategy on the frontier involved a town's location. Towns in the American interior were established at intervals (usually regular intervals) along transportation routes, like rivers and eventually railroads. Because river towns required ease of land access to the water's edge, and deep water was necessary for steamboats to land, founders usually built them on high ground: on a river terrace and/or along the base of a bluff. The towns whose sitings were the most successful enjoyed a broken bluff line, whose gentle slope to the river improved overland movement from the interior. Often river towns such as these were located at the confluence of a tributary stream that, if large enough, also facilitated the town's connection with the back country by boat.

Frontier towns were invariably laid out with regular street grids: streets meeting at right angles creating rectangular blocks that were divided into rectangular lots for sale. Width (front footage) and depth of lots varied from town to town, and even within towns. The overall simplicity of the grid survey made the conceptualizing and recording of real estate extremely easy. In general, planned street grids gave to towns a very similar look or appearance. Views up and down streets were open. That is, views were not interrupted or terminated close at hand, but extended indefinitely to far horizons. With buildings uniformly set back from streets and spaced more or less evenly these small-town thoroughfares bespoke a progressive, modern orderliness, at least to most nineteenth-century eyes. In the states of the Upper Midwest, town grids mimicked the survey of the public domain which itself encouraged in the rural countryside the evolution of a checkerboard landscape where roads, especially along section lines, oriented to the cardinal directions. As developers packaged real estate as a saleable commodity, town lots became something not only to be developed, but something to be speculated in. Many intended towns, of course, never developed beyond the speculative stage, and thus were stillborn as mere "paper towns" (towns surveyed only on parchment).

Everywhere in America seaport and river towns tended to precede inland towns. But the nation's most important era of town building was that which accompanied the building of the railroads. Railroad towns, often directly sponsored by the competing railroad companies themselves, were located along newly laid tracks at regular five- or six-mile separations (as was the case along the Chicago and Rock Island Railroad) to service narrow hinterlands that stretched eight, nine, or ten miles back into the country. Such spacing reflected the ability of farmers to haul crops to trackside by horse and wagon for railroad shipment. Along the Upper Mississippi, railroads were built along both sides of the river; most of the pre-existing river towns were sustained by rail rather than by river connection. The river towns that truly thrived were those where east-west railroads bridged the Mississippi. They became "river crossing towns." In general, those places had been the largest of the river towns — the cities that had been most fully energized by the north/south-oriented steamboat trade. Those were the places sought out by the railroads as western terminals. Initially, the railroads that radiated west out of Chicago and Milwaukee were intended to divert commerce away from St. Louis by tapping the Mississippi River trade at its most prosperous places.

In the steamboat era, river towns that were located farther north from St. Louis enjoyed the greatest urban growth. Convenience and the security of carrying farm products to market overland and/or by river made the difference. In 1845, the average cost of freighting a bushel of wheat by steamboat was approximately one-fifth the cost of land transport by wagon. St. Louis, the midcontinent's major city, cast a long trade shadow northward. Farmers upwards to 150 miles upriver found it expedient to ship crops by steamboat directly to merchants in St. Louis, or to carry crops to market themselves without any help from middlemen. Further upstream, however, it made more sense to use commission or forwarding agents who could ship in bulk with cost savings. As wheat prices decreased the farther one went north, the distances over which farmers could profitably forward or even take wheat to market decreased, inviting milling activities which, along with the work of the commission agents, proved more fully conducive to town growth. Incubated were larger-than-usual towns at forty-mile intervals beginning some 150 miles above St Louis: Quincy, Burlington, Muscatine, Davenport and Rock Island, Savanna, Galena, and Dubuque.[2] When reinforced by trade in corn (far more significant to the north than to the south), and by nonfarm products like lead, mined near Galena and Dubuque, economic energy enabled merchants, especially in Galena, to sustain steamboat fleets in competition with St. Louis. Galena boats provided connection not only upriver to St. Paul, but to river ports downstream even beyond St. Louis, especially Cincinnati. Arrival of the railroads, first at Rock Island and then within two years at Dunlieth (across from Dubuque) and at La Crosse, changed the geographical equation markedly. Commerce was then steadily reoriented eastward to Chicago by rail.

At the time of the Grand Excursion, territory above Dubuque was still largely unsettled. Urban development was largely absent, except at Prairie du Chien with its small military garrison. But that would quickly change. At least that was the thinking that prompted the Grand Excursion: an extraordinary publicity stunt intended to promote the region's developmental potential, especially at St. Paul. This northern city, with its trading link overland to Winnipeg and the promise of future linkage westward toward the Pacific, was already booming, its population doubling annually. The town, at the head of steamboat navigation on the Mississippi, had been selected as the capital for the new state of Minnesota. But what of the town sites below St. Paul? They needed to be evaluated also. St. Paul would not rise in a vacuum but would, like St. Louis, generate a hierarchy of urban places largely subservient to it. If not St. Paul, then Chicago or Milwaukee would do so. Clearly, it was time that eastern capitalists had a look. In later decades, subsequent travelers would continue to report on the region's progress largely by "reading" the landscape for the appropriate symbols (the landscape iconography) of success.

STEREOTYPING TOWNS

Travelers who came by steamboat invariably appraised a town from the waterside first, noting especially its profile or skyline. If given the opportunity, however, they usually climbed the bluff behind the town to enjoy the view down. Capsulized waterfront and bird's-eye descriptions often provided measures of the sole worth of a town. Attention, of course, focused on the larger towns with their stores, warehouses, and factories. The smallest places were largely ignored, or dismissed in summary statements that emphasized their menial commonalities. The regularity of street grids made looking at one American town very much like looking at another. Nonetheless, river towns, as a class of place, did have something that most other places did not — topographic relief. And with topography came something of the picturesque well beyond the merely utilitarian. Only with difficulty were street grids imposed on steep river bluffs, and as a result thoroughfares in river towns were often warped into unusual configurations. Their verticality constantly invited the traveler's eye to look down or up from one level of street to another — to glance down on roofs one minute and peer up at silhouetted rooflines the next.

Every river town at least initially faced the river, its business buildings concentrated along a street parallel to the levee or, if on an overly constricted site, along a street perpendicular to the river that led up the bluff or, more correctly, fed traffic downhill to the levee. Usually there was an improved landing with stone pavement and/or wharf boats, both of which served to facilitate the loading and unloading of steamboats. In the navigation season, it would not have been unusual to see sacks of wheat or other freight stacked out-of-doors along the wharves of even the smallest places. But when river towns became river crossing towns, substantial metamorphosis usually occurred. In some places, commercial activity shifted inland, there to generate a competing business district with passenger and freight depots offering a railroad focus. Of course, where a river terrace plain was sufficiently large, then new commercial infrastructure could expand along the river to substantially elongate a town.

What travelers saw of the very smallest villages, those places with only a few hundred people, was very easily stereotyped. Rarely actually seen, unless from mid-river, they were usually typified as having little if anything exceptional. Rather than describing separately each place, authors merely grouped them, often in opening remarks. "Above St. Louis, on each side of the Mississippi," Henry Lewis began in his 1858 description, "are a considerable number of . . . towns. In fact, every settlement that has as many as twenty houses, a tavern, and a store is honored by the name of 'city,' or at least 'town.'" Lewis was the creator of one of several Mississippi River "panoramas" painted onto lengthy rolls of canvas and carted across the nation to be unwound before paying audiences, theatrical events that simulated for viewers the act of travel. Lewis also published an illustrated travel book which, written in German (with an English translation), was probably the most widely read book (certainly in Europe) to focus on the mid nineteenth-century Mississippi River.[3] Travelers, especially journalists who themselves also expected to publish, studiously consumed previously published travel accounts, in the process developing expectations as to what they might, in turn, encounter and report upon. Much travel reportage, therefore, became little more than validation of these expectations. Lewis, among the earliest of the journalists, was widely emulated in his comments.

For that matter, not only geography, but also the history of these river towns could be stereotyped. A speculator, Lewis generalized, bought a piece of land where the riverbank was sufficiently elevated not to be frequently flooded. There he built a mill and a store and, as a proprietor, went into business, also hoping to attract others to engage in business nearby. "He provides the farmers with boots, shoes, manufactured goods, groceries, etc., and accepts their products in lieu of cash," Lewis wrote. "Oftentimes the owner takes [the] opportunity to make himself known to posterity by giving the town his own name, followed by 'ville' or 'burg.' Now the plan of the town is lithographed with mathematical exactitude and the 'magnificent buildings' (still to be erected) are drawn on it."[4]

Travelers expected to see more in the larger places, and came primed to do so. Large places invited more detailing as to specifics. How was it that towns became nascent cities? Who were the movers and shakers? Just how did their successes play out in the material culture of place? What set large towns apart from small was economic success that, in turn, could be described in terms of landscape or architectural features. Nonetheless, categories of things in landscape continued to receive stereotyped description, especially when travelers had little time in which to fully assess a place. This was especially true of the journalists involved in the Grand Excursion — a fast trip up and down the river that kept participants largely on the steamboats. Thus Catherine Sedgwick wrote of Galena and Dubuque: "We were amazed at the crowds that we saw lining the shores, and the glad social shouts of civilized men, at the warehouses and huge hotels, and continuous blocks of buildings."[5] But she described little else.

Even the best writers were not immune from generalization. Mark Twain, writing in 1881, stereotyped the rapid improvements along the Upper Mississippi in words that his readers surely found not only familiar, but fundamentally comforting. "There was this amazing region," he wrote, "bristling with great towns, projected day before yesterday, so to speak, and built next morning. . . . Winona, ten thousand; Moline, ten thousand; Rock Island, twelve thousand; La Crosse, twelve thousand; . . . Dubuque, twenty-five thousand; Davenport, thirty thousand; St. Paul, fifty-eight thousand." Such population figures spoke of grand developments actually realized, at least for some places. "They are all comely, well built, clean, orderly, pleasant to the eye, and cheering to the spirit," he assured his readers in disclosing little by way of claiming much.[6]

What made travel writing exciting, of course, was concern with the novelties of place. Places visited needed to seem memorable either for what was experienced, or, more importantly, for the very nature of the experiencing. The best travel writers had the ability to thrust themselves into seemingly novel situations and extract from them entertaining insights. Making places memorable was also the impulse that lay behind the publishing of lithographic and other prints, pictures rather than words used to describe places in terms of the specific if not the unique. The Grand Excursion was memorable for the scale of the enterprise, and the sophisticated logistical coordination it demonstrated. Indeed, describing the trip as a kind of experience diverted some attention away from town description.

QUEST FOR SENSE OF PLACE

Town descriptions tended to build on one another south to north when observers traveled upriver on steamboats. Davenport, already a city in 1854, was invariably described in some detail; neighboring Rock Island and Moline, because they were smaller and in the same locality, received little if any attention. In *Life on the Mississippi* (1883), Mark Twain used a description of Davenport to emphasize the theme of progress, since the book was substantially a reminiscence of his travel experiences on river during the early 1870s as contrasted against the 1880s. Following the fashion of the times, he tabulated the improvements he witnessed along the river — elements of landscape and place that could have been explored more fully had time permitted. "Davenport has gathered its thirty thousand people within the past thirty years," he wrote. "She sends more children to her schools now than her whole population numbered twenty-three years ago. She has the usual upper-river quota of factories, newspapers, and institutions of learning; she has telephones, local telegraphs, an electric alarm, and an admirable paid fire department, consisting of six hook-and-ladder companies, four steam fire engines, and thirty churches." Of Rock Island, he described only the "charming island" with its "national armory and arsenal." Of Moline, he offered only a single cryptic phrase. The place is, he wrote, "a center of vast manufacturing industries."[7] Some years earlier, editor William Cullen Bryant also referenced urban development along the river. He had included in *Picturesque America*, a heroic multi-volume compendium of engraved images and accompanying text, paired riverfront pictures of Davenport and Rock Island by Alfred R. Ward. The bridge of the Chicago and Rock Island Railroad figured prominently in both illustrations (fig. 14). Ward exaggerated the scale of warehouses and factories located along the waterfronts. Visible behind them are large commercial buildings, a hotel or two, and the spires of churches.[8]

Galena, as one of the largest places in Illinois, necessarily attracted attention. The town was nestled in the narrow valley of the Galena River only a short distance upstream from the Mississippi and was therefore

FIGURE 14. *Views of Rock Island, Illinois, and Davenport, Iowa. Reproduced in William Cullen Bryant, ed.,* Picturesque America; or the Land We Live In. A Delineation by Pen and Pencil, *vol. 2, p. 326.*

very much a Mississippi River town. An 1851 lithograph depicts the town from a bluff on the southwest (fig. 15). In Galena, the street grid was severely skewed — streets curving to conform to the shape of the valley. Thus churches and residences along the bluff, commercial buildings immediately below them, and riverfront warehouses beyond were made to appear jumbled together rather than regularly arrayed. Much of the architecture depicted in the engraving still exists. Lead mining's decline, the rise of nearby Dubuque (favored as a regional center), and the transfer of much of Galena's commercial enterprise to Chicago greatly depressed the town's economy. After the Civil War, Galena settled down to being a farm-service town with a modicum of light industry. For those wanting a sense of what late-nineteenth-century river towns were like in the Upper Mississippi Valley, Galena remains a good place to visit.

William Ferguson, an Englishman traveling in North America in 1855, described Galena in his journal. "We got up on the hill behind the town, ascending so far by a steep street, and then by a rough wooden stair of

FIGURE 15. *View of Galena, Illinois. Lithograph by A[dolphus F.] Forbriger in William Wells,* Western Scenery: or, Land and River, Hill and Dale, in the Mississippi Valley *(Cin[cinnati], O[hio], [1851], n.p.), reproduced in John W. Reps,* Cities of the Mississippi: Nineteenth-Century Images of Urban Development, *p. 256.*

105 steps. We sat down on a grassy bank, and had a superb view. . . . The city is built in a small crescent-shaped hollow, amidst the hills, and is very picturesque. Manufacturies and business-houses occupy the flat portion of the site; while dwelling-houses, with often little gardens attached to them, are perched on the sides of the hills, which surround it on every side." The Illinois Central Railroad had reached the town and, indeed, pushed beyond to Dunlieth, which contained a freight house and "abundant meadow land with ample space for an eventual town," Ferguson noted. Capturing and holding his attention there, however, was Dubuque on the Mississippi River's opposite bank.[9]

Often an unusual light, as at dusk or at dawn, could make experiencing a place memorable. Ferguson and his party witnessed such a sight when they crossed to Dubuque in the evening. "To crown all," he wrote, "the sun was going down behind the distant hills of Iowa, lighting up as he departed the few fleecy clouds that were floating in the sky, and imparting a sort of fairy light to the whole scene." The next day he strolled about the town, starting at the lead smelter at the riverfront. "The smelting-house stood at the mouth of a little gorge, leading from the river into the country, and the bluff between rose very steep and craggy. We climbed this, and were repaid by the view of a magnificent reach of the Mississippi, spread out with its islands below us. It was like looking down upon a map." Ferguson's expansive description notwithstanding, Dubuque was a small city, both in population and in function. Because it remained densely compacted or small in areal extent, it was possible to walk quickly out of town. From the bluff behind the town, as Ferguson emphasized, one could readily look out and over open countryside.[10]

A decidedly rural context characterized Guttenberg throughout the nineteenth century (fig. 16). As depicted in an 1869 engraving, a bird's-eye view from an imagined aerial position, the town stretched along the river for some ten blocks on a slightly elevated terrace. Nowhere were the streets built up more than three blocks inland. Albert Ruger, the creator of the view, was one of a score of itinerant artists who made a living traveling from town to town across the Upper Middle West producing and selling through subscription view maps designed to be hung in home parlors and business offices.[11] Such maps played directly to a town's pride of place. What they emphasized, of course, was the extent to which a town had prospered and hoped to prosper. They were ideal devices for town promotion. Ruger included in his Guttenberg view several steamboats and a float of timber, indicative that the river was an important artery of commerce. That Guttenberg, as the town's name suggested, was largely a German-speaking community, could be implied from pictures of the town's leading churches inserted into the map's title frame at the bottom. To Galena had come large numbers of Welsh to mine the lead, along with numerous Irish and Germans also. To the Dubuque and Guttenberg areas had come immigrants not only from Germany, but also from Switzerland, Austria, and Luxemburg.

Henry Lewis, whose moving panorama on canvas depicted each and every town on the Mississippi River, was not so all-inclusive in his books. He dismissed Cassville, Wisconsin, as merely the site of a former trading post. "The location is ideal for a picture," he wrote, "but less practical for a town because the prairie on which it is situated is too narrow." Cassville had suffered "a big town site speculation and swindle" in the 1830s: a large hotel had been built, but promoters were unable to find anyone to run it. In 1849, "the elaborate building was still unoccupied and was rapidly falling to pieces." Prairie du Chien, with some four hundred people, was more notable with its Fort Crawford, built some twenty years earlier, which still had a small garrison active in it. Although the old blockhouse had been demolished, a large barrack and adjacent parade

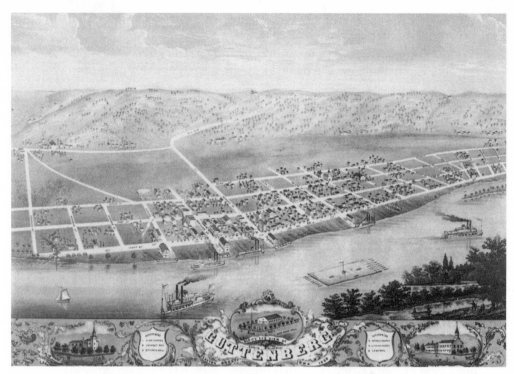

FIGURE 16. *View of Guttenberg, Iowa, 1869. From an engraving by Ruger, reproduced in John W. Reps,* Cities of the Mississippi, *p. 274.*

ground survived. Nothing remained worth mentioning from the French era, but the vicinity's numerous effigy and burial mounds of prehistoric Indian origin invited his lengthy comment.[12]

La Crosse, Wisconsin, was little more than a river landing when the steamboats of the Grand Excursion stopped to refuel (fig. 17). But in 1878, when Goldsmith B. West published *The Golden Northwest,* a promotional tome focused on the towns of the Upper Mississippi River, he described a thriving place. The town's good fortunes hinged on the bridging of the river by the Chicago, Milwaukee, and St. Paul Railroad. Indeed, the bridge was one of the town's major landmarks. Lumber and flour mills, as well as several farm implement factories, dominated the riverfront, but a four-story "white marble business palace" a few blocks away was, West said, "the most striking architectural feature of the city."[13] In 1854, Winona, Minnesota, was also an unassuming place, its rapid growth, as at La Crosse, still years away. "It consists of thirty or forty wooden houses, scattered over a perfectly level prairie eight or ten miles

FIGURE 17. *View of La Crosse, Wisconsin. Reproduced in William Cullen Bryant, ed.,* Picturesque America, *p. 336.*

long and about two in width, and backed by a range of well-rounded, partially-wooded hills," wrote Laurence Oliphant, another English visitor.[14]

Wabasha, Minnesota, called Pratt's Landing when E. S. Seymour visited the place in 1849, comprised only "two or three small houses . . . from which children, with strongly-marked Indian features, were seen gazing at the new-comers." Whereas Henry Lewis at Prairie du Chien had noted the Native American past through emphasis on the mound builders, at Wabasha Native Americans were still very much in evidence. Yet Seymour saw mainly the future. "It is natural for one who has lived many years in the West, and has seen cities, towns, and villages spring up, like magic, on spots but a few months previously dotted with Indian wigwams, to throw his mental vision into the future, and behold the beautiful country teeming with a dense population," he confided. At the site of what would soon become Red Wing, Minnesota (where a prominent bluff thrust out from a steep hill behind the town), a Native American village remained. It contained, according to Seymour, roughly a dozen lodges covered with buffalo skins, but also a log house occupied by a missionary.[15]

By 1880, travel writers reduced any mention of Native American presence in the region to "footnotes to history." Where their villages had once stood, Mark Twain saw nothing but towns, of course. Using the device of quoting the tour guide aboard his steamboat, he inserted a romanticized view of Native American life, albeit one conceived in the past tense. "Then Frontenac looms upon our vision, delightful resort of jaded summer tourists; then progressive Red Wing, and Diamond Bluff impressive and preponderous in its lone sublimity; then Prescott and the St. Croix [River]; and anon we see bursting upon us the domes and steeples of

St. Paul, giant young chief of the North, marching with seven-league stride in the van of progress, banner-bearer of the highest and newest civilization, carrying his beneficent way with the tomahawk of commercial enterprise, sounding the war whoop of Christian culture, tearing off the scalp of sloth and superstition."[16]

In 1849, St. Paul was but a place of some 150 people, and contained only a dozen or so log houses, a single hotel, a couple of stores, and a log Roman Catholic chapel, at least according to what locals told Laurence Oliphant. But the town that Oliphant saw a year later was anything but small. It was clearly booming. "There are four or five hotels, and at least half-a-dozen handsome churches, with tall spires pointing heavenward, and sundry meeting-houses, and a population of seven or eight thousand to go to them, and good streets with side-walks, and lofty brick warehouses, and stores, and shops, as well supplied as any in the union," he wrote. Included in his book was an illustration depicting St. Paul as the small place it had been but recently (fig. 18).[17] By 1857, C. C. Andrews thought the town contained at least ten thousand people. "Three or four steamers were tying at the levee," he noted. "Steam and smoke were shooting forth from chimneys of numerous manufactures; a ferry was plying the Mississippi, transporting teams and people; church steeples and domes and great warehouses stood in places which were vacant as if but yesterday; busy streets had been built and peopled; rows of splendid dwellings and villas, adorned with delightful terraces and gardens, had been erected."[18]

What became of the Upper Mississippi Valley was nothing less than what the organizers of the Grand Excursion assumed would unfold — towns would thrive, even where no towns had been before. Perhaps what the Grand Excursion accomplished was to hasten even more the self-fulfilling prophecies of land and town development along the river that visitors and investors foresaw. Positive publicity never hurt when it came to regional development. And the Grand Excursion, by the audacity of its scale, was something of a publicity breakthrough. Downstream from Dubuque, urban expansion favored the already well-established river towns of the pre-railroad era, as it did for sites upstream from that city, where the river was most easily bridged for railroading. The railroad was perhaps the most "civilizing" of all technologies, offering as it did very fast

FIGURE 18. *View of St. Paul, 1849.*
Reproduced in Laurence Oliphant, Minnesota and the Far West, *p. 281.*

and dependable year-round transportation that more firmly networked towns and their trade hinterlands across vast distances. In doing so, these urban linkages fostered larger-than-ever commercial exchanges between regions. Of course, not every town thrived. Most of the river landings became but minor station stops on the railroads that paralleled the Upper Mississippi. These places remained obscure, and hardly noticed by travelers who now rode the trains rather than the river steamers.

FIGURE 19. *This 1902 bridge was built to allow steamboats and their tall smokestacks to travel the Mississippi River unobstructed. Three-quarters-of-a-mile long, it was of a complicated, multi-style design and had a sharp turn near its middle. It was the first wagon bridge to connect Dubuque directly to Wisconsin. The Eagle Point Bridge was replaced in 1982 with a four-lane tied arch bridge, the second largest on the Mississippi of that design. Information from Mary Charlotte Aubry Costello,* Climbing the Mississippi River Bridge by Bridge, Volume One, From Louisiana to Minnesota, *p. 160. Postcard by B. B. Co.*

WHERE NATURE SMILES
THREE HUNDRED MILES
RAIL TRAVEL ALONG
THE RIVER *Jeff Crump*

At the time of the Grand Excursion in 1854, the scenery of the Upper Mississippi River presented the excursionists with a landscape that was seen as both picturesque and primitive. Yet even as they admired the untamed landscape of the Upper Mississippi, many of the travelers speculated on the future of the country and of the potential profits to be gained by its rapid settlement. Indeed, the Grand Excursion began as a railroad journey from Chicago to Rock Island and was sponsored and paid for by the Rock Island Railroad, a company that had a vested interest in promoting the development of the region. Even as the steamboats moved slowly upstream, railroad promoters planned to build tracks for the Iron Horse along the banks of the great river.

Not long after the 1854 excursion, railroads became the major engines of economic, social, and cultural change along the river. Eastern capital in the form of rails and trains funneled people and goods along its banks and the railroad formed the backbone of economic development of the region. Yet the railroad was more than just a way to get from one place to another. In its heyday, the railroad represented the finest achievements of modern engineering and technology. Railroad engineers were the most heroic figures of their time and the trains they drove caused many a young man's heart to beat faster, moving with the rhythm of the rails. As described by landscape historian John R. Stilgoe, "For the small boy, grasping his father's hand as the crack express thundered past . . . the train existed as fiercely directed energy, as power magnified almost beyond comprehension."[1]

Riding on the railroad gave passengers a new experience of time and space. First of all, the sheer speed of train travel brought places closer together. As the speed and comfort of rail travel increased, rural residents of the Upper Mississippi region found that the burgeoning cities of

Chicago and St. Paul were just a few hours away. Once aboard the train, passengers also experienced a new way of seeing the landscape. Viewing the landscape passing by at high speeds created a distancing effect for most passengers. As Stilgoe comments, "train travel provided a distinctive, almost cinemagraphic vision of the . . . environment beyond the plate glass windows."[2]

The passenger trains run by the Chicago, Burlington, and Quincy (CB&Q) were emblematic of modern rail travel. During the heyday of the streamlined passenger train (1935–1960), the scenic route of the CB&Q along the Upper Mississippi River carried the most modern passenger trains ever seen. Among the Q's most famous trains was the Twin Cities *Zephyr*, connecting the Twin Cities to Chicago and making the 427-mile trip in six hours and fifteen minutes. One chronicler concluded: "Of Burlington Route you can truly say, it had sizzle. And no trains exemplified the Q's hustle and glamour more than the Twin Cities *Zephyrs* . . . between Chicago and Minneapolis."[3]

Other fast and luxurious passenger trains traveled the scenic Mississippi River route as well. The Great Northern's *Empire Builder*, the Northern Pacific's *Mainstreeter*, and the Milwaukee Road's *Olympian Hiawatha*, which crossed the Mississippi at La Crosse and reached the Twin Cities by traveling along the west bank of the river, also carried their customers at high speeds in unparalleled style and comfort.

Although the streamlined passenger train was a new element in the landscape of the Upper Mississippi River Valley, the thrill of an excursion along the scenic valley remained timeless. Reflecting on the original 1854 Grand Excursion, William J. Petersen concluded that "promenading on deck and allowing the ever changing landscape to 'daguerreotype new pictures on the mind' formed the principle pastime for most of the travelers."[4] The attraction of the landscape along the river was much the same among rail travelers in later times.

This essay tells the story of passenger rail travel along the Upper Mississippi River at the height of the streamline era. It covers the years between the introduction of the streamliners in the mid 1930s to the end of the era in the 1960s. First, I discuss the development of the railway lines that paralleled the Upper Mississippi River, then, I examine the evolution of the streamlined passenger trains used by the CB&Q. To conclude, I present the voices of some of those who traveled and worked on the railroad.

Almost as soon as the steamboats of the Grand Excursion passed along the Mississippi River, railroad entrepreneurs sought to connect Minneapolis and St. Paul with the emerging metropolis of Chicago. The Milwaukee and Mississippi, one of the forerunners of the Chicago, Milwaukee, St. Paul and Pacific Railroad (the Milwaukee Road) reached the Mississippi in 1856 at Prairie du Chien. By 1859 passengers en route to Minneapolis and St. Paul were ferried across the river by a unique boat that operated on the water in the summer months and on the ice during the winter.[5]

Another ancestor of the Milwaukee Road was the Minnesota Central, which built a bridge across the Mississippi at St. Paul in 1869.[6] The line then headed south through Austin, Minnesota, where passengers headed to Chicago by going due east and crossing the Mississippi on the ferry at Prairie du Chien. They then transferred to the Milwaukee and Mississippi for the remaining journey to Chicago. Although this was a rather circuitous route, it was the first railroad connection between the Twin Cities and Chicago.

Recognizing the need for a more direct route, the St. Paul and Chicago Railroad constructed a line from Minneapolis and St. Paul down along the west bank of the Mississippi. A bridge across the river to La Crosse, Wisconsin, was completed in 1878. Once completed, this line cut across the state of Wisconsin to Milwaukee where it ran south into the city of Chicago. In 1888, the first daily fast-mail service between the Twin Cities and Chicago was inaugurated on this line and by 1900 these lines formed a single network under the Milwaukee Road rubric.

The Chicago and Northwestern Railroad (CNW) was another important early line. In 1871, the Winona and St. Peter Railroad (later absorbed by the CNW) crossed the Mississippi at Winona, Minnesota. This particular bridge did not last long, for when the first train approached it, the bridge tender neglected to properly secure the drawbridge. Once the train (carrying a heavy load of rock) was on the bridge, the structure collapsed, sending the train and its crew into the river. Fortunately, no one was seriously injured. However, it took several months before the bridge was once again ready for service. Much like the Milwaukee Road, the separate, smaller railroads such as the Winona and St. Peter were amalgamated to form a wide-ranging network of railroad lines under the banner of the CNW.

The CB&Q was a latecomer to the Mississippi River. By 1882 however, the management of the CB&Q could no longer ignore the economic potential of the Twin Cities. They began to consider the construction of a line that would connect their existing tracks that ran west out of Chicago with Minneapolis and St. Paul. Tracks were laid in Illinois, between the towns of Oregon and Savanna, and then northward along the east bank of the Mississippi. The tracks paralleled the river for 288 miles before reaching the line's terminus at Minneapolis/St. Paul.[7] To build and operate the new line, the Burlington founded a subsidiary railroad, the Chicago, Burlington, and Northern (CB&N). With adequate funds provided by the CB&Q, construction progressed rapidly and on October 24, 1886, the first passenger train to run on the line departed the Twin Cities and arrived in Chicago approximately twelve hours later. Following this successful demonstration, regularly scheduled passenger service began on October 31, 1886.

Because the new route hugged the eastern bank of the river, passengers had to be ferried across the river to reach major cities such as Dubuque, Iowa, and Winona, Minnesota. However, the train did pass directly through the Wisconsin cities of Prairie du Chien and La Crosse. Because La Crosse was a crew-change point and had a large locomotive servicing facility, it was a particularly important city for the Q. Interestingly, the important railroad functions of La Crosse were not mentioned in a 1951 Burlington route guide. The description instead focused on the activities of native inhabitants of the town: "Originally scene of winter camp of Indians and inter-tribal meets. Still has several Winnebago villages nearby, with annual pow-wow at La Crosse to this day."[8]

Although the Burlington's Mississippi River route was twenty-five miles longer than those of the Chicago and Northwestern and the Milwaukee Roads, by paralleling the Mississippi the Q's engineers laid out a line with very gentle grades, thus reducing the amount of motive power needed. The fast speeds that could be achieved more than made up for the slightly greater distance. This route had another important competitive advantage for the CB&Q: it provided passengers with the opportunity to view the spectacular scenery that exemplifies the Upper Mississippi River.

The beauty of the landscape along the Mississippi gave the Burlington a decided advantage in the cutthroat competition of the time. And there is little doubt that the scenic landscape qualities offered by the Burlington's Mississippi River Scenic Route did attract passengers to the line. The Q worked hard to highlight the thrill of a railroad excursion along the river. It advertised the scenic character of its route in numerous brochures, postcards, and advertisements, and passengers were provided with lavish pamphlets. In an early example from 1920, a cover image shows male passengers riding on the open platform of a passenger car. Equipped with binoculars and straw hats, they gaze at the steamboats plying the upper river. In the meantime, a young mother and daughter, safely ensconced within the comfortable coach, observe a slow-moving steamboat from the comfort of their overstuffed chairs as the train moves through the river corridor (fig. 20).

The Burlington also played up the route's allure in their brochure copy. The same 1920 issue proudly pointed out that "by those who know its charm, the Burlington Route between Chicago, St. Paul and Minneapolis has been titled . . . 'The Mississippi River Scenic Lines,' *Where Nature smiles — three hundred miles.* This will be readily understood when one comprehends that for almost the entire distance . . . the rails are within sight of the majestic Father of Waters. . . . a further charm is found in the quaint villages along the river. . . . Altogether, one may be sure of seeing something every hour of the journey, and if he should be so fortunate as to meet an old inhabitant, great will be his interest in the Indian legends and the tales of the pioneers." [9]

In this section of the brochure, the passenger's attention was drawn to the scenic beauty of the Mississippi. Yet the Burlington route guide also details the history of the area and emphasizes the historical continuity between the Native Americans, the pioneers, and the modern-day rail traveler. From behind the plate glass windows of the passenger train, railroad travelers were invited to imagine themselves as modern day explorers taking an adventurous excursion through a landscape that only recently had been the home to numerous Native Americans and intrepid explorers. In this manner, the Burlington juxtaposed historical continuity with the rapidly expanding modern system of transportation best represented by the beautiful trains of the CB&Q. As a representative of the latest in rail design and technology, the Burlington *Zephyrs* would have no peer. It is to the story of these famous trains we next turn.

THE TRAIN: THE DEVELOPMENT AND DESIGN OF THE BURLINGTON *ZEPHYR*

During the 1920s and into the depression years of the 1930s, patronage of passenger trains began to fall. There were several reasons for the loss of business. First, the growth of automobile ownership and the rapid

FIGURE 20. *From the safety and comfort of the* Zephyr, *a woman and her daughter look out over the picturesque Mississippi. From* The Mississippi River Scenic Line, Where Nature Smiles Three Hundred Miles *(1920). Courtesy of the Burlington Northern and Santa Fe Railroad.*

development of improved highways encouraged people to abandon trains for the fun and flexibility that automobile travel offered. Second, the widespread unemployment and loss of income during the Great Depression reduced the number of people able to afford train travel. Third, competition among the heavily regulated railroads was incredibly intense and strict government regulations made it almost impossible for railroads to abandon routes, even those that steadily lost money.

In response to these trends, Burlington President Ralph Budd (fig. 21) decided to embark on an ambitious program of modernizing the Q's passenger service. In late 1932, Budd traveled to Philadelphia to visit the plant of the Edward G. Budd (no relation) Manufacturing Company to examine the streamlined, lightweight passenger cars developed by that company. Using a patented welding technique called shotwelding, the Budd Company built passenger cars out of stainless steel.[10] Although stainless steel was more expensive than other materials, its strength and corrosion resistance made it an ideal material for a new type of passenger car. Attracted by the potential weight and cost savings offered by such designs, Ralph Budd ordered two sets of passenger cars, each consisting of three cars. The new locomotive and passenger cars were permanently attached using steel drawbars — a design that allowed the units to ride on shared sets of trucks and wheels. The unique articulated design was used to save weight and provide for a more stable and comfortable ride.

Having ordered the cars, Budd now had to decide on a power plant. Although diesel-powered switch engines were relatively common at the time, diesel engines were very heavy for the amount of horsepower they produced. Consequently, the dominance of steam locomotives remained unchallenged and steam power dominated the "high iron" of the railway mainline. The ultimate challenge to steam power was close at hand, however. The Electro-Motive Corporation (EMC), a subsidiary of General Motors (GM), was developing a new type of two-stroke diesel engine. Constructed out of newly developed lightweight materials, the EMC diesel greatly improved the power-to-weight ratio of diesel engines and clearly had the potential to provide economical and reliable power for the streamline train then being constructed.

Needing to quickly decide on the motive power for the new streamliners being constructed, Budd traveled to the GM exhibit at the 1933–1934 Century of Progress Exhibition in Chicago. Impressed with what he saw, Budd was all ears when Hal Hamilton, the head of EMC engi-

FIGURE 21. *In this 1934 photo, Burlington President Ralph Budd enjoys the view from the cab of the first* Zephyr. *Photo taken by the* St. Paul Daily News, *from the Minnesota State Historical Society.*

neering in Detroit, approached him about using a new power plant then under development to power the three-car train ordered by the CB&Q.[11] Hamilton told Budd that if he could wait an extra three months to put the new trains into service, he would provide him with a diesel locomotive that would prove to be the answer to the need for more reliable and economical motive power. Ever the risk taker, Budd was happy to wait.

Now that the decision had been made to purchase the train with the new diesel engine, Budd faced the question of what to name the new train. Because it would be the last word in passenger train comfort and speed, Budd thought he would use the last word in the dictionary to name the train.[12] When a dictionary was consulted, however, the last word turned out to be "zyzzle," meaning to sputter — hardly an appropriate name for the most modern of passenger trains. The next word he found was "zymurgy," meaning to distill or ferment wine. Temporarily stymied, it just so happened that Budd was reading the Canterbury Tales by Chaucer in which Zephyrus (the god of the west wind) symbolizes rebirth.[13] Shortening the name, Budd christened the new train the *Zephyr.*

The train consisted of a locomotive that included a baggage and mail section, a car that contained the diner and smoking area, and a third car that was devoted to seating.[14] The little train, designed to accommodate only seventy passengers, was initially envisioned for use on the Lincoln-Omaha-Kansas City run. Before the new *Zephyr* went into regular service, the gleaming, stainless steel streamliner toured the United States. Wherever the *Zephyr* was displayed, large crowds turned out to marvel at the bright, shining train powered by the clean-running diesel engine. The *Zephyr*'s most famous achievement was a demonstration run from Denver, Colorado, to Chicago, Illinois. It completed the run nonstop in just over thirteen hours. Considering that a regular passenger schedule over this route took over twenty-six hours, this record is even more impressive. The excitement elicited by the *Zephyr* was evident throughout the country as Depression-weary Americans turned out to view the silver train.

Now that the feasibility of the new design had been amply demonstrated, Budd ordered two more sets of articulated three-car units to be used on the Twin Cities-to-Chicago route. Christened the *Twin Zephyr*s, the new trains entered into service on April 21, 1935, and completed the journey to St. Paul in a little over six hours (fig. 22). Not surprisingly, the new trains were very popular with the traveling public. They were almost always filled to capacity and many passengers rode standing up just to experience the thrill of riding the *Twin Zephyr*.

To be sure, the *Zephyrs* offered an unprecedented level of speed and comfort. Traveling at an average speed over seventy miles an hour, they were completely air-conditioned. Passengers were able to relax into the comfortable seats and enjoy the beauty of the Mississippi Scenic Line, "Where Nature Smiles 300 Miles!" Local newspapers commented: "The two trains are all steel and powered with diesel engines. They are completely streamlined. . . . Although high winds filled the air with dust the effect was not felt within the trains due to complete air conditioning."[15]

Since the three-car *Zephyrs* proved unable to meet growing passenger demand for seats, two new six-car trains were soon ordered. In 1936 the new *Twin Zephyrs*, comprised of one power car equipped with an eighteen-hundred horsepower diesel engine and six articulated passenger cars, replaced the original three-car trains that were then relegated to service between St. Louis and Kansas City. As *Zephyr* service caught the public's imagination several additional train sets were ordered and put into service. The *Denver Zephyr*, *Texas Zephyr*, and *Mark Twain Zephyr* were all implemented using the diesel-powered streamlined cars.

FIGURE 22. *Route and timetable for the morning* Zephyr *trains connecting Chicago and Minneapolis, 1944. From "Burlington Route Time Tables."*

In keeping with the *Zephyr* theme, the two *Twin Zephyrs* were named after Greek and Roman gods and goddesses. The so-called "Train of the Gods" included the locomotive *Zephyrus*, followed by *Apollo, Neptune, Mars, Vulcan, Mercury,* and *Jupiter*.[16] Its twin, the "Train of the Goddesses," was powered by *Pegasus* and passengers traveled in *Venus, Vesta, Minerva, Ceres, Diana,* and *Juno.* In September of 1937 one more car was added to each train, named *Cupid* and *Psyche,* respectively. With the new cars, each of the trains had a capacity of 160 passengers and a dining car that could accommodate forty-eight customers.

In every way these trains provided the latest in passenger comfort and convenience. In particular, the windows were designed to provide the best possible view of the Mississippi River. As railroad historian J. W.

Schultz notes, "To provide *Twin Zephyr* passengers with unobstructed views of the Mississippi River Scenic Line, side windows of the new *Twins* were comprised of two thicknesses of Pittsburgh shatterproof glass with a dehydrated air space hermetically sealed between them."[17]

The implementation of the new trains doubled patronage on the Twin Cities-to-Chicago line. As passenger traffic improved, the Burlington initiated many other enhancements. For example, a new station was constructed in La Crosse, opening in January 1940. The location of the station allowed the trains to bypass busy downtown streets and cut fifteen minutes off the Twin Cities-Chicago schedule. The *Twin Zephyrs* now made the journey in just under six hours and achieved the fastest average speed of any regularly scheduled passenger train service in the nation.

A Burlington advertisement heralded them as the "Wonder Trains." As writer Roger Reynolds described the new trains: "Today the newest of new trains runs along this road — a glistening, streamlined train. Lightweight cars of stainless steel, and lightweight engines with diesel power, give this train the name of *Zephyr*. Twice a day these *Zephyrs* leave for the Twin Cities, one in the morning and its twin in the afternoon. What could be more natural than to call these twin trains . . . the *Twin Zephyrs?*"[18]

The six-car *Twin Zephyrs* were frequently supplemented with additional cars when the traffic warranted, which it often did. However, efforts to increase the capacity of the trains pointed out one of the major failings of the articulated train design. Because the cars were permanently connected, it was difficult to add additional capacity when needed, and when one car required service the entire train had to be withdrawn. These limitations led the Burlington to design its next generation of passenger trains as separate cars rather than as articulated train sets.

One of the major changes ushered in by the *Zephyr* and its diesel-powered locomotives was a tremendous reduction in the maintenance required to keep the trains on the main line. Instead of the regular watering, coaling, and firing required by steam locomotives, the diesels needed little service beyond regularly scheduled maintenance. The new technology greatly reduced the labor needed to maintain and service the locomotives.

Railroad management argued that a single engineer could safely operate diesel locomotives. Not surprisingly, railroad unions objected to this notion, demanding that each locomotive employ an engineer and a fireman. As the *Zephyrs* came on line in 1935, management and the Brotherhood of Locomotive Firemen and Enginemen reached an impasse over this issue.[19] Although a strike was threatened, in the end the union and railroad management compromised. Diesel freight and passenger loco-motives would carry both an engineman and fireman, while diesel switch engines would be operated with a single engineman.

VOICES: RAILROAD WORKERS AND PASSENGERS

Despite their apprehension over the impact of the new diesels on employment prospects, Burlington employees were particularly proud of the *Zephyr.* As Bob Franke of La Crosse commented, "A passenger run was the best job. . . . It was a great life, even though you could get called all hours of the night. Firing the *Zephyr* was the best job you could have!"[20]

In 1947, the six-car *Twin Zephyrs* were retired from the Twin Cities-Chicago run and replaced by stainless steel cars that featured the newest innovation in passenger rail design, the *Vista Dome* (fig. 23). In yet another example of innovation on the Mississippi River Scenic Line, the new *Twin Zephyrs* featured the very first trains in the nation to be so equipped. With five dome cars, these trains were explicitly designed to allow passengers to get the best possible view. As a 1951 Burlington Route advertisement put it: "Here is America's latest travel thrill — the new *Twin Zephyrs,* offering that most delightful travel innovation, the *Vista-Dome.* Yes, you'll find a real thrill riding in an air conditioned 'penthouse on wheels' with an unobstructed view as you glide along the enchanting Upper Mississippi River."[21] Passengers loved the *Vista Domes.* Even pro-fessional observers such as writers for *Trains* magazine were impressed, saying that as "a new dimension in travel . . . it lends the impression of being outdoors at 60 miles per hour and provides a full sweep of vision: ahead, behind, on both sides and straight up."[22]

Traveling on the Burlington *Zephyrs* was an exciting experience for many people. The gleaming, streamlined trains bespoke modernity and progress. Indeed Burlington's ads proclaimed that the new *Zephyrs* were the "Wonder Trains of Tomorrow Today" bringing new standards of com-fort, reliability, and speed. The sheer speed of the journey was a major topic of conversation. As one of his friends wrote on a postcard to a (then) young Curt Roseman in 1948, "Saturday night on *Zephyr.* Can't write very well because the train is going so fast."

The stainless steel trains traveled through a narrow corridor where the speeding railroad cars were controlled by sophisticated electrical signal systems. Representing the latest in engineering technology, the railroad created a space of modernity that sliced through the countryside. Clearly

VISTA DOME TWIN ZEPHYRS

TWICE DAILY VIA THE BURLINGTON BETWEEN CHICAGO AND ST. PAUL-MINNEAPOLIS

FIGURE 23. *In a classic postcard view, the* Twin Zephyrs *meet just north of East Dubuque along the scenic Mississippi River. From a postcard published by the Burlington Route. Courtesy of the Burlington Northern and Santa Fe Railroad.*

the railroad lines came to represent more than just utilitarian transportation. Stilgoe concurs, arguing that because it "reach[ed] from the very hearts of great cities[,] . . . the metropolitan corridor [created by the railroad] objectified in its unprecedented arrangement of space . . . a wholly new lifestyle. Along it flowed the forces of modernization."[23]

The modern, streamlined *Vista Dome* was represented as another step in a long line of transportation improvements that linked the modern traveler of the Mississippi corridor with those of earlier times. In a typical example, a 1951 Burlington Route guide proclaimed that "progress goes forward along the Mississippi, but the new does not cloud the old. The scenic route today is what it always has been — a route of natural loveliness, a route of history. . . . This is the route to which every American thrills as he follows it on the Burlington Lines. . . . The long-drawn-out whoop of the *Zephyrs* echoes from cliff to cliff across the valleys and rivers which once echoed to the whoops of . . . Indians."[24] Even though passengers rode in air-conditioned comfort, the *Vista Dome* still allowed the traveler to absorb the beauty of the landscape, one that was enlivened by the colorful history of the area — an experience not so very different from the experiences of those who traveled on the Grand Excursion of 1854.

Throughout the 1950s, the *Vista Domes* attracted many travelers. Passenger trains, however, began to face increasingly stiff competition from automobiles and airplanes. Beginning in the late 1950s, ridership on the *Twin Zephyrs* started to decline and by 1960 the trains were not what they had been. When Louis Menk took over as the CB&Q's president in 1965, he was determined to eliminate the *Zephyrs*.[25] A 1966 Burlington report found that the tarnished trains were losing $121,608 per year.[26] In 1967 the Burlington went to the Interstate Transportation Commission (ITC) to ask it to allow the Q to discontinue the *Twin Zephyrs*. The ITC, however, found that the trains carried 155 passengers per train mile so it only allowed the Burlington to discontinue the morning *Zephyr*, leaving the afternoon *Zephyr* to carry on. Despite this reprieve, the handwriting was on the wall, and when the Burlington merged with the Northern Pacific and Great Northern in 1970, the trains were discontinued. Finally, when Amtrak was formed in 1970 to run the nation's passenger rail network (what was left of it, anyhow), it chose to follow the route of the original Milwaukee Road, which reaches the Mississippi at La Crosse then crosses to the west side of the river at Winona. Today its *Empire Builder* takes eight hours and fifteen minutes to make the trip from Chicago to the Twin Cities. This is a painfully slow schedule when compared to the six hours it took the *Twin Zephyrs* to make the run.

Many people still fondly remember the *Twin Zephyrs*. As one former passenger said, "I always traveled by train. . . . I'd take the *Zephyr* . . . the food service was just super. You always got a good meal. The coaches were comfortable and very clean. I loved travel by train . . . still do!"[27]

Tremendous changes have occurred in how people travel since the mid nineteenth century. In the late nineteenth century the steamboat was replaced by the whistle of the steam locomotive and by the 1940s, steam power had been superseded by the diesel locomotive. In the post–World War II era, the passenger train was replaced by the automobile as people discovered the convenience and flexibility of automobile touring.

Yet whether we travel by steamboat, train, or car, the magic of the Upper Mississippi River endures. Today many thousands of tourists take leisurely excursions along the Mississippi and the tour books issued by the American Automobile Association recount some of the same stories and legends found in the Burlington pamphlets of fifty years ago. On any given weekend the scenic two-lane roads are filled with automobiles and recreational vehicles, and groups of motorcyclists tour the valley, the roar of their engines filling the void left by the *Zephyr*.

The Mississippi River provides a connection between our past, present, and future. Yet it also exudes a sense of timelessness as it flows ceaselessly toward the Gulf of Mexico. Perhaps it is the unique combination of continuity and change that gives one the inescapable feeling that to travel next to or on the Mississippi is no ordinary journey. Rather, it is to undertake an adventurous excursion of the highest order. As it has for hundreds of years, the Mississippi still exerts a powerful pull on many of us. As author Tom Weil has noted, "Over time the river slowly seeps into your very being."[28]

FIGURE 24. *This 2,481-foot-long two-lane bridge, completed in December 1932, crosses both the Burlington tracks and the Mississippi River just north of Savanna, Illinois. Its metal grid roadway makes for a "squeaky" car ride, as well as a disconcerting "view of the river" through the floor of the bridge. Information from Mary Charlotte Aubry Costello,* Climbing the Mississippi River Bridge by Bridge, Volume One, From Louisiana to Minnesota, *p. 150. From a 1942 postcard in "Souvenir Folder of Mississippi Palisades State Park, Savanna, Illinois." Postcard 2B79 from the Lake County (Illinois) Discovery Museum, Curt Teich Postcard Archives.*

HIGHWAY TO EMPIRE
REMAKING THE RIVER
John O. Anfinson

It seems appropriate that former president Millard Fillmore led the 1854 Grand Excursion. The excursionists paddled up a mostly natural river. To the extent it was not natural, Fillmore had played a role. Fillmore and his Whig Party supported federally funded navigation improvements for the Mississippi and other rivers. And, ironically, Fillmore and the Grand Excursion celebrated an event that both undermined river shipping and helped justify the Upper Mississippi River's transformation for navigation. While the Grand Excursion celebrated the railroad, the railroad heralded the end of most steamboat traffic on the Upper Mississippi.

As railroads quickly captured the region's freight and passenger traffic, farmers and business interests protested that the Midwest needed a more navigable river to compete with railroad monopolies. They found the natural river too fickle and began pushing Congress to remake the Mississippi. Since the Civil War, at the request of these interests and others, America has radically altered the Mississippi's physical and ecological character in order to facilitate navigation. Two other factors have also shaped the upper river's appearance and function: the agricultural levee system and the establishment of the Upper Mississippi National Wildlife and Fish Refuge.

THE NATURAL RIVER
Grand Excursionists thought they ventured onto a pristine wilderness river. In many ways it was, but important changes had occurred. Father Louis Hennepin, who ascended the river from the mouth of the Illinois River in 1680, encountered herds of buffalo wading across the Mississippi.[1] In 1806, Zebulon Pike discovered dense rookeries of the now extinct passenger pigeon. So many birds inhabited the rookeries that, he claimed, "the most fervid imagination cannot conceive their numbers."

He compared their cackling to the "roaring of the wind."[2] Millions of beaver and muskrat also swam through the river's backwaters. By the time the excursionists arrived, however, the buffalo had retreated west and most of the passenger pigeons were gone. So few beaver and muskrat remained in or near the Mississippi that the fur traders and trappers, which included the Dakota and other Native American tribes, had moved west. The Dakota and other tribes had also been forced to leave their villages along the river. In May 1854, only a month before the excursionists reached their destination, the Minnesota Territorial government escorted the Mdewakanton Dakota out of their ancestral villages in the Twin Cities area to a reservation far up the Minnesota River.

Physically and ecologically, however, the river remained largely natural at the time of the Grand Excursion. Uncounted side channels, backwaters, snags, islands, sandbars, and wide shallows characterized the natural Upper Mississippi, delaying, stranding, and sometimes sinking steamboats. Spring floods spread into the river's vast floodplain and slowly receded during the summer and fall, until the river reached its low-water stage. This great annual cycle or pulse renewed backwater and main channel habitat. During low water, no continuous channel existed. The channel might flow along one side for a short reach and then cross to the other or skip in short segments down the middle. The Des Moines Rapids, which extended 11.3 miles upstream from present-day Keokuk, Iowa, and the Rock Island Rapids, which ran for almost fifteen miles near Rock Island, posed two of the most dangerous obstacles.

Sandbars presented the most frequent and difficult problem for navigation. As the 1820 expedition under Territorial Governor Lewis Cass headed down the Mississippi, one member reported that from St. Anthony Falls to Prairie du Chien they found "sand bars without number" and complained that they struck fifteen to twenty per day. They were traveling in birch bark canoes, which drew only a few inches of water. For steamboats, shallow bars could separate one end of the river from the other. According to George Byron Merrick, whose family steamed upriver from Rock Island to their new home at Prescott, Wisconsin, in 1854, three of the worst bars lay between Prescott and St. Paul.[3]

The Rock Island Rapids and sandbars should have worried the Grand Excursion's organizers. In the fall of 1853, just eight months before the excursionists departed Rock Island, Horace Ransom Bigelow, a thirty-three-year-old teacher and law student, left Utica to visit the Upper Mississippi. He arrived in Rock Island on October 19, where he spied two steamboats trapped on the rapids. He too became trapped, in a sense, as the captain refused to run the rapids until the wind died down. Because the river often became shallow, the boats had small rudders that made steering in a strong wind difficult. Despite extremely low water, Bigelow arrived in St. Paul on November 1. He hoped to stay a few days and return on the *Nominee*, which he expected within days. The *Nominee*, however, grounded on Pig's Eye bar, over three miles below St. Paul, on November 5, forcing the captain to unload his passengers and cargo. The river froze shortly after, compelling Bigelow and the *Nominee* to stay for the winter. Neither the Grand Excursion organizers nor the citizens of St. Paul were prepared to cart the excursionists and their baggage into town from Pig's Eye bar.[4]

Fortunately for the Grand Excursionists, the river remained deep and constant during their trip. Where Bigelow had recently seen two steamboats stranded on the Rock Island Rapids, the excursionists, the *Albany Argus* reported, "crossed without any difficulty, as the water is quite high." Although the *New York Tribune* reported a strong current, the steamboats easily pushed upriver. Misled by the excellent conditions, some writers encouraged easterners to flock to the Mississippi for the short and inexpensive trip to St. Paul. They did not see the river in flood or at low water. Floating trees and other debris found in the river at high stages did not assault them, and they did not get stranded on sandbars. Those who opposed Fillmore, the Whig Party, and federal navigation improvements must have questioned the need for government projects.[5]

NAVIGATION IMPROVEMENTS

Before the Civil War, the American government generally rejected federal projects for roads, harbors, canals, and rivers. Many Americans believed that states should fund their own internal improvements. They recognized the benefits of good roads and navigable waterways for commerce and security, but they feared a powerful central government even more. Some Americans, however, supported a stronger federal role. They insisted that the government had the "implied power" under the constitution to undertake internal improvements to promote commerce and public safety.

Navigation boosters won some victories in Congress during two periods before the Civil War. The first began in 1824 and lasted until 1838.

During this era, the government sponsored surveys of many of the country's rivers, harbors, and coasts. On the Upper Mississippi River, the U.S. Army Corps of Engineers began working on a wing dam to keep the river flowing past St. Louis and undertook two surveys of the Des Moines and Rock Island Rapids. Lieutenants Robert E. Lee and Montgomery Meigs undertook the second survey in 1837. Progress on the Upper Mississippi River and on most internal improvement projects ended with the economic panic of 1837 and Martin Van Buren's inauguration as president in 1838. The Dubuque harbor represented one exception. While Congress authorized $7,500 for deepening the harbor, the Corps did not finish the project, as the Mexican War (1846–1847) siphoned funds and engineers away.[6]

In 1848, however, waterway advocates celebrated the election of Zachary Taylor, a Whig, to the White House. Although Taylor died on July 9, 1850, Vice President Millard Fillmore pushed the Whig agenda and initiated the second period of national waterway projects, which lasted only for the duration of his presidency, from 1850 to 1853. Shortly after taking office, Fillmore declared that the federal government had the authority and responsibility to undertake navigation improvements. At his recommendation, the House passed the Western Rivers Improvement Act in 1852, which contained $2.25 million for navigation improvements. The Upper Mississippi River received $90,000 for work between St. Louis and the Des Moines Rapids, $100,000 for the Des Moines and Rock Island Rapids, and $15,000 for the Dubuque harbor. Contractors began blasting and chiseling a channel through the Rock Island Rapids in August 1854 and continued work on the two rapids and Dubuque harbor until 1856.[7]

Overall the Corps made little progress before the Civil War. The large boats of the St. Louis-to-New Orleans trade could not operate on the Upper Mississippi River. The Corps simply did not have the funding or equipment to make substantial navigation improvements. While the Midwest gained political strength, slavery divided northern and southern Whigs. As a result, the Whigs lost control, and with the ascendancy of Democratic Party presidents Franklin Pierce (1853–1857) and James Buchanan (1857–1861), the economic panic of 1857, and the Civil War, further work on the river became impossible. Serious navigation improvements had to wait until after the war.[8]

In 1866, Congress authorized the four-foot channel project, the first of four major navigation projects to transform the Upper Mississippi

River into a commercial highway. The other projects were known as the four-and-a-half, six, and nine-foot channel projects. The Corps set each number, representing a depth, against the low-water year of 1864. So under the four-foot project, Congress charged the Corps with creating a continuous channel at least four feet deep for the Upper Mississippi, if the river fell as low as it had in 1864. The four projects employed three radically different approaches.[9]

The Corps pursued the four-foot channel by snagging (pulling trees out of the water), clearing away trees that overhung the river where the navigation channel hugged the shoreline, removing sunken vessels, and dredging. These measures, however, proved temporary. Sandbars quickly returned and each flood undercut the river's banks and delivered more trees into the water. For the Corps to make significant and permanent changes, Congress would have to authorize a much more aggressive program.

Railroads, in part, spurred the call for a new project by raising their rates. As the Midwest's agriculture and businesses boomed, railroads increasingly monopolized the region's shipping. To protest high rail rates, farmers joined an organization called the Patrons of Husbandry, or Grange, by the hundreds of thousands. Business interests in the Midwest and around the country attended cheap transportation meetings and lobbied for railroad regulation. Yielding to this pressure, Congress approved the four-and-a-half-foot channel project in 1878. While only one-half foot different, this project called for a new and more radical approach.

Under this project the Corps was to engrave a permanent channel, at least four and a half feet deep, in the river's shifting sand and gravel between the Illinois River and St. Paul. To create the channel, the engineers continued the dredging and snagging begun in 1866. More importantly, they started constricting or narrowing the river with wing dams and closing dams of rock and brush. Working like the nozzle of a garden hose, wing dams focused the river's current into a single channel, so it flowed faster. By flowing faster the river cut through sandbars and carried more suspended sediment. As water ran around the ends of the wing dams and into the space between or behind them, it slowed and the sediment dropped out. In this way, wing dams moved sandbars to places where they would not obstruct navigation. This project initiated the major transformation of the Upper Mississippi River's physical and ecological character (fig. 25).

FIGURE 25. *Wing dams below Nininger, Minnesota, 1891, by Henry P. Bosse. From the Rock Island District, U.S. Army Corps of Engineers.*

Wing dams depended upon the volume of water in the river. Without enough water, they could not scour the channel. To deliver more water to the main channel, the engineers built closing dams extending from the shore to an island or from one island to another. While the river could flow over them when high, for most of the year the dams directed water to the main channel.

Despite the navigation improvements made under the four-and-a-half-foot channel project, steamboat traffic declined. Too often the river fell so low that the wing dams and closing dams could not work. And as more and more sediment entered the river from lands ploughed up for agriculture and denuded of trees by the lumber industry, the wing dams and closing dams had to work harder. By the 1890s, timber rafting remained the only significant river traffic.

More than passenger or grain traffic, the four-and-a-half-foot channel project served the timber industry. Because it floated, timber emerged as the only significant commerce of the Upper Mississippi River during the last decades of the nineteenth century and first decades of the twentieth century. Raft boats pushed timber to mills all along the upper river. A typical raft of 2.5 million board feet carried enough timber to build 125 houses and covered three to four acres. Overall, 1.6 to 2.1 billion feet of lumber moved into and on the Upper Mississippi River each year between 1892 and 1900. After turning out two billion feet in 1901, mills along the river steadily declined. As the forests of Minnesota and Wisconsin began to disappear, so did sawmills and raft boats on the river. In 1915, the *Ottumwa Belle* guided the last lumber raft down the St. Croix and Mississippi rivers from Hudson, Wisconsin, to Fort Madison, Iowa. Without timber, the river ceased to be a meaningful part of the Midwest's transportation network.

In 1902, hoping to end river competition, railroad baron James J. Hill declared the Upper Mississippi River no longer worth improving for navigation. Hill scared cities and business interests along the river and triggered the first sustained navigation improvement movement by midwesterners. Backers of the new movement contended that a deeper channel, a six-foot one, would provide the depth, reliability, and economies of scale needed to restore river commerce and compete against railroads.

To fight for river transportation, upper river business and civic organizations formed the Upper Mississippi River Improvement Association in 1902 and began lobbying Congress for the deeper channel. Cities along the river dominated the organization. The decline of timber shipping and milling and the loss to railroads of most other commodities that might have been shipped via the river undermined the economies of many river cities. Farmers, enjoying unusual prosperity and therefore not as concerned about shipping costs, did not join in large numbers. For the next five years, the association steadily pushed for a six-foot channel. Responding to this lobbying, but more so to other national forces and to a railroad car shortage from 1906 to 1907 — which left midwestern grain rotting at terminals and the region short of coal during the winter — Congress authorized the six-foot channel in 1907.

Under the six-foot channel project, the Corps intensified channel constriction, narrowing the river even more. They did this by extending, raising, and adding wing dams. By 1930, the Corps had ribbed the river between St. Louis and St. Paul with wing dams and had closed many of the upper river's side channels. The reach from La Crosse to St. Paul contained over one thousand wing dams.

During the channel constriction era, the Corps completed one lock and dam on the Upper Mississippi River and a private interest erected another. In 1913, the Keokuk and Hamilton Power Company finished a hydroelectric dam at Keokuk, Iowa, at the base of the Des Moines Rapids, flooding it over. In 1917, the Corps completed Lock and Dam No. 1 between Minneapolis and St. Paul. The Corps built Lock and Dam No. 1 because, from St. Anthony Falls to the mouth of the Minnesota River at Fort Snelling, the river dropped through a deep, narrow gorge. The river descended faster between Minneapolis and St. Paul than anywhere else along its course, falling more than one hundred feet in under fifteen miles. Most of that drop occurred in the eight-and-one-half miles of the gorge. During high water, a fast and turbulent rapids boiled through the gorge. During low flows, it became a quick, rocky, and shallow stream that a person could wade across. In either condition, navigation ranged from treacherous to impossible. Zebulon Pike had ascended the gorge on September 26, 1805. He arrived at the foot of St. Anthony Falls, "after," he complained, "much labor in passing through the rapids." From the Minnesota River to St. Anthony, he wrote, "there is almost one continued rapid, aggravated by the interruption of 12 small islands."[10] Due to the rapids, the Grand Excursion's steamboats stopped in St. Paul, and the excursionists boarded whatever overland transportation they could find to visit St. Anthony Falls.

These locks and dams altered the river's physical and ecological character in new ways and presaged a bigger project, one that would replace channel constriction. Overall, the period from 1878 to 1930 was the era of channel constriction, a time when the river became increasingly narrow at low and medium flows. By 1930, however, the Upper Mississippi was evolving into two distinct reaches. While channel constriction was resculpting the whole upper river, agricultural levees had begun redefining the river between Rock Island and St. Louis.

LEVEES

Outside of navigation interests, flood plain farmers had the greatest initial impact on the Upper Mississippi River and its environment. Individual farmers had begun building the Upper Mississippi River's levee system before the Civil War by reinforcing and adding to the river's natural levees. Following the war, they started forming levee districts and inaugurated a campaign to capture much of the river's flood plain for agriculture. They raised, extended, and connected their levees and began draining the lands behind them. Reflecting the mentality of the time, they called this process reclamation, turning what they saw as useless swamps into productive fields.

During the 1880s, individuals and organizations occupying the flood plain began pushing for federal help and convinced Congress, over Corps objections, to authorize several levee projects under the guise of improving navigation. By 1900 Congress had directed the Corps to build or protect some of the most important agricultural levees on the Upper Mississippi River, but Congress balked at further federal help.

In 1917 Congress finally passed an official flood control act for the Mississippi River. The country's first such act, it allowed the Corps to work on levees from the Head of Passes, in Louisiana, to Rock Island. Through this act, the federal government assumed an official role in capturing the Mississippi River's flood plain wetlands. While channel constriction narrowed the whole Upper Mississippi River at low water, farmers and the Corps increasingly squeezed the river below Rock Island at high water. Reclamation there eliminated some of the river's natural flood storage capacity and destroyed thousands of acres of habitat for fish and wildlife. What would prevent farmers from isolating the flood plain above Rock Island behind levees?[11]

PARK AND REFUGE

By the early 1900s, reclamation, channel constriction, pollution, siltation, and resource overuse threatened the river's fish and wildlife. In response, conservationists mounted two campaigns to reserve large parts of the Upper Mississippi for native plants and animals and for recreation. Their success would determine the number of acres lost to reclamation above Rock Island.[12]

Beginning in 1909, conservationists in Iowa tried to establish a national park around Guttenberg in northeastern Iowa. Although they fought for more than a decade, they failed. Then, in 1922, Will Dilg, the Izaak Walton League's co-founder, thought of a new plan while fishing for bass off a wing dam near Wabasha, Minnesota. He suggested that Congress create a 260-mile-long national fish and wildlife refuge between Wabasha and Rock Island. Refuge proponents warned Congress that the Upper Mississippi River Valley faced an environmental crisis.

Under Dilg's leadership, conservationists focused on the dangers of reclamation to justify the refuge's formation. After landowners in an area called Winneshiek Bottoms proposed in 1923 to drain much of the thirty-mile-long, 28,000-acre wetland above and below Lansing, Iowa, for farming, refuge proponents went into action. In their testimony before Congress on the refuge bill and in their many writings, they detailed what losing the river's wetlands would mean, not only to the region but to the country. Refuge boosters insisted that destroying the wetlands would eliminate North America's most important flyway for migratory waterfowl. Dilg touted the proposed refuge as the greatest bass fishery in the country. He predicted bass would become extinct in the Upper Mississippi River unless Congress established the refuge soon. Other proponents argued that losing the Upper Mississippi's wetlands menaced not only the river's ecosystem but the Midwest's economy, which relied on tourism, the river's sport and commercial fisheries, and its mussels and waterfowl. The *Saturday Evening Post* joined the call for the refuge, arguing that "it is time for America to wake up and to call a halt on waste and our haste to develop every resource regardless of conditions. These great swamps . . . may conceivably be a better national asset in their natural state than under cultivation."[13]

To some refuge backers, losing the river's fisheries went beyond simple recreation; it affected the country's moral character. Missouri representative Harry B. Hawes, the bill's sponsor, argued: "We are going to make mollycoddles of our kids if they don't know how to use a fishing rod and a gun. We are going to lose the best American traditions if we do not have a place for our boys to play." He believed that the refuge would draw children from all over the country.[14]

Not only men and boys cared about the upper river's future. Frances E. Whitley, chair of the General Federation of Women's Clubs' Conservation Division, argued that a faster-flowing river would reduce mussel populations already threatened by pollution, silt, and overcollecting. Her organization supported the refuge, but not as a place for hunting or fishing. Its members were not sportsmen, she stressed. They backed the refuge idea because it "stands for one of the things that we have been working for ever since this division was organized in 1894, which is to try to conserve for the future some of the resources of this country both for the material prosperity and for the natural beauty that we believe is just as great a heritage which we ought to pass on to our children."[15]

Responding to these pleas and to national support for the refuge, Congress passed the refuge bill and President Calvin Coolidge signed it on June 7, 1924, creating the Upper Mississippi River National Wildlife and Fish Refuge. Where park proponents had failed, Dilg succeeded in making the refuge a national concern, not just a regional boon. Conservationists gained more than the refuge. They established an organization that could bring their vision for the river to life, and they now had something to protect and foster. They had established the foundation for future environmental efforts to protect the river. The refuge largely removed the river above Rock Island from reclamation and established Rock Island as the physical and ecological divide between two different Upper Mississippi Rivers. Above Rock Island the river could spread into its flood plain, whereas it could not below. Yet even greater changes were coming.

NINE-FOOT CHANNEL

By the time conservationists secured this victory, navigation on the upper river had died. Despite decades of building wing dams and closing dams, virtually no through traffic moved between St. Paul and St. Louis by 1918. Recognizing the lack of river competition, in 1922 the Interstate Commerce Commission put the Midwest on a dry-land rate basis (a rate for goods that only railroads were allowed to carry) and ordered railroads operating along the Mississippi River to sharply increase their rates. Midwestern business and civic organizations fought the decision for three years, but it took effect in 1925. In response, navigation boosters initiated another movement to revive navigation, a movement that surpassed all previous efforts. Between 1925 and 1930, they fought to restore river traffic and persuade Congress to authorize a new project for the river, one that would allow the river to truly compete with railroads. This movement would draw support from various entities: the largest and smallest businesses in the valley, most of its cities, the Midwest's principal farm organizations, and major political parties.

Through their efforts, navigation boosters convinced Congress to authorize Lock and Dam No. 2 at Hastings, Minnesota, in 1927, and the nine-foot channel project in 1930. The Corps completed Lock and Dam No. 2 in 1930. Under the nine-foot channel project, Congress directed the Corps to build twenty-three locks and dams from near Red

Wing, Minnesota, to Alton, Illinois. By 1940, the Corps finished the project. Subsequently, Congress added two locks and dams, allowing traffic to move above St. Anthony Falls. Known as Lower and Upper St. Anthony Falls Locks and Dams, the Corps completed these structures in 1956 and 1963, respectively. Together with Lock and Dam No. 1, which the Corps finished in 1917, these locks and dams made Minneapolis the head of navigation on the Mississippi. In 1973, the Corps finished Lock and Dam No. 27 above St. Louis, bringing the total number of locks and dams on the Upper Mississippi River to twenty-nine.

MODERN ISSUES ON A MODERN RIVER

In 1854 the Grand Excursionists anticipated America's economic manifest destiny without question. Whatever America needed to do to the Mississippi River to make it a vehicle for reaching this end, they applauded. The Grand Excursion of 2004 highlights how much we have changed and how diverse our visions for the river and the nation have become. This diversity is most apparent in the current controversy over the upper river's future. While a new generation of navigation boosters is calling for more navigation improvements, Will Dilg's heirs are insisting that the river's ecological qualities should come first.

The excursionists experienced the river during the packet boat heyday. Despite the threat posed by the Rock Island Railroad, most would have been surprised to know that river traffic died by the 1920s. They might have been even more surprised to know how much commerce now moves on the Upper Mississippi. In 1940, the upper river drew some 2.4 million tons of goods. By 1960 this number multiplied by more than ten to over twenty-seven million tons, and by 1970 the total doubled to about fifty-four million tons. In 1980, towboats pushed just over seventy-six million tons on the upper river. Although commerce declined during the mid 1980s, by 2000 shipping jumped to more than eighty-three million tons. The excursionists also would have been amazed to see towboats pushing fifteen barges (the standard upper river tow), and they would be flabbergasted to know this tow equaled the quantity carried by 250 railroad cars.[16]

Grain returned slowly to the river but eventually dominated. Wheat, corn, and soybeans accounted for less than 10 percent of the total commerce shipped on the upper river until 1958, when these crops reached

14 percent. By 1964 grain comprised 30 percent of the total tonnage shipped, but grain exports began booming after 1972. Between 1986 and 1995, grain shipping averaged 42.9 million tons or about 52 percent of the total annual tonnage. Corn and soybeans are the two principal crops moved on the upper river.[17]

The river transports many other commodities. Coal and petroleum products are the most important after grain. Between 1986 and 1995, barges carried an average of 9.8 million tons of coal or about 12 percent of the total. Petroleum products averaged 9.2 million tons (11 percent of the total) for the same period. Nonmetallic minerals and metals and industrial and agricultural chemicals accounted for most of the remaining tonnage.

The nine-foot channel project's success for navigation and its mounting adverse effect on the river's ecosystem is one source of the present debate about the river's future. Navigation boosters complain that demand for shipping on the river has exceeded the ability of the lock and dam system to carry it. Most lock chambers are 110 feet by 600 feet. As the standard tow is just shy of twelve hundred feet, it has to break apart to pass through a lock, causing costly delays and backing traffic up at some locks. Navigation boosters have cited eight of the twenty-nine upper river locks as among the twenty worst for delays in the country. These delays, they contend, cost shippers as much as $35 million per year. A fifteen-barge tow costs about $250 per hour to operate. The boosters want twelve hundred foot locks at some sites to eliminate the delays.

Environmentalists, however, contend that the navigation system, even without longer locks, is destroying the river's ecological health. Among the most striking changes from the natural river are huge open areas of water at the downstream end of each reservoir. Due to wave erosion, the reservoirs have eaten away many of the forested islands, so that the size of the open water area has expanded dramatically over the last sixty years. Today the maze of channels observed by the Grand Excursionists exists only at the upper end of the reservoirs.

As the river can still flood to its natural level above Rock Island, the Grand Excursionists might have seen the river as deep as the dams now hold it. The Corps built the dams (except Dam 19, which a private company erected for hydroelectric power) to serve only navigation; none of the dams control floods. When the river gets high, the Corps raises the dam gates, and the river flows freely. The dams prevent the river from falling below the minimum nine-foot depth. In doing so, they have eliminated the low end of the river's pulse.

While steamboat pilots might have viewed a permanently deep channel as an advantage, biologists today know that the river's pulse supported many ecological processes. Because the dams hold the river artificially high, large areas no longer dry out, keeping the sediment soft and loose. The sediment's condition has prevented seeds of important emergent aquatic plants from germinating. Since wind and boats stir the sediment, little light filters to the river bottom. With loose sediment and reduced light, submerged aquatic plants do not root firmly and have difficulty growing. Without these plants, waterfowl have to alter their migration route or face starvation. Furthermore, due to siltation in the generally placid reservoirs, the river's bottom is leveling out, which has altered fish habitats. Bass and other fish need deep holes outside the main channel to winter over, and the holes are disappearing. The more scientifically minded excursionists might have noticed that the flood plain forest is less diverse, since only a limited number of species can stand the constant moist conditions created by the reservoirs.

Ecological impacts also result from the elevation difference (the lift) above and below the nine-foot channel locks and dams. Most have lifts between five and sixteen feet, but those at Locks and Dams 1, 19, 26, 27, and those at Upper and Lower St. Anthony Falls exceed twenty feet. Because of the elevation differences and other factors, the dams prevent fish migration to varying degrees. Below Rock Island, where agricultural levees have limited how high the Corps could raise the reservoirs, the river cannot spread out as widely across its flood plain as it previously did. As a result fish and wildlife that depended upon lateral migration, or moving back and forth between the main channel and the backwaters, have lost their opportunity to do so. Above Rock Island, where farmers had constructed few agricultural levees, owing to the establishment of the refuge, the river spread into its natural flood plain and covered much of it permanently. These are only a few of the physical and ecological changes. There are many more; some obvious and some not.

The current debate about the river's future concerns whose priorities are the most important and which ones should take precedence. Representatives of both sides are looking at ways to stop and fix the worst problems without hindering navigation. It is likely that the attention brought to the Upper Mississippi region as a result of the 2004 Grand Excursion reenactment will broaden the discussion. Hopefully, decisions made over the river's future will consider all of its roles and assets.

Author's note: Much of this essay represents a synthesis of my book *The River We Have Wrought: A History of the Upper Mississippi,* published by the University of Minnesota Press in 2003.

THE GOVERNMENT BRIDGE AND ROLLER DAM BETWEEN DAVENPORT, IOWA AND ROCK ISLAND, ILL.

FIGURE 26. *This 1896 structure is the most recent of four bridges to have been built at the location of the first railroad bridge to span the Mississippi (1856). Trains are carried on the upper deck while cars and pedestrians use the lower deck. Unique to this bridge is the 366-foot swingspan that can revolve 360 degrees. Information from Mary Charlotte Aubry Costello,* Climbing the Mississippi River Bridge by Bridge, Volume One, From Louisiana to Minnesota, *p. 116. The adjacent Lock and Dam No. 15 was completed in 1934. From postcard 4A-H685, the Lake County (Illinois) Discovery Museum, Curt Teich Postcard Archives.*

PRESERVATION AND MANAGEMENT OF THE RIVER'S NATURAL RESOURCES *Gary C. Meyer*

The Upper Mississippi River's natural resources are vast, varied, and unique. These resources provide benefits — ecologic, economic, recreational, educational, inspirational — enjoyed by many millions of people annually. These benefits have contributed to the perception in the United States that the Mississippi is a national treasure, and to its recognition internationally as one of the world's great rivers.

Journalists traveling with the Grand Excursion of 1854 documented some of the river's inspirational qualities by stressing the abundance and diversity of natural resources in the Upper Mississippi region. They referred to "its remarkable features and resources," to "hills . . . [with] the appearance of cultivated pleasure grounds or parks," to "majestic rocks," to "delightful valleys, blooming in luxuriant herbage," to "scenery of the most beautiful description," and to "boundless prairies . . . in all their wildness and loveliness."[1] Incomplete as they are in providing a full appreciation of the richness and variety of the river's natural resource base (including its aquatic and wildlife resources) these accounts describe resources that the region's settlers, in this era of essentially unbridled resource exploitation, had already haltingly begun to conserve and preserve.

Hundreds of government agencies and numerous other organizations, commissions, and committees engage today in one or more management-related activities aimed at preserving, protecting, regulating, and enhancing the Upper Mississippi's natural resources. The focus of this essay is on a set of entities — federal, state, and local government agencies — that have major responsibilities in the management of parks, recreation areas, refuges, preserves, and other land and water units. This essay examines the units managed by these agencies by placing their formation into four historical eras or periods — beginning before the

Grand Excursion and extending to the present — and by considering each unit's natural attributes, management objectives, recreational facilities, and other uses. It also provides context for the various management units by first introducing the natural resources of the river from St. Paul to Rock Island, with emphasis on their diversity and distinctiveness.

NATURAL RESOURCES OF THE UPPER MISSISSIPPI[2]

The U.S. Congress formally recognized the value of the Upper Mississippi River's natural resources in 1986 in the Water Resources Development Act, which designated the Upper Mississippi River system — defined as the river extending from Minneapolis to Cairo, Illinois, and its drainage basin — as a "nationally significant ecosystem" (a biological community of different species interacting with one another and with their environment). Although shorter than the river's reach as defined by Congress, the Upper Mississippi region considered in this book is a vital part of the larger river system and contributes ecological benefits to downstream portions of the ecosystem, including water and material transport, migration routes, and nutrient cycling.

Important plant communities of the Upper Mississippi River include submersed and emergent aquatic vegetation and floodplain forests. Each provides critical and varied benefits to the river ecosystem. Submersed and emergent aquatic vegetation produces dissolved oxygen, filters suspended particulates, stabilizes bottom sediments, and provides food and shelter for fish, aquatic invertebrates, and migrating waterfowl. Floodplain forests furnish essential habitat for many bird species and for fish and wildlife during floods, and they reduce erosion, enhance water quality, and provide scenic and recreational landscapes.

Fish rank near the top in any appraisal of the river's most cherished biological resources. The Upper Mississippi is home to about 120 species of fish, an exceptionally large number for a river in a temperate climatic zone and far more than the fifteen or fewer species found in a typical midwestern lake. The river's wide-ranging aquatic environments and north-south orientation create conditions favorable for sustaining sturgeon, paddlefish, and several other species with ancient lineages; bass, panfish, catfish, and other popular sport fish; and buffalo, carp, drum, and other species that contribute to the commercial fishing industry.

About thirty-five species of freshwater mussels and many species of macro invertebrates (river fauna) such as insects, worms, and some crustaceans and mollusks, are widely dispersed in the Upper Mississippi. The river's diverse aquatic habitats, ranging from soft, bottom substrates of mud and sand to aquatic plants and hard substrates such as rocks and woody debris, provide the varied environments needed to support these organisms. Freshwater mussels furnish food for mammals, birds, and fish, and macro invertebrates serve as a major part of the diet for some fish and birds.

In addition to fish and other aquatic organisms, the Upper Mississippi River's habitats, including wetlands and floodplain forests, support about sixty species of mammals, forty-five species of amphibians and reptiles, and nearly three hundred species of birds. The river is especially critical to North American bird and waterfowl populations. It shelters and provides feeding and resting places for millions of birds migrating through the Mississippi River corridor or those remaining permanently. Mallards and other dabbling ducks, as well as geese, wading birds, and songbirds, use shallow backwater wetlands. Swans, cormorants, and diving ducks depend on the river's deep, open pools. Raptors and songbirds nest in bottomland forests.

Waterfowl are the river's most economically important migratory birds. Expenditures on travel and equipment associated with the hunting of waterfowl in the Upper Mississippi flyway produce economic impacts on the region of many millions of dollars annually. And bird watching, a popular nonconsumptive use of waterfowl, generates additional economic impacts.

The Upper Mississippi and its adjacent upland environments harbor numerous rare, endangered, or threatened plant and wildlife species. Such varied species as the pallid sturgeon, Higgins eye mussel, and least tern are included on the federal list of endangered species. Other species are, or have been, candidates for federal listing as endangered or threatened. Many additional species have been given endangered or threatened designations, or are considered rare or of special concern by one or more of the four states that adjoin the river.

The bald eagle, national symbol and perhaps the country's highest-profile wildlife species, was proposed amid much fanfare in 1999 for delisting as a threatened species from the federal register in the lower forty-eight states. Bald eagle populations had plummeted in the 1950s and 1960s because of reproductive failure caused by pesticides (particularly chlorinated hydrocarbons such as DDT) in fish, their primary diet, as well as habitat loss and illegal hunting. President Clinton and other government officials heralded the recovery of the bald eagle as a dramatic success story, attributable in part to actions initiated under the landmark Endangered Species Act of 1973. As in a number of other regions in the country, bald eagle populations in the Upper Mississippi have soared over the past twenty-five years, and eagle watching has become an eagerly pursued recreational activity.

BEFORE THE GRAND EXCURSION OF 1854

Efforts by government agencies to manage the Upper Mississippi's natural resources prior to 1854 were minuscule. Federal and state agencies did not allocate land for recreational uses until the twentieth century. But a handful of towns and cities set aside for public use a few parcels of land or open space as commons or squares. Consistent with national trends of the time, these parcels were seldom envisioned initially as spaces for parks or recreation areas. The provision of public space for recreation (especially outdoor recreation) was still in an embryonic state. Workers commonly endured long workdays and workweeks and they had little leisure time and discretionary income that could be applied to recreation. Only later, if at all, would these commons or squares become recreation spaces.

In 1836 the federal government designated four parcels of land in Dubuque to be reserved for public use. The directive helped to establish the park system of this modest settlement of one thousand people. At about the same time, when the community was originally laid out, Davenport dedicated two public squares. A few years later, in 1849, the first public squares or parks in St. Paul (and in the Twin Cities area) resulted from donations of three pieces of land to the city by civic-minded individuals. By the end of this period, Moline and Rock Island had also dedicated public squares.

The region's first public spaces received varied uses early in their history. A log structure built in one of Dubuque's public spaces served as a meeting place for a Methodist congregation and as a schoolhouse and courtroom. Another Dubuque public space served as a cemetery for more than thirty years, and still another as a city marketplace. An early square or park in St. Paul provided pasture and a place where women of the neighborhood could shake their rugs.

1855–1915

Land allocated to public use and to parks and other recreational uses increased greatly across the Upper Mississippi region between 1855 and 1915, but this growth was entirely at the local level. More and more cities and towns that before the date of the Grand Excursion had not designated land for public use began to do so, while others that had, like Dubuque and Davenport, expanded their public land holdings. What occurred in the Upper Mississippi at the local level matched national trends, but the region lagged behind the country in the formation of park and recreation areas at the state and national levels.

Scanty funding for development and maintenance of the region's public lands and parks characterized much of this period. In 1889, forty years after dedicating its first public squares, St. Paul had thirty-seven parcels of land, totaling 367 acres, that had been donated or acquired for "public park purposes." But 257 acres, or 70 percent of the city's total park acreage, were in only one park (Como Park), which had been largely neglected and undeveloped for fourteen years after its acquisition in 1873. Most of the remaining parcels were small, and some did not survive as public space. In 1907, nearly seventy-five years after land in Dubuque was first dedicated for public use, Charles Robinson, an eastern park specialist, said of the city's parks: "I have never seen a place where the Almighty has done more, and mankind less, than Dubuque."[3] Although some of Dubuque's citizens took offense at his comments, Robinson's candid remarks did serve to stimulate the city to expand and improve its park system. In 1908 Dubuque purchased a one-hundred-acre tract of land on which it developed one of its foremost parks, Eagle Point Park.

With a location overlooking the Mississippi, Eagle Point Park was one of a slowly growing number of the region's parks that later in this period were sited on or close to the river. Previously, most municipal public squares and parks had been located in or near downtown areas but not adjoining the river, even though early in this period a few visionary individuals argued that the river and its bluffs provided scenic beauty meriting preservation. In 1872, for example, Horace Cleveland, a nationally prominent landscape architect, proposed that St. Paul and Minneapolis create a joint plan to preserve their river bluffs and create a system of parks and parkways along the Mississippi in order to discourage unwise development.

The latter part of this period also witnessed the appearance of park boards or commissions, organized park systems, and a wider acceptance of using public funds for developing parks. The beginning of St. Paul's park "system" is sometimes dated to 1887 when the state legislature authorized the creation of a Board of Park Commissioners and gave it control of a city park fund whose revenues came from the issue of bonds. Also in 1887, Rock Island appointed its first park commissioner. Davenport adopted an ordinance in 1890 providing for the election of park commissioners and for levying taxes for parks. Dubuque elected its first park board in 1910. Again, these developments and trends were congruent with those at the national level.

1916–1950

This period marks the emergence and rise to prominence of state and federal agencies in the acquisition and development of parks, refuges, and recreation areas in the Upper Mississippi region. In 1917 Wyalusing State Park became Wisconsin's fourth state park and the Upper Mississippi's first such park. Initially named Nelson Dewey, after Wisconsin's first state governor, the park's name became Wyalusing in 1937 when Dewey's homestead was purchased and made into Nelson Dewey State Park. The creation of Wyalusing followed a recommendation by nationally acclaimed landscape architect John Nolen in 1909 that the state preserve the best of its scenic wonders by acquiring land for four additional state parks (Wisconsin already had two), including this one at the confluence of the Mississippi and Wisconsin rivers.

Seven state parks in the region were dedicated in the 1920s and 1930s: Mississippi Palisades in Illinois; Bellevue and Pikes Peak in Iowa; John A. Latsch in Minnesota; and Merrick, Nelson Dewey, and Perrot in Wisconsin. The 1920s and 1930s were especially active decades nationally for the formation of state parks. States developed and expanded their park systems, inspired in part by the recommendation of Stephen Mather, influential director of the National Park Service, at a national conference on state parks in 1921. Mather noted that the resources of the Park Service would permit it to acquire and administer only areas of prime national significance, and he recommended that sites of lesser significance that had been promoted by citizens and politicians for inclusion in the national park system be considered for state parks. Mather promised the states that the Park Service would assist them in undertaking park development.

The creation of state parks in the 1920s and 1930s also received a vital boost from the generous donations to the states of land or money by individual benefactors. In this regard, the Upper Mississippi's experience paralleled the nation's. John A. Latsch, a Winona, Minnesota, businessman and conservationist, donated land near Winona for two Wisconsin parks (Perrot and Merrick) and one Minnesota park (John A. Latsch).

Latsch also donated much of the land that today comprises Winona's extensive city park system.

Merrick was the only one of the state parks formed on the Upper Mississippi before 1940 to be sited essentially on bottomlands along the river. The other parks included bluffs overlooking the river. Several park bluffs today provide breathtaking and (for this observer) occasionally vertiginous views of the Mississippi from elevations that rise more than five hundred feet above the river. Perhaps the most stunning views are those from Pikes Peak and Wyalusing, from which one can see Wisconsin's longest river, the 430-mile Wisconsin, join the Mississippi. Pikes Peak possessed more than a scenic view to Zebulon Pike (for whom the park is named), who extolled its strategic assets. Sent by the U.S. government shortly after the Louisiana Purchase to explore the Mississippi Valley in 1805, Pike's objectives included selecting locations suitable for military posts and searching for the headwaters of the river. Pike endorsed a towering bluff in the park that carries his name for a military post, but nearby Prairie du Chien was chosen instead.

More than a century before Pike's expedition, Europeans had first viewed the meeting of the Wisconsin and Mississippi rivers. On June 17, 1673, Father Jacques Marquette and explorer Louis Joliet completed their famous journey across Wisconsin and steered their canoes from the lower course of the Wisconsin River into the Mississippi. Readers of *Midwest Living* magazine in 1992 rated the sweeping vision of the rivers presented from atop Pikes Peak as the prettiest overlook view in a twelve-state Midwest region. The equally dramatic view of the rivers from Wyalusing was ranked by *Wisconsin Trails* magazine in 1997 as Wisconsin's most scenic.[4] Partly because of its blufftop vistas, but also because it provides outstanding recreational opportunities, Wyalusing was voted Wisconsin's fourth most popular state park and the best for watching wildlife by readers of Wisconsin's largest newspaper, the *Milwaukee Journal Sentinel,* in 2000.[5]

In addition to scenic panoramas, the sites selected for the region's state parks often incorporate other extraordinary natural features. Mississippi Palisades includes a line of bold, lofty cliffs along the river, reminiscent of the Palisades of the Hudson, for which it is named, as well as caves, sinkholes, deep ravines, and unusual rock formations. Perrot includes 425-foot-high Trempealeau Mountain, the only geological feature of its kind on the Upper Mississippi River: a mountain or bluff completely surrounded by water. The mountain serves as a navigational landmark and as a sacred place for Native Americans. Bellevue contains a butterfly garden, unique to the Midwest and one of only a handful of such sanctuaries in the United States.

In 1935, midway through the Great Depression, Iowa established the Yellow River State Forest, one of two state forests in the Upper Mississippi region. Sited on land adjacent to the Yellow River near its confluence with the Mississippi, the great majority of the forest's land — fifteen hundred acres — was transferred in 1949 to the National Park Service to form the Effigy Mounds National Monument. Later land acquisitions increased the state forest's area to almost eighty-five hundred acres, including islands and sloughs in the Mississippi and uplands close to the river.

The federal government's role in managing the Upper Mississippi's natural resources began in 1924. At this time it established the Upper Mississippi River National Wildlife and Fish Refuge, which came nearly two decades after the dedication in 1903 of the country's first national wildlife refuge in Florida. Indisputably one of the country's most important refuges, "Upper Miss," as the refuge is often called, consists of 233,000 acres of wooded islands, sloughs, marshland, and winding channels. Extending continuously for 261 miles from the mouth of the Chippewa River just north of Wabasha, Minnesota, almost to Rock Island, Upper Miss is the longest refuge in the lower forty-eight states. Since it includes over 70 percent of the Upper Mississippi's length from St. Paul to Rock Island, Upper Miss incorporates most of the biological diversity of the river and its flood plain.

Managed by the U.S. Fish and Wildlife Service in cooperation with the U.S. Army Corps of Engineers and state and local units of government, Upper Miss is considered an overlay refuge. It includes land owned by the Fish and Wildlife Service and by the Corps of Engineers. On land owned by the Corps, the Fish and Wildlife Service assumes management, but the Corps retains certain other rights, especially related to forestry.

Although the primary management objective for Upper Miss is to protect and nurture habitat for fish, migratory waterfowl, and other wildlife, recreational use of the refuge has risen substantially over the years, and especially since the 1950s. Upper Miss now receives more recreational use than any other national refuge: about 3.5 million visits annually, a number comparable to Yellowstone Park. Boat and bank anglers comprise about half of the refuge's annual recreation participants, followed by sightseers and nonfishing boaters, but visitors also pursue many other recreational and educational activities.

The next benchmark for federally managed refuges in this region occurred in 1936, when Trempealeau National Wildlife Refuge was established. Also managed by the Fish and Wildlife Service, the refuge has been called one of Wisconsin's best-kept secrets. Located within the flood plain of the Mississippi where the Mississippi and Trempealeau Rivers meet, its history began with the setting aside of 706 acres as a refuge for migratory birds and other wildlife. About five thousand acres were added to the refuge in 1979 with the purchase of most of an adjoining fish and fur farm. The refuge includes three principal plant communities: sand prairie, backwater marsh, and hardwood forest. An upland portion of the refuge is surrounded by backwater wetlands that have been protected from floodwater sediment of the Mississippi and Trempealeau Rivers by railroad and diversion dikes. The dikes have helped foster a variety of marsh plants, some of which are unique to the Upper Mississippi. Birds and other wildlife species abound. Open year-round, the refuge provides abundant water- and land-based recreation opportunities.

Although best known for its long history of participation in navigation projects on the Upper Mississippi, the Corps of Engineers also has had a prominent, but briefer, role as a provider of recreation opportunities. Significant recreation use of the Corps's properties can be dated to the 1930s, when the locks and dams associated with the nine-foot navigation channel unexpectedly began drawing visitors. The Corps did not initially encourage recreational use of these properties; it merely responded to such use by building guardrails on dams and constructing other facilities designed to ensure visitor safety. In 1944, with the passage of the Flood Control Act, the Corps was authorized, but not required, to construct, maintain, and operate public park and recreation facilities at water resource projects under its control or to permit local agencies to assume responsibility for such projects. But it was not until the early 1960s, as recreational use of its properties continued to grow, that the Corps sanctioned many of its facilities on the Mississippi as official recreation sites.

With thirteen project sites located mostly along the Illinois and Iowa portions of the river, the Corps today manages parks and recreation areas that generally emphasize multiple recreation activities. The Corps also owns a number of other recreation sites along the river that are managed wholly or partly by counties or municipalities. Typically small (on average fewer than thirty acres), the Corps's recreation sites provide facilities ranging from Spartan to modern. Most provide opportunities for both water- and land-based activities, including camping. Several of the larger sites offer interpretive programs and other nature-oriented activities. A few sites also incorporate outstanding views of the river and opportunities for visitors to view wildlife and birds, including bald eagles at Wisconsin's Blackhawk Park in the winter.

The depression of the 1930s impacted recreation in the country and in the Upper Mississippi region both negatively and positively. Reduced tax collections associated with the distressed economy produced cuts in government appropriations for parks and recreation. Conversely, Roosevelt's New Deal program pumped large quantities of money into public works projects. The Civilian Conservation Corps built and improved recreation facilities, ranging from trails and campgrounds to recreation centers and picnic shelters. The legacy of these programs can be seen across the Upper Mississippi region in parks and recreation areas at all levels of government.

Near the end of this period, in 1949, the National Park Service dedicated Effigy Mounds National Monument, located near Marquette, Iowa. Formed after about forty years of an on-again, off-again campaign by Iowans to create a national park and, after that effort failed, a national monument in northeastern Iowa, Effigy Mounds preserves 195 known ceremonial and burial mounds of prehistoric peoples. Most of the mounds have geometric shapes, but the shapes for which the monument is named take the form of bear and bird effigies (images). The monument contains thirty-one effigy mounds, built between 450 B.C. and A.D. 1300 by Native American tribal people often categorized as the Effigy Mounds culture, whose geographic domain focused on what is now southern Wisconsin and smaller parts of Iowa, Minnesota, and Illinois.

Comprising 2,526 acres, Effigy Mounds National Monument recently has received about eighty thousand visitors a year. Although the monument has no roads or facilities for picnicking or camping, it has eleven miles of trails. The monument also incorporates diverse plant and animal life, and its trails lead to several overlooks that provide striking views of the Mississippi River.

1951 TO THE PRESENT

Several national trends related to the management of land and water impacted the Upper Mississippi region in the 1950s and 1960s. One trend emerged from a growing recognition and concern among ecologists and conservationists that forces of development were increasingly threatening the area's organisms and ecosystems. State and federal agencies responded to this concern by establishing various natural areas preservation programs. At the state level, Wisconsin led the way by creating the country's first state natural areas program in 1952. Illinois initiated a program in 1963, followed by Iowa in 1965 and Minnesota in 1974. In the Upper Mississippi region, the four states collectively managed about twenty-five natural areas or preserves. These ecologically sensitive areas generally receive little publicity, in part to minimize potential human disturbance. In fact, the use of some of these areas is reserved mainly for scientific purposes, an intent made explicit in the naming of Wisconsin's areas as "scientific" until 1985, when "natural" was adopted, and in the designation "scientific and natural" that is presently applied to Minnesota's areas.

Five state natural areas in the Upper Mississippi are sited in state parks. Most, but not all, of the other state-designated natural areas are on state-owned land. Natural areas vary greatly in size — from about three to more than three thousand acres — and incorporate a wealth of geological, ecological, and archaeological diversity. Each of Iowa's three preserves protects geological and archaeological resources, including prehistoric Native American mounds. Minnesota's natural areas include nesting sites for water birds and for wintering bald eagles, two sites with rolling sand dune topography on terraces of the Mississippi, and a goat prairie. Natural areas in Wisconsin include two nearly pure stands of black walnut, and dry, lime prairies with many native plants. Natural areas in Illinois include a loess hill prairie, a sand hill prairie, and an upland forest.

Management strategies for state natural areas vary somewhat from area to area, depending upon such factors as the area's ownership, size, and ecological characteristics. In some instances managers concentrate on protecting these generally fragile, unexploited areas by instituting rather passive measures designed to control and restrict public access. In other cases, management includes active ecosystem intervention focused on restoring and maintaining natural conditions. Controlling invasive woody plants in prairie environments by using prescribed burning, designed to emulate the role of natural fires in the ecology of pre-settlement prairies, illustrates this more hands-on management approach.

Three areas in the Upper Mississippi — two in state parks (Mississippi Palisades and Wyalusing) and one located outside a park — have been designated National Natural Landmarks. Begun in 1962 by the Department of the Interior, this program identifies and encourages the preservation of ecological and geological features, on either public or private land, that represent nationally significant examples of the country's natural heritage. The Mississippi Palisades landmark includes both geological and ecological features (prominent rock formations and varied plant life), and the Wyalusing landmark delimits an old-growth, hardwood forest climbing a slope from the Wisconsin River. State park agencies manage the two landmarks so as to preserve their distinctive natural attributes and to minimize human impacts.

The third National Natural Landmark, the Nelson-Trevino Bottoms, is one of Wisconsin's (and the Upper Mississippi's) truly remarkable natural areas. Occupying 3,740 acres just south of the confluence of the Chippewa and Mississippi rivers near the village of Nelson, this natural area is part of the Upper Mississippi River Wildlife and Fish Refuge. Basically road-less and pristine, the bottoms are a maze of channels and aquatic and terrestrial vegetation, rich in rare bird species and other wildlife. Although the Nelson-Trevino Bottoms also has been designated a Wisconsin natural area, the U.S. Fish and Wildlife Service manages the area. Its management plan, developed in concert with the Wisconsin Department of Natural Resources, affirms the area's wilderness character.

Socioeconomic changes in American society that intensified after World War II have produced another important trend impacting the allocation and use of recreation-related areas in the region. Recreation demand and participation increased dramatically in association with shorter working hours, larger blocks of leisure time (especially two-day weekends), growing prosperity, and more discretionary income. Greater access to recreation resources resulted from expanding ownership of automobiles, boats with outboard motors, and other mechanized recreation equipment. The creation of new parks and recreation areas in the Upper Mississippi has been one response to these changes.

Minnesota added three new state parks (Frontenac, Fort Snelling, and Great River Bluffs) between 1957 and 1976, and Iowa dedicated the Mines of Spain State Recreation Area in 1981. The intriguing name Mines of Spain is a legacy of the lead-mining era in northeastern Iowa. In 1796 a land grant of that name was given to Julian Dubuque by the Spanish governor of Louisiana to mine a 189-square-mile area that includes

FIGURE 27. *State parks and major federal reserves on the Upper Mississippi.*

the present-day recreation area. Although it differs in some ways from an Iowa state park — notably in its provision of facilities for day-use only and in its greater emphasis on interpretive activities — Mines of Spain also has many elements in common with a state park, and materials publicizing the area often refer to it as such.

Agencies managing the state parks in the Upper Mississippi region have experienced changes in name and organization over the years. A Department of Natural Resources now administers the state parks of each of the four states, and the states have adopted an analogous approach to developing and managing their parks. The parks preserve areas of statewide significance because of scenic, geologic, ecological, archaeological, historical, or wildlife featues, and they also help the states meet the needs of their residents for outdoor recreation, both active and passive.

The Upper Mississippi's eleven state parks and one state recreation area incorporate more than 20,500 acres, with a range among the parks from about thirty-four hundred acres (Fort Snelling) to 320 acres (Merrick). Partly reflecting their average size of more than seventeen hundred acres, the parks typically incorporate substantial topographic variation and a rich and diverse ecological environment. Many contain heavily wooded bluffs, flood plains, and a wide array of birds, mammals, and other wildlife. Some have grassland environments, including high "goat" prairies that usually form on south- or west-facing slopes in areas inhospitable to trees because of site conditions that include rapid temperature transitions, accelerated freezing and thawing cycles, and soils with relatively poor moisture retention.

The parks provide varied, year-round recreation opportunities. Hiking and picnicking are universally available, and campsites (often ranging from modern to primitive) are provided in all of the parks but Fort Snelling and Mines of Spain. Hiking trails vary in length among the parks from more than twenty miles to less than a mile. In most of the parks, the trails provide the best access to scenic vistas overlooking the river and to plant and animal life. In several of the Wisconsin and Iowa parks, the trails pass prehistoric Native American burial or ceremonial grounds.

Although a few of the region's state parks are lightly used, several receive rather heavy visitation. Annual visits have ranged recently from about ten thousand at John A. Latsch, a park with no developed facilities, to about 600,000 at Mississippi Palisades and at Fort Snelling, Minnesota's most-visited state park (to no small degree because of its location in the Twin Cities). Two other parks — Pikes Peak and Perrot — receive more than 200,000 visits annually.

Minnesota established in 1961 the Upper Mississippi region's second state forest, the Richard J. Dorer Memorial Hardwood Forest. Portions of this expansive, 43,000-acre forest extend discontinuously along the Mississippi for more than one hundred miles, from north of Red Wing, Minnesota, to the Iowa border. Great River Bluffs State Park lies within this forest. Like Iowa's Yellow River State Forest, Dorer Forest is managed for multiple uses: the production of forest products, the protection of wildlife habitat, the maintenance of watershed integrity, and the provision of a diverse array of facilities and opportunities for outdoor recreation.

In 1988 the National Park Service began collaborating with numerous partners in the management, operation, and administration of the Mississippi National River and Recreation Area (MNRRA), a unique type of park. The MNRRA is a seventy-two-mile corridor on either side of the Mississippi stretching southward from the cities of Dayton and Ramsey, Minnesota, through Minneapolis-St. Paul to just south of Hastings, Minnesota. Of the approximately fifty-two thousand acres included in the MNRRA's boundaries, only forty-five acres — all islands — are owned and managed by the Park Service. County and municipal governments as well as the state of Minnesota manage the vast majority of the acreage, which includes city, county, regional, and state parks.

The MNRRA was formed to serve three primary purposes: (1) to protect, preserve, and enhance nationally significant resources in the Mississippi River corridor in the Twin Cities area; (2) to coordinate local, state, and federal programs in the corridor; and (3) to provide a framework to assist the state of Minnesota and local government units to develop and implement integrated resource management programs to ensure orderly development in the corridor. The National Park Service provides educational and interpretive programs, services, and products focusing on the corridor, and it helps enhance the corridor's many recreation opportunities.

County governments in the Upper Mississippi region (and in the nation) have shorter histories than cities and towns in the development of parks and recreation areas. The role of counties as recreation providers has grown substantially since 1950. As in other parts of the United States, counties in this region typically operate parks intermediate in size and concept between smaller, more developed municipal parks and larger, less developed state parks. Nationally, county parks often center on a resource such as a forest, lake, or river, whereas municipal parks tend to be less resource-oriented. But the river and bluffs in this region present appealing opportunities for cities as well as counties to capitalize on a resource in creating a park.

As a result of state legislation in the 1950s that enabled counties to establish conservation boards, Iowa has the most extensively developed system of county parks and recreation areas in the region. Each Iowa county now has a conservation board that can acquire, develop, and maintain public parks, preserves, parkways, county forests, and conservation areas. The programs of conservation boards are supported by county tax funds, supplemented by user fees, grants, and donations. Iowa counties along the Mississippi participate variously in county board programs. Their participation depends on such factors as the amount of their land in state and federal ownership. Several of the counties have numerous river-oriented parks. The Jackson County Conservation Board, for example, manages six parks near Bellevue and Sabula. Ranging in size from forty-three acres to less than one acre, most of these parks provide opportunities for fishing and picnicking, and two parks, each on land leased from the Corps of Engineers, have campgrounds.

County parks in other states in the region range from urban-based county or regional parks in the Twin Cities of Minnesota and the Quad Cities of Iowa and Illinois, to rural sites similar to those of Jackson County, Iowa. A few sites are larger than several of the region's state parks, as exemplified by Goose Island County Park, a few miles south of La Crosse. Created in 1960 and leased by La Crosse County from the Corps of Engineers, this 717-acre park provides striking views of bluffs along the Mississippi and extensive facilities for camping, picnicking, and other recreation activities.

Today, virtually every city, town, or village along the Upper Mississippi has at least one park or recreation area, and even small villages sometimes have several. Common references to "riverside," "riverview," "riverfront," and "river valley" in the names of municipal parks and recreation areas attest to the importance of the river as a site factor in the location of these facilities. River parks are typically small, often only an acre or two, and provide facilities for two or three recreational activities such as picnicking, fishing, swimming, and boat launching. Some parks are much larger — occasionally more than two hundred acres — and offer a greater array of recreation activities. A few communities, notably Guttenberg and Clinton, Iowa, feature attractive linear parks with lengthy walkways along the river.

Other communities have taken advantage of blufftop sites to develop parks. Among the best examples are Alma, Wisconsin (Buena Vista Park), Winona, Minnesota (Garvin Heights Park), Lansing, Iowa (Mt. Hosmer), and La Crosse, Wisconsin (Grandad Bluff). Accessible by car or on foot (for more adventuresome individuals with healthy cardiovascular systems), each of these parks provides commanding views of the Mississippi from elevations approaching or exceeding five hundred feet above the river. A twisting, tree-canopied road leads to the summit of Mt. Hosmer, where a sign declares: "Mt. Hosmer City Park [dedicated in 1923] was named after Harriet Hosmer, a noted sculptress who won a foot race to the summit during a steamboat layover in 1851." Grandad Bluff, a 150-acre park from which visitors can see parts of Wisconsin, Iowa, and Minnesota, presents "the most scenic view in Wisconsin," according to a 1992 vote by readers of *Wisconsin Trails* magazine; the confluence of the Mississippi and Wisconsin rivers as viewed from atop the bluffs in Wyalusing State Park was a close second in that poll.[6]

Several municipal parks feature wildlife observation. Riecks Lake Park, located on a slough just north of Alma, Wisconsin, hosts waterfowl that regularly pass through the area. An observation platform, funded by the U.S. Fish and Wildlife Service and Alma area patrons and maintained by the City of Alma, provides visitors with a splendid opportunity to watch migratory birds, notably tundra swans (formerly known as whistling swans). Other parks and observation sites along the river from the Quad Cities and Clinton, Iowa, to Genoa, Wisconsin, and Wabasha, Minnesota, present opportunities to observe wintering bald eagles. Areas of open water just below the river's locks and dams, where fish congregate, provide some of the best eagle-viewing sites.

A multitude of government agencies now manage the Upper Mississippi River's bountiful and unique natural resources. Early management efforts, dating to the 1830s, were minimal, geographically spotty, and concentrated only at the local level. Involvement of state and federal agencies occurred much later, beginning near the entry of the United States into World War I — when the preservation and management of land and water resources in the United States were taking on greater importance — and intensified in the 1920s and 1930s. In the several decades following the end of World War II, as demand for outdoor recreation grew sharply, a number of new parks and recreation areas were created, and natural areas were established to preserve and perpetuate natural features and rare resources of exceptional ecological, scientific, and educational value.

Federal, state, and local government agencies clearly have made some wise and prescient decisions to conserve and preserve some of the best, most distinctive, and most representative of the Upper Mississippi's extraordinary resources. These agencies also have provided abundant opportunities for residents of the region and visitors alike to access these resources and to derive recreational, educational, and inspirational benefits from them. In their combined and largely successful efforts to preserve these resources and to make them available for use, these agencies have contributed immeasurably to the quality of life in the region.

FIGURE 28. *"A far reaching view from Fire Point, Effigy Mounds National Monument, near Marquette and McGregor, Iowa." Off in the distance are the confluence of the Wisconsin and Mississippi Rivers, Pikes Peak (Iowa) and Wyalusing (Wisconsin) State Parks, and the 1932 suspension bridges connecting Marquette, Iowa, with Prairie du Chien, Wisconsin. Color photo by Margery Goergen. From a postcard published by Goergen Studio, McGregor, Iowa, made by Dexter Press, Inc., West Nyack, New York.*

A RIVER OF LOGS
Gayle Rein

"Tim-ber-r-r-r!" This cry reverberated through the last half of the nine-teenth century, both in northern forests and in company boardrooms along the Upper Mississippi River and its Wisconsin and Minnesota trib-utaries. Pine lumber and log rafts — some four acres in size — floated to lumberyards and sawmills along these rivers. During the years from 1850 to 1869, the populations of Illinois, Iowa, Wisconsin, and Minnesota more than doubled. To supply the burgeoning settlements with afford-able lumber, loggers and lumber barons performed feats comparable to those of legendary lumberjack Paul Bunyan and turned the Upper Mis-sissippi into a river of logs.

Earlier trailblazers like Willard Keyes, James Lockwood, and John Shaw in the Wisconsin Territory had tried to establish sawmills from 1810 to 1837. At that time, however, they lacked both a market and, more impor-tantly, the right to cut on government or Native American land. The Panic of 1837 also prevented financial speculation. But by the middle of the nineteenth century things were different. Future lumber barons Freder-ick Weyerhaeuser, F. C. A. Denkmann, Chancy Lamb, Thomas B. Walker, Orrin Ingram, John Knapp, William H. Laird, Isaac Staples, Dorilus Mor-rison, and others parlayed the need for lumber into financial dynasties. Despite a precarious economy, they set up logging camps in Wisconsin and Minnesota and built sawmills. When the century ended, more than fifty sawmills could be found on the Upper Mississippi and its tributaries.

It was not an easy way to make a fortune. Sawmill owners could expect to face catastrophes such as logjams, flooded streams, or low water that impeded delivery to the mills. Fire threatened timber sites and sawmills, many of which had to be rebuilt frequently, and the Civil War created a worker shortage. As editor Horace Greeley, who had traveled extensively in the West, reported in an 1865 *New York Tribune* article:

> Like all hazardous pursuits . . . [the lumber business] attracts thou-sands by its possibilities of sudden wealth — possibilities which are seldom transmuted into realities. The poor lumberman fails to get out

his logs promptly, and is made bankrupt by the delay or he gets them out, saws and runs them, only to find the market so glutted with boards that must be sold, that he cannot meet his liabilities. Only a great capital and shrewd, far-seeing management can ride safely the wild billows which sweep across the lumberman's course; and this region [of Minnesota and Wisconsin] will breath [*sic*] freer when its last pine tree is cut, run, sawed, rafted and sold.[1]

Despite these problems, many did succeed and shared with Astor, Carnegie, and Rockefeller the Gilded Age's fevered drive for wealth.

"TIM-BER-R-R!"

Beginning in 1830, when people referred to timber they meant pine, and preferably white pine. The profit came from harvesting white pine trees one hundred feet or taller, trees prevalent in the northern pineries. Historian William Rector describes the spatial extent of the North American pinery before serious logging began:

If satellites had existed in 1781, a camera mounted in one of them would have sent back a far different picture of North America than they do today. If focused upon the northern United States and southern Canada during the winter, the picture would have shown a band of dark green stretching from the cliffs of Labrador and the coasts of New England westward, on both sides of the St. Lawrence including the Appalachians of New York and Pennsylvania. The green belt would have covered most of Quebec and southern Ontario, and it would have engulfed Michigan, the northern two-thirds of Wisconsin and the northeastern third of Minnesota. This huge green band was the North American pinery; the darker greens were the white pines growing on the clay loams, and the slightly lighter greens were the Norways or red pines on the sandier soils. To the south, the green belt would have merged into the gray, shadowy snow — the shadows being cast by the defrocked hardwoods. To the west of the belt, the snow would have been whiter, as few trees would have interrupted the windswept prairies.[2]

This vast pinery provided the means for American expansionism. Historian Robert Fries estimates that originally it contained a hundred billion board feet of commercial lumber.[3] (A board foot is one square foot in area and one inch thick.) Pines that were three to six feet across grew so densely in the pulverized loamy and sandy soil left by the glaciers that the marshy land never saw sunlight. To start the logger's day, the traditional cry was "Roll out — Daylight in the Swamp."

Some white pine stands were five hundred years old, essentially dating back to the pre-Columbian era. Buoyant, strong, and easily cut straight, this wood did not warp, shrink, splinter, or decay. It floated down streams and rivers from the Wisconsin and Minnesota forests to mills along the Mississippi tributaries: the Chippewa, Wisconsin, Black, and St. Croix. Sawn boards were rafted from here to lumberyards along the Mississippi as far south as St. Louis.

The pine stands did vary. Timber cruisers, who estimated the board feet in a tract of timber, always searched for trees from which they could cut five sixteen-foot log lengths (eighty feet) before branching. Four pines eight feet in diameter could provide enough lumber to build a good-sized house.[4]

Harvesting these titan pines demanded lumberjacks and raftsmen with Paul Bunyan's legendary strength and spirit. Even the Mississippi River's origins have been tied to his heroic character. One story had Paul Bunyan spraying the skidding road (built to move logs to the river) in western Wisconsin one night, when the sprayer on his massive watering wagon went out of control and flooded a huge, deep, north-south valley. The onrush was so powerful that it cut the country into two sections. By filling this valley, Paul created the Mississippi River and thus provided a passage for the lumber needed to build the nation.

LIFE IN THE LUMBER CAMPS

Come all ye gallant lumberers, that range the wild woods through,
Where the river flows and the timber grows we're bound with a jolly
    crew;
For the music of the mills is stopped by the binding frost and snow;
So we'll take our packs upon our backs, and a-lumbering we'll go.[5]

Each year when lumberjacks arrived in the camps to start cutting the pine, a well-organized system was in place. In early summer, the timber cruiser was sent to find the best tract of pine located close to a stream for log navigation. Based on his report, the lumber company had three options: purchase the logs already cut, purchase land, or purchase standing trees, referred to as "stumpage." When negotiations to cut timber were finalized, the lumber camp boss, along with a few men, headed to the site in July and August to build the camp, cut marsh hay, create a road to the stream, and make the stream navigable. In September and October supplies arrived; from November through April the lumberjacks harvested trees; and from April to July, logs floated to sawmills. As the eastern pineries were depleted, this cycle, which was first established in Maine, moved west with the loggers to Wisconsin and Minnesota.[6]

When the Maine loggers went west they joined forces with Irish-Scotch New Englanders, French Canadians, freed slaves, and a few Native Americans who also helped to subdue the vast pinery. The Germans swelled the ranks in the 1850s, and the Poles, Finns, and Scandinavians — called "Scowegians" by the Minnesota loggers — came to the camps a few years later. The lumber camps became a home base for these men, some of whom relied on the logging camp's remoteness as a way to evade the law. Most, however, were honest, seasonal workers. Many were farmers with families, or young men planning to get their own homesteads, and the one hundred dollars they earned during the winter became seed money.

To survive the northern winters, the right clothes were a must: a fur hat and layers of wool — long johns, heavy socks, pepper-and-salt Malone (wool) pants, mackinaw shirt and coat, woolen mittens covered by moosehide chopper mittens, and German socks (footless woolen hose pulled

FIGURE 29. *Here shanty boys sit on a raised fireplace in an early timber shanty and wait while the cook prepares the evening meal. Notice the clothes hanging to dry and the hole in the roof that allowed smoke to escape.* Reproduced in Peter Adams, Early Loggers and the Sawmill, *p. 37.*

down over boots to keep out dry snow). The early logger put his things in a wheat sack called a "turkey" that also served as a pillow. Except for his ponderous wardrobe, he traveled light.

Before the 1870s, lumberjacks were called lumbermen, woodsmen, pinery boys or, most commonly, shanty boys. In 1850 a campsite included seven to eight shanty boys and four to eight oxen. In the late nineteenth century, twenty-five to one hundred men competed in teams to see who could harvest the most board feet per day. By this time, they used horses rather than oxen because they were easier to shoe.

> Oh, a shanty-man's life is a wearisome life, although some think it
>   void of care,
> Swinging an ax from morning till night in the midst of the forests
>   so drear.
> Lying in the shanty bleak and cold while the cold stormy wintry
>   winds blow,
> And as soon as the daylight doth appear, to the wild woods we
>   must go.[7]

Early camps only had a stable and one log building, the latter called a State of Maine shanty, first created in the Maine pinery and used only one season. Probably it had been named by the Irish loggers since the Gaelic for "old house" is *sean+tig*. These early one-room shanties, generally twenty-four to forty feet long and twenty-four feet wide with four-foot-high sides, contained both kitchen and sleeping quarters. In the center, providing the only heat, was the caboose[8] or kitchen fire pit. It was eight feet square and a foot high with a crude funnel to direct smoke to the hole in the ceiling. Under the fire pit was the bean hole, where a pot of beans, molasses, and salt pork cooked all night for the next day's breakfast, lunch, and supper (fig. 29).

The logger's menu in these early 1840s camps consisted of salt pork, beans, biscuits, and tea — gallons of hot, steaming tea. They drank tea rather than coffee as late as 1915 in the Minnesota camps, probably a carry-over from the Maine camps. Eventually the Scandinavians demanded coffee. Butter or oleo, vegetables, fruit, and fresh meat were added as farms nearby were established. And loggers required stacks of flapjacks to be able to work from daylight to dark — upwards of ten to twelve hours a day in the harsh northern winters.

The cook demanded silence at the table to avoid fights. Alcohol was forbidden in the logging camps; even lemon extract and liniment were kept under lock and key to prevent the kind of trouble that often erupted in a river town when loggers celebrated the end of a cutting season. Many fights ended with someone getting a bad case of "Logger's Small Pox," the lumberjack's name for pockmarked scars left from caulked or spiked boots.

The only door in the shanty faced south and the only window was located in the wall opposite the door, thus making the early shanties crowded, "ill-ventilated, odoriferous, and pestiferous."[9] Wet woolen clothes were dried overnight by the fire and were only occasionally washed on Sunday; consequently, lice were a logger's constant companions. The logger bored a hole at the head of the bunk for ventilation while sleeping and plugged it with a sock when it turned really cold. By the end of the nineteenth century, living conditions had improved greatly, but a logger still needed a hearty constitution. These men were used to living under Spartan conditions, but if a camp were very poorly run, they labeled it as one gone "haywire," because it appeared to be barely held together with hay bale wire.

Between the evening meal and nine o'clock, the shanty boys sharpened their axes or sat on the deacon seat — a bench that extended the length of the shanty — to smoke, play cards, and brag their personal tall tales. Originally, the men slept on the dirt floor. By the 1850s one long bunk, six or seven feet deep, was situated along one side of the shanty. Here the loggers slept side by side covered with hay, straw, or pine boughs. An 1855 journalist described the scene: "Nine o'clock came, and . . . we all tumbled in. . . . A blanket was spread from one end of the row of bodies to the other. It was a laughable sight to see so many heads 'all in a row,' presenting all colors of hair and whiskers, with as many different kind[s] of noses."[10] Later in the century, this common bed was replaced with tiered, individual bunks.

In January of 1876, Frank W. Gould, the son of Moline (Illinois) lumberman J. M. Gould, wrote a letter to the company's general agent about his challenging experiences at a Wisconsin logging camp: "We have 30 men in our camp now, and they are of most every nationality. I am bunking alone at present and manage to keep warm, though I would suffer if it were not for the buffalo robe Mr. Hill sent me. We have had four cooks already and three of them were miserable, and I was forced to starve myself before I could stand their grub, but now we have a pretty fair one and all are happy. Still, it is not much like home."[11]

With Sundays off, these hardy laborers enjoyed Saturday night by telling stories and singing and stomping the ballad "The Jam on Garry's

Rock" about the death of logger Young Munroe. A fiddle or harmonica accompanied their rounds and reels called "stag dances." And, of course, it was around these early shanty cabooses with pipe tobacco smoke and the smell of drying wool socks that the legendary Paul Bunyan tall tales were passed on from camp to camp. The loggers carried these yarns west with them to each new logging site, bragging — in many different dialects — about the brawn needed to survive in the wilderness. On Sundays they rested, washed clothes, prepared equipment for Monday, and sometimes heard Young Men's Christian Association (YMCA) or Women's Christian Temperance Union (WCTU) temperance lectures from itinerant preachers.

The foreman maintained law and order in a logging camp. His physical stature and strength settled many a conflict in this true Darwinian setting where the fittest and the strongest survived. Some of the loggers tested the foreman's authority, but few succeeded. The cook remained if the loggers liked the "vittles." If not, he packed his "turkey sack" and hit the road. The cookee, someone who was too young, too old, or too infirm to log, peeled potatoes and blew the five-foot tin horn at 4 A.M. to awaken the loggers. The men bought on credit clothes and snoose (damp chewing snuff, a.k.a. "Scandihoovian dynamite") from the company store (the wanigan), which began as a locked box and later became a separate building where the foreman and his clerk (the ink slinger) stayed.

A distinctive name was also applied to the job each lumberjack performed. The most prestigious lumberjack was the chopper. In the early camps choppers used a double-edged axe that by 1880 was replaced with the two-man crosscut saw the loggers called a "Swedish fiddle." Once the tree was felled, barkers trimmed branches and removed bark from one side for easier sliding. Sawyers cut the trunk into sixteen-foot lengths. Branches and treetops were left to rot or, tragically, to fuel forest fires.

When the logging was close to the stream, skidders and oxen hauled a log to the landing using a wishbone-shaped hardwood the loggers called a "go-devil." This device was used during the winter cutting season and then discarded. Later in the century, when the cutting was farther from the landing, a log was dragged to the logging road maintained by a man called the road monkey. Here with block and tackle the log was loaded onto a sleigh that held from five to seventeen thousand board feet. A teamster with oxen or horses then pulled the sleigh to the rollway landing by the stream. At night, swampers sprayed sleigh-runner ruts with water to form ice, thus making it possible to move the sleigh with tons of logs. At the landing, the scaler calculated the number of board feet. Since many different lumber companies used the same streams, each log was branded with two company marks: a bark mark made with an axe and a hammered-end mark. These logs sat by the stream until spring when the ice melted.

When sleighs could no longer slide, the lumberjacks were done for the season. Many headed home to plant spring crops, some to work in the sawmills. Others collected their wages and headed to Stillwater, Minnesota, Eau Claire, Wisconsin, and other river towns to celebrate. The saloons in these towns awaited the sound of spiked boots booming on the wooden sidewalks. With their wages spent, the loggers were forced to stay in the run-down skid row, named for these men who had skidded the pine.

Those left in the logging camps waited for the ice to break, rounded up their peaveys (a pole with a hook), filed the spikes on their caulked boots, and headed to the river for the log drive, singing

> Come, all ye gallant shanty boys
> An' listen while I sing;
> We've worked six months [hip]-deep in snow
> But now we'll have our fling . . .
> Oh, it's break the rollways out, me boys,
> An' let the big sticks slide;
> File yer caulks an' grease yer boots
> An' the river we will ride.[12]

RIDING THE RIVER

The cowboys or riverpigs rode a river of sixteen-foot logs hundreds of miles to a mill or a boom, which is a floating log corral. Crews steered the fast-moving monsters with peaveys, unlocked any jams, and rounded up the strays. Behind the logs and crews floated the cook shanty raft (the wanigan) that provided a place to sleep and the five meals a day needed to sustain wet, cold, tired men. The French Canadians' "devil-may-care attitude" suited them for this grueling task. From dancing on logs for miles and miles, these men walked on land with a graceful, easy assurance.

Getting logs to the sawmills or booms quickly was financially crucial. Logjams devastated not only the lumber industry but also the river towns waiting to be paid for supplies. The Great Logjam of 1869 in the Chippewa River involved 150 million board feet of logs covering fifteen miles, some thirty feet in the air. In 1886 another jam of the same magnitude on the St. Croix River took two hundred men six weeks to break.[13] Unclogging a stream sometimes required dynamite, with unpredictable results. Often the men had to use fancy footwork to herd the rolling logs in a life-or-death birling contest with the fast-moving river. Many a river-pig died during a drive, but work could not be stopped for the men to mourn. Their only memorial might be to hang the victim's caulked boots in a tree along the bank — if the boots could be found.

When logs arrived at the boom, they were sorted into separate holding pens according to each owner's registered bark mark and end mark. They were then organized into raft sections or strings, typically sixteen feet wide and two hundred to four hundred feet long. Several strings could be combined into a rigid raft forty to sixty feet wide that floated to sawmills along the Minnesota and Wisconsin tributaries of the Upper Mississippi: the Black, Chippewa, St. Croix, and Wisconsin Rivers.

Before 1844 only Wisconsin and Minnesota sawmills processed the pine into lumber. From these mills rafts of lumber, containing from three to five hundred thousand board feet, floated to lumberyards along the Mississippi, going as far south as St. Louis. Delivering the sawn lumber to markets downriver depended upon the Mississippi raft pilot and his crew. To maneuver the huge free-floating rafts down the swift current of the Mississippi, crews of ten to fifteen manned thirty-five-foot oars called sweeps at both the bow and the stern. The pilots of these early rafts — men like Buckskin Brown, Sailor Jack, and French Fred — were highly regarded for their ability to navigate a wild and dangerous river. The pilot's outfit reflected his silver-studded sense of importance: "French calf boots, black cassimere [sic] trousers, red flannel shirt of extra fine knitted goods, a large black silk necktie, tied in a square knot with flowing ends, and a soft wide-brimmed black or white hat."[14]

Among the crews on the early rafts, the fiddler led the group in songs that often ran to the risqué: "One-Eyed Rily, whom the women loved most dearly"; "Dandy, handy Raftsman Jim"; and "Buffalo Gals, can't you come out tonight and dance by the light of the moon." Men sang along and stomped to the beat on the wooden rafts, probably catching the attention of girls and their wary fathers on the shore. Mark Twain called these early raftsmen "fiddling, song-singing, whisky-drinking, breakdown-dancing rapscallions."[15]

Until 1844 only rafts of sawn lumber could be found on the Mississippi floating to the lumberyards downstream. But in that year, Stephen Beck Hanks, a first cousin of Abraham Lincoln, floated the first raft of pine logs down the river. Hanks, who lived and farmed in Albany, Illinois, had driven cattle to a Wisconsin timber camp where he worked during the winter. In the spring of 1844, when the logs were floated to the mills, a flooded stream pushed the logs beyond the sawmill. Hanks purchased the strays, assembled a raft six hundred feet long, and then rode it to sawmills at St. Louis. After that, sawmills downstream in Clinton and Davenport, Iowa, Rock Island, Illinois, and many other towns processed their own lumber, and log rafts dominated the river economy.

Pine log rafts for the Mississippi were created primarily at Beef Slough, Wisconsin, and West Newton, Minnesota, at the mouth of the Chippewa River, and at Stillwater, Minnesota, and the St. Croix confluence. The participants on the Grand Excursion flotilla to St. Paul in June 1854 would have passed towns that lined the Mississippi and thus would have seen hundreds of logs in booms ready for the sawmill. James F. Babcock, editor of the *New Haven Palladium* and a participant on the 1854 Grand Excursion to St. Paul, reported that they "met several immense rafts, some guided by five or six men each, others by twice that number. They cheered our boats, swung their hats, and one of them, for the want of artillery, fired his rifle several times in the way of a salute."[16]

When log rafts floated through water with no current, such as Lake Pepin, which is twenty-eight miles long and three to five miles wide, the raftsmen often had to kedge to move the raft forward. In kedging, a small boat went several feet ahead of the raft and dropped an anchor. Then men or horses on the raft pulled the raft forward to the location of the anchor. This was a very time-consuming procedure that was repeated over and over until the raft could catch the river current again. Eventually steamboats towed rafts for short runs, but they were not powerful enough to move the raft tonnage on the Mississippi. In 1870, J. W. Van Sant from Le Claire, Iowa, created the first stern-wheeler able to push a log raft to the Weyerhaeuser & Denkmann mill in Rock Island. At first, sweeps (large oars) were used with steamboats; eventually steam-powered bow boats replaced sweeps (fig. 30).

Major problems for the raft or steamboat pilots were bridge piers and the Rock Island Rapids, which ran 14.7 miles from Le Claire to Davenport, Iowa. Moving downstream, pilots stopped at Le Claire to hire a rapids pilot who could maneuver the seven dangerous chains of rocks in the rapids. Capt. Walter Blair lists sixteen Le Claire rapids pilots working from 1840 to 1915: among them three Dorrances, two Rambos, and six

FIGURE 30. *After the Civil War steamboats pushed log rafts, while men at the front of the rafts steered with large oars, or sweeps. Earlier, rafts had been guided with sweeps at both the front and rear, but later the sweeps at the front were replaced by small bow boats.* Reproduced in George W. Wickstrom and Charles P. Ainsworth, Always Lumber: The Story of Dimock, Gould & Co., 1852–1952, *opposite p. 25.*

generations of Suiters.[17] The rapids piloting business ended when the last raft floated down the Mississippi in 1915, nearly two decades before the U.S. Corps of Engineers finished their seventy-five-year project to correct this navigational problem.[18]

A NIGHT AT THE GREEN TREE HOTEL

When rafts docked at Le Claire to hire a rapids pilot, some of the deck crew roustabouts headed for refreshments at local saloons and occasionally missed the raft's departure. Waiting for the next raft, they slept, cooked, ate, bragged, and spun river yarns along the riverbank under a rock elm tree sixty-five feet high with a 110-foot branch spread. This tree, jokingly named the Green Tree Hotel, was an important part of river lore. It died of Dutch elm disease in 1964. A plaque marks its location and records an additional claim of historic significance: "In Memory of the Green Tree That Was Used as a Playground by Buffalo Bill." (Buffalo Bill Cody was born and raised in the Le Claire area.) Dick Stahl, Quad Cities' Poet Laureate, wrote the poem, "Under the Green Tree Hotel, An Invitation," to capture the essence of this legendary tree.

All guests stay free
as the Mississippi's drift
at the Green Tree Hotel,
Le Claire, Iowa. The river bends
west so the channel's nervous
as a firefly. Look at the head
of the Rock Island Rapids,
the newest stretch of the river,
while you relax
like a weary raftsman waiting
for a Rapids pilot. Toss
your reservations over
the last log raft
docking here, and see them spin
down fifteen dizzy miles
like an elm leaf riding
an eddy. The air's always cooler
under the shade
of the green canopy,
and the talk's straight
as soft white pine. No posted
weekly rates or room service
bother you here; revel
in some good outdoor
hospitality that leans
like this hotel a little
toward the river
but stays
solid as a rock elm.[19]

GLORY DAYS OF THE LUMBER KINGS

Most of the lumber barons of the Upper Mississippi Valley came from the East in the 1850s. Filled with the rugged individualist's spirit and limited in funds, these young men created sawmill empires. Their resulting fortunes allowed them to build sumptuous Victorian homes and also gave them the means to improve their communities and states.[20]

Chancy Lamb, who came to Iowa from New York, dominated the lumber industry in the Clinton, Iowa, area with four sawmills. At one time Clinton (including Lyons and Camanche) had twelve sawmills, thirteen millionaires, and was known as both "The Saw Dust City" and "The Lumber Capital of the Mississippi Valley." According to the *Clinton Herald* in March of 1880: "On Tuesday, C. Lamb & Sons sawed in twelve hours 408,209 feet of lumber, 73,000 lath, 69,000 shingles and planed 50,000 feet. This was probably the biggest day's work at any point on the Mississippi River."[21] Through the years, Chancy invented many laborsaving devices. Some he patented, but many others he simply made available to the entire lumber industry. His most important invention was the double-spooled winch, which helped pilots steer log rafts around river bends and through bridge spans. This same device was then adapted as a cargo winch on seagoing merchant ships and used until 1960. Gifts from the Lamb family include the Clinton Public Library, an addition to the YWCA, the Jane Lamb Hospital, and improvements to public parks. The importance of logging to the city can be found in the name of their minor league baseball team, the Clinton Lumber Kings.

Orrin Ingram, like Chancy Lamb, came from New York and resided sixty years in the Wisconsin Chippewa Valley. In 1857 he established the first of his sawmills along the Chippewa River and became one of the main players in the logging saga. He was director of the Chippewa Logging Company, vice president of the Chippewa Lumber and Boom Company, president of the Rice Lake Lumber Company, president of the Empire Lumber Company of Eau Claire, principal stockholder in the Empire Lumber Company of Minnesota, vice president of the Standard Lumber Company of Dubuque, and a heavy stockholder in the Weyerhaeuser Timber Company. Ingram invented and generously did not patent the gang edger, a device that quickly finished the edges of a sawn board. Throughout his life, Ingram was dedicated to improving Eau Claire and gave funds to the YMCA, which in the 1880s sent itinerant representatives through the north woods to conduct religious meetings in lumber camps. He also donated money to the Eau Claire Public Library, the local Children's Home, the Eau Claire Sanatorium, and Ripon College to create a new Ingram Science building.

With inherited money, John H. Knapp, also a New York native, started a sawmill in Menomonie, Wisconsin, in 1846, having a daily capacity of five thousand board feet. He weathered the financial panic of 1857 and developed with his partners a lumber company that claimed in 1871 to be the largest in the United States and in 1900 to be the largest in the world. The Knapp family mansion reflected the lumber barons' desire to create true nineteenth-century Victorian splendor to rival anything built in the East. Their "mansion with its ports-cochere stood on the brow of a hill in Menomonie above the mill town. It contained ten good-sized rooms on two floors, plus many small service rooms such as butler's pantries, the maids' rooms, and the ice room. The upstairs was finished in pine, the downstairs in oak [with] . . . a garland panel frieze[,] . . . Brussels lace window draperies[,] . . . rosewood piano[,] . . . stucco bead chains and pendants[,] . . . [and a] chain and pendant frieze."[22]

The Knapp family donated many objets d'art to the Wisconsin Historical Society.

In 1857 William H. Laird, along with his cousins James and Matthew Norton, built their first sawmill in Winona, Minnesota. By implementing both the muley saw and the circular saw, they were able to cut 25,000 feet of lumber in ten hours, a feat that led to their great success. Laird's legacy includes recognition for his efforts to improve the lives of the men who worked in the forests. He actively solicited money from all of the logging and lumber companies to send YMCA missionaries to logging camps. Most companies gave twenty-five dollars to fifty dollars; the Laird, Norton Company of Winona contributed $150. Besides being involved in church activities, Laird contributed financially to Carleton College and served on its board of trustees. The Norton family gave generously to Hamline University. Even though their sawmills had closed, they all remained in Winona.

The entrepreneurs who established sawmills at St. Anthony (now Minneapolis), Minnesota, were primarily from Maine and had brought with them lumber and logging expertise. Dorilus Morrison was among this group and set up his first gang saw in 1854, the year the railroad reached Rock Island. He would have been in St. Anthony when the Grand Excursion arrived in June of that year and may have witnessed the event. The steady influx of immigrants to Minnesota required lumber, and Morrison's sawmill, which was the best equipped at that time, kept continuously busy with a capacity of twenty million feet a year. The top price for lumber at that time was $25 per 1,000 feet, so Morrison was making a sizable income. He was able to pay cash for pine lands. With early access to $12,000 worth of government warrants, he acquired 11,000 acres of Minnesota pine and established himself as a key Minnesota lumber baron. In 1867, when Minneapolis was chartered, Dorilus Morrison was chosen as its mayor, and through the years he backed the Athenaeum Library. When he died, the Morrison family donated the land on which the Minneapolis Institute of Arts is located.

The person who made the most lasting and greatest impact on the industry was Frederic Weyerhaeuser, an immigrant from Germany. According to Richard G. Lillard, "Frederic Weyerhaeuser . . . was the most powerful single lumberman in the history of the American forests."[23] In 1856 he arrived at Rock Island, Illinois, via a short stay in Erie, Pennsylvania. He started as a laborer who stacked slabs at the Mead, Smith and Marsh Lumber Company and shortly became manager of their nearby Coal Valley, Illinois, lumberyard. An astute businessman during trying economic times, he traded lumber for horses, oxen, hogs, and eggs and then exchanged these items for logs to repeat the process. When the company went bankrupt during the panic of 1857, Weyerhaeuser and his brother-in-law F. C. A. Denkmann purchased it in 1860, beginning what would become one of the largest U.S. industries that is still in existence.

In 1864 Weyerhaeuser, with two mills in Rock Island, decided that he wanted to control all aspects of the process: logging, rafting, and sawing. In order to acquire Wisconsin pine logs, he organized seventeen down-river mill owners in 1870 to form the Mississippi River Logging Company. To control the logging of the pines, this company bought Wisconsin timberland. Likewise they built Beef Slough Boom at the mouth of the Chippewa River to control the rafting of the pines. When these downriver mill owners and the Chippewa mill owners fought over the rights to the Wisconsin logs, Weyerhaeuser argued his company's case in the courts and political arenas and won. Eventually he found a solution that benefited everyone: In 1881, he formed a syndicate that included the mill owners from downriver and those from the Chippewa area. That nearly every one of the associates in this enterprise became a millionaire is a reflection of its financial success. When the writer Lincoln Steffens asked Weyerhaeuser how rich he was, Weyerhaeuser said that neither he nor his banker knew for sure, but it is believed that his syndicate was one of thirty groups controlling the nation's economy during the last half of the nineteenth century. He remained in Rock Island until the 1890s when, to be closer to timber sources, he and his family first moved to St. Paul, Minnesota, and then to Seattle, Washington, establishing new headquarters in nearby Tacoma. While in Minnesota he provided leadership and money to Macalester College in St. Paul. Both the Weyerhaeuser and Denkmann families contributed to Vassar, Harvard, Yale, and Rock Island's Augustana College, as well as making donations for museums, civic centers, and libraries. When Weyerhaeuser died in 1914, his friend James J. Hill, railway promoter and financier, said: "His place cannot be filled. He was a national force among men who have helped to build up the country."[24]

SUNSET ON RIVER RAFTING

Lumber and log rafting dominated the upper river's commerce from 1870 to 1910 with some rafts carrying two million board feet covering three to four acres, the rough equivalent of three to four football fields and enough lumber to build 125 houses (fig. 31). But then it abruptly ended. Weyerhaeuser's mill in Rock Island closed in 1905, and his company in Minnesota sawed its last board in 1919.

On July 1, 1915, the last raft was towed to Fort Madison, Iowa. The *Ottumwa Belle*, piloted by Capt. W. L. Hunter from Hudson, Wisconsin, stopped at Albany, Illinois, to pick up Lincoln's cousin, Stephen Beck Hanks, for this last raft ride. In 1844, Hanks, at age thirty-three, had created the first log raft, and on this occasion at age ninety-four, he rode the last lumber raft as far as Davenport, Iowa. The end of timber rafting left the Upper Mississippi River with very little through commercial traffic for the next two and a half decades. In the late 1920s business and civic groups in the region lobbied the U.S. government to make improvements to navigation to stimulate the river economy.[25]

Some of the lumber barons expanded to other businesses such as banking, railroads, mining, steamboats, and grain milling. Most of these men remained to help build their respective cities by serving in civic and political posts. Samuel Van Sant, for instance, served two terms as governor of Minnesota. Historian Robert Fries assesses the lumber barons as

> not, for the most part at least, hedonists. They did not believe that the world existed solely to afford them wealth and pleasure. The worthiest of them manifested the highest sense of duty to their communities and high ethical principles in their business dealings. These they measured, of course, by the standards of the day; if some of them had trespassed on government land, it was not an offense for which their communities blamed them. Their neighbors were more likely to observe that they were conscientious church-goers and that they met all their financial obligations promptly. More than that, they spent philanthropically at least part of the wealth that Providence and their own ability amassed for them.[26]

Weyerhaeuser, Denkmann, Ingram, Stout, Laird, Stephenson, Sawyer, Shevlin, Morrison, Steele, Norton, and Young generously endowed col-

FIGURE 31. *Rafts of logs arrive at their Rock Island destination. Notice the building-high stacks of lumber onshore. Photo from the Rock Island County Historical Society, Moline, Illinois.*

leges and universities. Libraries, museums, YMCAs, and art/music centers were created with donations from the Weyerhaeuser, Denkmann, Hauberg, Washburn, Gardiner, Morrison, Walker, Carpenter, Young, Ingram, and Knapp families.

FINAL LEGACY

There is, of course, a darker side to the story. Besides the glory of Bunyanesque loggers and the financial success of the lumber kings, it cannot be ignored that the legacy of both also involves the loss of great stands of primeval forests. The early settlers encountered a wall of huge, overwhelming impediments to creating farms and settlements. From their perspective, the trees had to go. In the nineteenth century, what chance did the pines have against the steam-powered sawmills and the railroads that in the decade after the Civil War extended harvesting well beyond the skidding roads to streams?

Although William Penn had advocated as early as the seventeenth century that for every four acres of timber cut one acre should be saved for forest preserves, few listened to his advice. Two hundred years later, Americans took this resource for granted and expected it to last forever. The timber industry kept cutting until they conquered the pineries and left them battlefields filled with gigantic stumps, making the land virtually unusable for farming. The rivers filled with silt from sawmills and land erosion. Charles

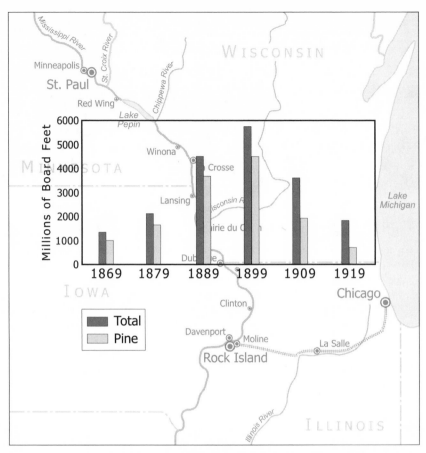

FIGURE 32. *Lumber production, Wisconsin and Minnesota, 1869–1919. Data from Henry B. Steer,* Lumber Production in the United States, 1799–1946.

Edward Russell, who chronicled the pine story along the Mississipppi, astutely observed that "in the literature of waste, this is the *Iliad.*"[27]

By the 1860s and 1870s, many were crying against the waste and fires caused by lumbering. If lumber mills would have had more efficient band saws rather than muley and circular saws, a billion more board feet could have been available between 1872 and 1905. Also, loggers cut young trees for roads, left high stumps, windfalls, partly decayed trees, and the tops of the pine, all of which provided fuel for massive forest fires. Robert Fries makes a startling statement that "perhaps more good pine timber was burned than ever reached the sawmills."[28]

Driven by reforestation concerns, Congress passed the Timber Culture Act of 1873. Under this legislation, homesteaders could apply for an additional 160 acres if they planted trees in at least one-fourth of their acreage within four years. The act's fifteen-year run was beneficial. But by 1891, when Weyerhaeuser's timberland acquisitions had expanded to more than two million acres, Congress reacted by passing the Forest Reserve Act, setting aside thirteen million acres of timberland. Other conservation-minded activity by the federal government quickly followed. In 1902 Chippewa National Forest in Minnesota became the first national forest established east of the Mississippi River. President Theodore Roosevelt created in 1905 a Bureau of Forestry in the U.S. Department of Agriculture, naming Gifford Pinchot as chief forester, a position designed to protect public lands from private interests. Today conservationists and the lumber industry continue to battle over the 191 million acres of national forests and 50.2 million acres of state-owned forest lands.

The pineries are gone, the old-growth pines transmuted into houses and barns, many still standing. The loggers have moved on to other forests. The Mississippi remains.

Rafting on the Mississippi, Passing through Pontoon Bridge, Marquette, Iowa

51099-N

FIGURE 33. *The origins of this unusual railroad bridge date to the 1870s when John Lawler, a local railroad agent, built approach bridges on either side of the navigation channel and used barges to connect the two sides. Occasionally railroad cars fell from this cumbersome structure into the river. To solve this problem Lawler hired Mike Spettel who, in 1874, built two pontoon bridges, each 276 feet long and 55 feet wide. This ingenious design, which accommodated variations in river conditions and weights of the trains, was used until 1961. Information from Ed Brick, "Mike Spettel's Better Bridge — Part Bridge, Part Pontoon." From postcard 51099-N, the Lake County (Illinois) Discovery Museum, Curt Teich Postcard Archives.*

FISHING THE FATHER
OF WATERS

Malcolm L. Comeaux

Surprisingly, a person on the Mississippi River today would see commercial fishing almost exactly as it was done during the era of the Grand Excursion. Few truly new techniques have been introduced. Traditions and fishing knowledge continue to be handed down from one generation to the next, and fishing culture remains as it was 150 years ago.

Since the beginning of human habitation of the Mississippi Valley, fishing has been practiced in the river. Native Americans fished, as did trappers and explorers. As the frontier moved westward, early European farmers supplemented their food supply by fishing. This was mostly subsistence fishing, however. Commercial fishing had to wait until a market developed as the result of urban growth along the nation's inland waters in the 1850s and early 1860s.[1]

Commercial fishing practices have not changed much since the nineteenth century. Most fishing techniques were introduced directly from Europe, then quickly spread far and wide. Up to the early 1960s many fishermen moved from one place to another by houseboat, bringing their ideas and techniques with them and introducing them to new areas. One can travel today from Louisiana to above Lake Pepin on the Upper Misssissippi and find little variation in the use of techniques and gear. The only variations are caused by laws (e.g., Iowa may outlaw a particular fishing technique or type of gear, while it would be legal on the Illinois side), and by environmental situations (e.g., fishing under ice is well-known in the Upper Mississippi but not in the South).

Commercial fishing allowed fishermen freedom and independence, but it never provided a lucrative living. Traditionally low on the socioeconomic scale and barely eking out a living while working long and arduous hours, fishermen have always supplemented their income by gathering other resources along the river — almost anything that they could sell. They would harvest turtles, gather driftwood and logs, trap for hides, hunt for wild game, gather mussels, and the like. Some full-time fishermen would seek employment off the river during the winter months.[2] Almost always ignored by "higher" society, fishermen were seldom mentioned by writers or reporters, thus remaining a largely forgotten and ignored underclass.

Commercial fishing is an occupation that is passed from older fishermen to younger men, usually from father to son, but it is not unusual for a fisherman to take an unrelated young man under his tutelage. The business can be learned no other way. Because it is dangerous and arduous work, women are usually excluded, but they do play a role. Women often make the nets, and they help in various other ways, such as in gathering bait, baiting hooks, and repairing gear.

Large-scale commercial fishing began in the Upper Mississippi only after railroads reached the river. Fish begin to deteriorate as soon as they die but if packed in ice they can be kept "fresh" for about seven to nine days, depending on the weather. Ice was cut in the winter from lakes and ponds, stored in icehouses, and then used in packing fish in wooden boxes for transport by rail to cities in the East. Chicago was the main market, but fish were shipped all the way to the East Coast. The first refrigerated car of fish sent from the Mississippi River to New York, in 1896, was a financial success.[3]

The productivity of the fishing industry in the region is difficult to gauge. The total commercial fish production in the Mississippi River over the last fifty years for the states of Iowa, Minnesota, and Wisconsin is a generalization, as it is hard to gather accurate data from independent fishermen at isolated spots along the river.[4] On average, the Upper Mississippi produced 6.89 million pounds of fish a year, which is close to the averages taken for the 1990s. Good or poor years, however, are not dependent on the abundance of fish, as other factors beyond the river have a great influence. For example, fluxuations in the price of fish or a recession can encourage people to turn to the river for a living or extra income. Surprisingly, while the catch has remained rather steady, there has been a definite decrease in the number of fishermen over the years. But they obviously are catching more per capita in order to maintain their living standard, especially since the price of fish remained virtually unchanged (except for catfish, which declined) between 1979 and 1999.[5] Furthermore, international producers that freeze and then ship their fish products to the Midwest, as well as producers of pond-raised fish, have also helped to lower the price that local fishermen can get for their catch.

HOOK-AND-LINE FISHING

Hook-and-line fishing has long been important in inland waters. Native Americans successfully used hooks when fishing. Long before the coming of Europeans, however, they had learned more efficient techniques, and had largely given up hook-and-line methods in some areas.[6] Hook-and-line remains important today because it is used to catch catfish, which bring a relatively high price in the market. Also, hook-and-line fishing is in some ways similar to the use of traps because both hooks and traps can be set and checked daily and catch fish while unattended.

Sometimes fishermen will use a line with a single hook. Such a line can hang from a bush or branch (hence a "bush line" or "branch line") in overflowed lands in the spring, or near the bank at high water just before or after a flood. This technique remains unchanged from the early 1800s except for the use of nylon twine.

Another example of a single hook on a line is the jug line. In this type of fishing, a hook and a line are tied to a bottle or some other floating object and set afloat in the river. The fisherman will send several of these lines slowly floating downstream with the current, following in his boat and retrieving them when they catch a fish. It is reportedly an efficient way of taking large catfish. Jug fishing was a technique commonly used in the 1800s, but while all fishermen know how it is done, it is seldom practiced today.[7]

In inland waters hooks are most commonly used on trotlines. The typical trotline consists of a "mainline" with smaller lines (known by many names, such as "stagings," "droppers," "offshoots," etc.) extending down, with hooks on the ends. In the days of cotton or linen twine, mainlines were tarred, but the stagings would not fish well if tarred, so they would be replaced quite often. Swivels (which allow lines to turn freely) are always put on the stagings, because otherwise the fish would twist and yank out the hook. In the past fishermen would bend two nails to form a swivel, but today they purchase them already made. In fact, all trotlines are made by fishermen from purchased twine, swivels, and hooks.

Trotlines are usually set diagonally across a stream, and during the summer months they are fished deep. During the springtime, trotlines are often set near the surface along the bank or in overflowed areas. At other times of the year, fishermen will use their trotlines in whatever manner they think will catch fish. They are almost always used at night, however, with the fisherman baiting his line in the evening and checking the catch in the morning. A trotline usually lasts for one year of use, although its hooks must be replaced periodically.

Trotlines can be fished in two ways. The first is called a set line or stationary line. In this setup, the fisherman leaves the line out and checks and re-baits it twice a day, only infrequently moving it. Such a line, usually consisting of one hundred hooks or some multiple of one hundred, is placed in an open body of water and can be over a mile in length.

The more common way to use a trotline is as a jump line, commonly called a box line along the Upper Mississippi. It resembles the stationary line, except it is removed from the water every morning and reset each evening. This method of fishing began in early days to help preserve cotton or linen twine. If removed from the water and allowed to dry, the twine lasted considerably longer. If fished continuously, it lasted a few weeks at best. Laws also played a role in the development of the jump line. Illinois, for example, had a law that no line could be left unattended during daylight hours. The jump box evolved to help further solve these problems.

Still in use today, a jump box, which is always used with jump lines, is a small and shallow box with one hundred grooves cut into the sides. After a fisherman pulls in his jump line in the morning, he removes the fish, and puts the trotline in a large tub. Later that day, the jump lines are placed in the jump boxes (they are "shipped up"), with the hooks hanging over the edges in consecutive order and the mainline in the bottom. Fishermen then bait their hooks in the late afternoons, and set them out at various locations in the water in the evening, by allowing the hooks to come out of the box as they cross the water body. There are two types of jump boxes, a square one with twenty-five hooks to a side, and long ones with fifty hooks to a side. The long boxes were developed first and worked well with oar-powered boats. Once outboard motors were widely accepted in the 1950s, the long box became awkward to use in the rear of the boat because it was hard for a fisherman to work the motor and handle the box at the same time. Because square boxes were easier to handle, their use spread widely. In the Upper Mississippi, however, the long jump box remained the favorite, and techniques were developed to allow its use with outboard motors. For example, fishermen can place the box on a frame above the motor or on a swiveling apparatus hanging over the side of the boat.[8]

One of the main tasks of hook-and-line fishermen is acquiring bait. The average full-time commercial fisherman uses about twelve hundred hooks, and getting enough bait each day for all of these hooks is a chore. Several baits can be used; if one does not work, the fisherman will try another the next day if at all possible. A listing of bait recorded in 1902[9] shows that fishermen still prefer the same kinds of bait. The most common bait used in the spring is young crawfish, gathered in ponds, sloughs, and roadside ditches. Earthworms are used when they can be acquired, as well as catalpa worms (larva of the American hawk moth). Grasshoppers, a common bait in the summertime, can be gotten by simply driving through tall grass in the early morning with a butterfly net dragging through the grass. Several more innovative techniques have been developed by some fishermen, such as a scoop-like arrangement on the sides or in front of a vehicle to catch grasshoppers when driven through tall grass. Some of these techniques can gather several days' worth of bait in a few minutes. Young shad, called minnows, are another popular bait, and if all else fails, cut bait (the cutting of trash fish into small cubes) is used. The meat from mussels is sometimes an option, and almost anything that a fisherman can acquire for free, or almost free, will be used. Whatever bait a fisherman ends up using, he usually baits his hooks late in the afternoon. Often aided by his wife and children, the fisherman places the bait on hooks along the edges of the jump box (fig. 34).

FISHING WITH NETS

The use of nets allows fishermen to catch greater numbers of fish and a greater variety of fish, as some commercial fish (buffalo fish in particular) will seldom bite on a hook. The most common net type used in the Mississippi River is the hoop net.[10] A hoop net is a long, tubular net with a series of "throats"—openings in the nets that are held open by the hoops, once made of white oak but now more commonly of fiberglass or iron—that lead fish to the rear of the net. Whereas fishermen or members of the community made hoop nets locally, the hoops themselves were usually purchased. Hoop nets were introduced into the Mississippi River system very early, and a picture of one being used opposite Memphis, Tennessee, was published in 1868.[11]

Hoop nets are kept outstretched by the current, with an anchor on the end of a rope holding the tail of the net (the throat must always face downstream to catch fish who are swimming upstream). The nets are placed in the natural pathways of fish. If there is no current, as in a lake,

FIGURE 34. *John Diehl of Ferryville, Wisconsin, baiting his jump boxes. Photo by Malcolm L. Comeaux, July 1971.*

hoop nets can be anchored at each end to hold the net outstretched. The net is collapsible, and relatively easy to move from site to site, although a large net can weigh over one hundred pounds (fig. 35). If the fisherman wants to catch "fiddlers" (immature channel catfish), he will use a particularly small net, with a diameter of about a foot and a half, but if he wants to catch buffalo fish, he will use a very large net, which may be six feet in diameter. Most hoop nets between these two sizes are primarily used to take catfish, and are about fourteen to sixteen feet long. One other type of hoop net, used to capture turtles, is very short and wide and has only one throat.

Hoop nets can be used in many ways, depending on the circumstances. They are usually fished deep in the river during summer months when the water is warm and the river low. In the spring and fall fishermen place their nets in shallower water near the shore, and when water is in flood, they place the hoop nets in overflowed land. In this circumstance, they normally place another net in front of the hoop net to lead fish into the net (at which time the net is given another name, such as pound net or wing net). At some times of the year hoop nets must be baited, often with female catfish, cottonseed cake, soybean cake, or stale cheese. One man

FIGURE 35. *Brothers Paul and Chester Gibbs of Lansing, Iowa, raise a hoop net. They were the only fishermen I could find in 1971 who were still working as a team (as done in the early days, when each fisherman typically had partners). They still used a launch, the only serviceable one remaining in the Upper Mississippi. Photo by Malcolm L. Comeaux, July 1971.*

can handle a hoop net, making it a popular piece of equipment for inland fishermen. Full-time commercial fishermen will often have thirty to fifty of them set out at any one time.

Hoop nets are usually fished blind (fished with nothing visible on the surface). Using handmade grapples (large hooks or other devices used to grasp nets), fishermen will locate and raise their nets. In the center of a deep river, like the Mississippi, a long line with a buoy on the end (usually a plastic jug) tied to the front of the net will be used, as it may be too deep to grapple. The net can be emptied simply by inverting it and shaking out the fish through the front, or emptied through the tail of the net, where it can be opened using a drawstring. One type of gear that also has throats is not a net at all. The basket trap, which fishes like a fiddler net, is made of wooden slats, and is either round or square. The traps are about eighteen inches across and five feet long, have two throats, and will catch only catfish, as catfish enter them thinking they are hollow logs. Basket traps are set with the mouth facing downstream, and often do not need baiting.

Another popular method of fishing in the Upper Mississippi uses a seine, a long net having floats on its top line and weights on its bottom line. Crews of from five to eight men work seines using several boats, called a fleet. In operating a seine, the water bottom must be clear of stumps or other snags that might hang up the net. Fishermen will therefore make sure that an area is clear by dragging a weighted line. Once a site is successfully used, it will be given a name, and everyone will use that same name for the spot as long as it is fished.

A crew will put out the seine in a semicircle and pull the net toward the shore or toward a backstop made of webbing, thus encircling the fish. Small motors will sometimes be used if it is a long seine, but there is always much hard work in pulling in the net (fig. 36). Very large catches have been made in single seine hauls. In Iowa hauls of up to eighty thousand pounds were recorded in 1876.[12] Seines typically take buffalo fish, drum (or sheepshead), and, most commonly, carp. Traditionally much of the seining for carp was done in winter under ice, but because recent winters have been rather warm, this type of fishing has declined.

When large amounts of fish are caught with seines, fishermen use either a live-car or a dead-car to get fish to market. A live-car is a boat made of slats, about thirty feet long, usually with a bulkhead at the front and rear, which allow it to float or partially sink to the gunwales (fig. 37). When sunk, water moves through the live-car, allowing the fish to remain

FIGURE 36. *The William Steele crew at the "Apple House" haul near Lake Pepin, Wisconsin, are using a long seine (2,300 feet). A motorized winch is used to pull in the lead line, although small seines are still pulled by hand. The lead line is connected to a reefer line (to the right) every fifty feet. The man in the foreground pulls in the lead line, and will unhook the reefer line when it approaches the shore. The man in the background pulls in the cork line. All of the gear was owned by the Lake Pepin Fisheries, which received a percentage of the catch. Photo by Malcolm L. Comeaux, August 1971.*

alive as the boat is towed to market. They can even be left in the live-car at the market for several days. Live-cars were once widely used in the South, but after ice plants were established they ceased to exist, and the last one was used in south Louisiana about 1920. Live-cars survive and are important only in the Upper Mississippi, because the water is cooler, and it provides an efficient way of moving carp. The aptly named dead-car, however, is just a large boat (fig. 38). No effort is used to keep the fish alive in a dead-car, although ice will usually be thrown on top of them if the weather is warm. Fish are loaded in a dead-car with dip nets after sport fish and under-sized fish are removed, but they can be loaded directly into a live-car.

Other net types found in the Upper Mississippi include the cast net, a circular net sometimes used in catching bait. Two other net types, however, are important in commercial fishing — gill nets and trammel nets. Gill nets are very light nets made of fine twine with a wide mesh. They are designed to catch fish by their gills as they swim into the net without their noticing it. Since the nets are light and delicate, they cannot be used where there is a current, as they could be easily carried away or ruined by large floating objects. Therefore they are usually set in sloughs and backwaters.

FIGURE 37. *The Earl Breitung crew loads a live-car a short distance above Lake Pepin at the "Roberts" haul. The catch is almost all buffalo fish. The man in the boat is discarding undesired fish before they enter the live-car. The cork line is attached to the boat, while the man in the foreground pulls in the seine, concentrating the fish into a smaller and smaller area. This net was not pulled to shore, but to a net called a backstop. Photo by Malcolm L. Comeaux, July 1971.*

Trammel nets are somewhat like gill nets except that on either side of this light net is a net with heavier twine of very large mesh. Fishermen set out this net in the hope that fish will run into it, but they also will resort to driving fish toward this net by beating the water with paddles, toilet plungers, or whatever. The fish are startled by the noise and stampede into the net. The trammel net does not gill fish, but rather fish hit the inner net with such force that they pass through the outer net, and are caught in a pocket as they twist, spin, and turn. Another way of using the trammel net, now seldom done, is to have it drift downstream with the current. Two "mules" made of wood, attached to both ends of the net with rope, keep the net outstretched as it moves with the current. The net can be fished at the surface or at the bottom of the river, while the fisherman floats along to make sure all is well with the net.

OTHER WAYS OF EARNING A LIVING

Fishermen on the Upper Mississippi are literally "scratching for a living," and earning money on the river in any way they can. Sometimes they

FIGURE 38. *The William Steele crew loads a dead-car. The fish are concentrated near the car, while the men in the net remove the unwanted fish, as does the man standing in the car. They load the fish into the dead-car with a dip net. Ice, in boxes on the boat's rear, will be thrown over the fish. Photo by Malcolm L. Comeaux, August 1971.*

take turtles by catching them in short and broad-baited hoop nets, with part of the net above water. Sometimes they take them by placing a very large baited hook just above the water level. Fishermen also trap other animals. Although they traditionally trapped fur-bearing animals in the late fall, the price of fur has been so low in the last few years that today few fishermen trap these animals. They also hunt for game in the fall, especially for deer, in order to fill their freezers with venison.

Fishermen have also been involved in the gathering of mussels. Musseling was done for two distinctive purposes: the production of buttons and the production of cultivated pearls. The first button factory on the Upper Mississippi was established in about 1889 in Muscatine, Iowa. Soon that city was the undisputed "button capital of the United States." By 1899 sixty button factories on the Upper Mississippi, including forty-one in Iowa, employed 1,917 persons — in a booming industry.[13] Musseling expanded up and down the major rivers from Muscatine, but soon the beds were depleted, leading to a curtailment of the industry. The last button factory in Muscatine closed in 1967, a casualty of the popularity of plastic buttons, which are much stronger, cheaper to make, and whose shape and size is more amenable to standardization. Beginning in the 1950s, the industry revived somewhat when an export market developed for shells to be used in Japan as "seeds" in oysters for the production of cultivated pearls. Some musseling for this industry continues to the present.

Fishing for mussels was done in a variety of ways, none of them expensive or requiring much skill. Mussels were taken with large rakes in shallow water and in deeper water with long-handled tongs. The invention of the brail in 1897, however, ultimately led to extensive overfishing. Brails consisted of eight to ten-foot boards or iron bars, on which were four-prong wire hooks. By lowering them into the water and dragging them across the mussel bed, fishermen hoped to lodge the hooks between the open valves of the mussels. By the 1960s the few beds remaining were being harvested by scuba divers. Today, laws protect mussels, but surviving beds are still threatened for they are under attack by zebra mussels, an exotic species that has caused much damage in inland waters.

CHANGES IN COMMERCIAL FISHING

The vast majority of changes in commercial fishing have occurred as a result of technology, not new fishing ideas or techniques. Probably the best example is in the use of nylon. Before nylon, fishermen used cotton or linen twine that would last, at most, for one season. It had to be dipped into hot tar if it were to last that long, and nets needed re-tarring every two weeks. Today's hoop nets are still darkened, but rarely with hot tar. Some fishermen use a commercial product, Texaco *Netcoat*, while others use less expensive roofing coating, diluted 50 percent with gasoline. Darkening the net helps hoop nets in fishing (catfish will enter a dark net thinking it is a log). Other nets, such as gill and trammel nets, become too stiff to catch fish effectively when they are tarred.

Another technological change in fishing came with the use of engines in boats, which were widespread by the mid twentieth century. In the early days, boats had to be rowed. This meant that fishermen usually worked in pairs, as it took two men to row the boat a long distance and one to hold the boat steady while the other raised nets. The boats used were expensive commercially produced skiffs that would row easily.[14] When the first motors were introduced, they were used as inboard engines. Fishing boats became about twice as long as earlier boats, were oblong in shape with a scow (square) bow, and were known as launches. With the introduction of outboard motors, the commercial fishing boat's appearance changed again. They became shorter, broad-beamed, and straight from the mid-section to the rear, so that the boat would plane over the water. This new boat type allowed fishermen to go much greater distances and made teamwork obsolete or optional. Known as a flatboat or john boat, this type is now ubiquitous. Today many are made locally of heavy-gauge aluminum, and they seem to last indefinitely.

The changes in twine and boat engines allowed commercial fishermen to be more efficient. Even with relatively fewer fishermen working the Upper Mississippi, the catch remains high. Now they need not share the income that comes from working in teams, and they can fish over much greater distances. Using nylon nets that last much longer, today's fishermen can more efficiently use their time, and fish many more nets than could a fisherman in the past.

We have also seen some changes in the types of fish caught commercially. In the early days all fish were fair game, but in the early part of the twentieth century laws began to limit some fish types to sport fishing only. Another change was the introduction of carp. How and when the first carp got into the Mississippi River is a mystery, but the first ones taken from the river were in 1883 at Hannibal, Missouri, and Quincy, Illinois.[15] After that date, the catch of carp rose dramatically for use in Jewish markets to the east. Carp is well-known in Europe, where it is traditionally used to make gefilte fish (cakes made of deboned and ground-up fish, mixed with eggs and seasonings) eaten at Jewish holiday and Sabbath meals. By the early twentieth century carp had become a mainstay of commercial fishing in the Upper Mississippi River, because it had become important in the Jewish trade, a status it still maintains today. Traditionally the fish were moved by rail, but beginning in about 1960 shipments by truck started to dominate.

The increase in the number of carp, however, had an adverse effect on buffalo fish. Filling the same ecological niche, carp were more successful and became more numerous. The numbers of buffalo fish caught by commercial fishermen fell dramatically, and a big disadvantage resulted from the relative price paid for the two fish. In 1977, the last year for an extensive study by the federal government of the Mississippi River system, carp sold for 6.9 cents per pound, while buffalo fish sold for 19.7 cents (by comparison, catfish sold for 45.3 cents).[16]

Another change in commercial fishing was caused by the building in the 1930s of locks and dams to aid navigation on the Upper Mississippi. This action created vast areas of open water and extensive backwaters behind most of the dams. In many of these areas the river did not flow as freely and tended to flood less often and less severely. While this modified fishing environments, fishermen adjusted and catches remained high.

One change as a result of these pools was in the use of gill nets and trammel nets. They were generally not used in the earliest era of commercial fishing,[17] but with the lack of a strong current, their use has increased. Dam construction, however, had detrimental effects on musseling. Silting behind the dams covered many of the mussel beds, destroying them and thus killing the mussels.

Commercial fishing in the Upper Mississippi River region probably began when towns were first established in the nineteenth century and expanded as improved technology facilitated long-distance shipping. It was big business by the end of the nineteenth century and it remains important to the economy of the region to this day. Yet surprisingly little has changed in commercial fishing since the late 1800s. Practically none of the techniques have changed, although advancing technology (such as nylon twine and engines) has greatly aided commercial fishermen. There is virtually no other difference, however, between a commercial fisherman working today from those who worked during the era of the Grand Excursion. The chief similarity is that commercial fishing remains a marginal occupation. Just a few full-time fishermen remain, with many part-timers supplementing their other income by fishing.

None of these men will retire wealthy. The rewards to commercial fishermen obviously go far beyond the little money earned. It is an occupation that offers freedom, independence, and a meaningful livelihood. All fishermen state how they love to be "on the river." With that attitude, fishing will probably remain basically unchanged for the next 150 years.

FIGURE 39. *Part-time commercial fisherman Louie "Catfish" Spinner pictured under the Black Hawk Bridge in Lansing, Iowa. The bridge was planned and financed by private investors and opened in 1931. In 1945 floating ice dislodged by the* Fern, *a U.S. Coast Guard ice cutter, damaged parts of the slough bridges on the Wisconsin side. Since funds were not available to repair it immediately, the bridge did not re-open until 1956 after purchase of and repairs made by the Iowa and Wisconsin Highway Commissions. The name "Black Hawk" was chosen for the bridge because of its proximity to Bad Axe in Wisconsin, where the last battle of the Black Hawk War was fought. Information from William J. Burke,* The Upper Mississippi Valley: How the Landscape Shaped Our Heritage, *pp. 233–236. Photo by William J. Burke.*

RENEWALS AND REINVENTIONS
RIVER TOWNS ON THE
UPPER MISSISSIPPI
Norman Moline and Charles Mahaffey

In the nineteenth century Mark Twain wrote of the Mississippi River: "The face of the water, in time, became a wonderful book. . . . And it was not a book to be read once and thrown aside, for it had a new story to tell every day."[1] He was describing the river itself, but the same notions of change and pleasant landscapes currently apply to the cities and towns along the Upper Mississippi River. Established because of their riverside sites, these places have been transformed in varying degrees over the past two centuries. National and regional economic shifts and transportation developments, including changing dependence on the railroads, the arrival of the automobile and good roads — including the Great River Road and Scenic Byway and the Interstate Highway System — have modified the region's economic geography and local landscapes. Similarly, successive river modification schemes, particularly the current lock and dam system constructed in the 1930s, have had a major impact. The setting aside of public land along the river, notably the establishment of the 261-mile-long Upper Mississippi River National Wildlife and Fish Refuge in 1924 and the water quality acts of the 1960s and 1970s, have been crucial to improving the potential of the region to meet growing demands for outdoor recreation opportunities.

In recent decades the severe loss of manufacturing jobs that resulted from industrial restructuring and the demands and opportunities of the postindustrial economy have complicated the realities of life in the region. The tendencies for new commercial developments to prefer locations on the suburban fringes of cities and towns and for municipal governments to accommodate those preferences have made it difficult to give high priority to older sections near the river. Still, their proximity to the river remains a central feature of these Mississippi Valley cities and towns. Collectively and individually, they make a "wonderful book" with new stories unfolding every day.

These river towns have been using, planning, and reshaping their waterfronts as they renew and in some cases reinvent their relationships with the Mississippi. We analyze these activities to shed some light on the place-making processes by which the region's towns and cities hope to secure their own future. We conclude by offering suggestions about how these processes contribute to an emerging long-term Upper Mississippi regional vision.

THE GEOGRAPHER'S PERSPECTIVE

To understand the character of the towns and cities located along the Upper Mississippi River and their plans for the future, we visited all seventy-eight incorporated places adjacent to or near the river between Rock Island and St. Paul — the beginning and end points of the Grand Excursion.[2] Even though the largest ten cities represent seventy-five percent of the over 900,000 people who live in these places, the smaller towns and cities are also important parts of the region's character and were worthy of study. We identified some of the more notable details in these urban landscapes and looked for general themes. Our goal — and we think a goal of any such excursion — is to enhance awareness about the region's visible urban features, improve understanding about life in these settings, and thus provide an informed assessment of future prospects.

We observed current uses of waterfronts: the relative proportion devoted to industrial, commercial, and recreational activities; evidence of beautification projects; presence of nature interpretative centers and river-related festivals; and any development of quality new housing at riverside or river-overlook locations. We tried to get a sense of who uses these facilities and services. We looked for links between waterfronts and other urban activities, such as community and economic development, preservation and restoration of historic sites and districts, adaptive reuse of buildings, and new uses of abandoned industrial land. To get a sense of their connections with adjacent lands and towns, we looked both for functional or promotional linkages with nearby federal and state water-related facilities and for land and water trail links with other towns. Finally, we looked at descriptions and symbols in signage, promotional materials, planning documents, regional publications, and web sites for evidence of the degree to which cities and towns emphasize their river locations.

Many natural and cultural factors contribute to the development of settlement patterns and to differences in cultural landscapes from place to place that, in turn, influence the character and prospects of any future plans. In the specific context of this valley, the following questions are pertinent for inquisitive travelers and researchers:

What are the influences of local topography (e.g., steep bluffs, flood plains, terraces, riparian wetlands) on the present character and future plans of a given town?

How is each town situated relative to the main channel of the river and/or island-dotted backwaters?

Which towns are "protected" by levees that provide protection from flooding but also block some visual and physical access to the river?

Do railroad lines, which often run parallel between the river and the core downtowns, present some problems of continuity between the towns and the river?

To what extent is the river frontage consumed with private residences?

What are the impacts of street alignment, especially for the smaller towns? Do streets parallel the river at the base of the bluffs, giving many properties good river frontages or river views, or are they in a T-pattern with the major axis extending perpendicularly from a relatively narrow frontage on the river?

Which towns benefit from locations near state or federal facilities such as lock and dam visitor centers, wildlife refuge overlooks and access points, or parks?

How have the beauty and recreation functions of waterfronts impacted evaluations of the quality of these places and been used as additional selling points to reinforce the historical character of these towns and cities?

Do the cumulative effects of buildings, street layout, economic activities, resident comments, signage, and future plans convey a sense that the river is the "front door" or the "back door" in the life of each town or city?

To what extent does the nearness of other towns and cities with their waterfront development efforts and environmental policies present opportunities or problems for economic and community developments?

What are the impacts when long-term working waterfront commercial and industrial activities continue to function effectively and, thus, may limit a city's ability to develop more public waterfront uses?

What are the agendas of the commercial and political leaders and citizen groups in these towns and cities, and how do these agendas shape the evolution of the cultural landscape?

What local factors determine the relative weight given to any foci on the river and waterfronts (e.g., do smaller- or medium-sized towns and cities where the river to some extent is "the only game in town" emphasize their waterfronts and river character more than do the bigger cities that have many agendas and future opportunities)?

For each town and city a unique story can be told about how these characteristics and factors combine to give character to place and shape the hopes and plans for the future. While each story deserves to be told in detail, for this essay we discuss three types of places: cities in the four metropolitan areas (St. Paul, the Quad Cities, La Crosse, and Dubuque), medium-sized cities and towns, and finally the smallest incorporated places.

ST. PAUL, MINNESOTA

St. Paul (population: 287,151),[3] now paired with Minneapolis, comprises the core of a metropolitan area that in 2000 had a population of almost three million. St. Paul was the primary destination for the Grand Excursion of 1854 and is the inspirational locus for its 2004 reenactment. Although many urban projects were on the drawing board back in 1994, the discovery of the 150th anniversary of the Grand Excursion by a St. Paul urban planner prompted some civic leaders to perceive it as the perfect vehicle around which to plan the city's renaissance.[4] St. Paul hoped to reinvigorate its riverfront and its image in the national and even global consciousness and allow it to shine as brightly as its twin, Minneapolis. The slogan of the Grand Excursion 2004 — "Commemorate, Celebrate, and Educate" — suggests a multifaceted role for the spectacle. For some, the booster notion of bringing tourists and businesses to the region is paramount; other groups, however, want the event to help the city meet a broader set of objectives, those that are more associated with the renaissance of the riverfront and adjacent office districts and neighborhoods;

still others wish to see an overall improvement of the Mississippi River itself and an improved relationship between the city and the river in current activities and future plans to reinforce the historical importance of this connection.

One of St. Paul's twenty new developments, West Side Flats, a neglected forty-five-acre and former river's edge industrial site, was initiated in 1997 as a mixed-use urban village. Featuring the latest environmental planning concepts, it is a key part of St. Paul's vision of a city of neighborhoods in vital relationship to the Mississippi River.[5] Indeed, the Mississippi will provide the spine around which the renaissance is centered. The construction of the new Science Museum of Minnesota near the river was an important early step in the city's efforts to refocus on the river. River greening projects and urban village developments such as Upper Landing, the Minnesota Centennial Showboat, and other Harriet Island improvements are central in converting these working sites into landscapes of pleasure and models of sophisticated urban living (fig. 40). In total, over fifty-eight projects can be identified within about a half mile of the river that will enable St. Paul to function effectively as a "twenty-four hour city."

Locating urban amenities such as restaurants, theaters, recreational facilities, and other entertainment in the heart of the city, along with urban transport that integrates walking, biking, and future streetcar systems, are much more indicative of European cities. By utilizing this cosmopolitan approach, St. Paul provides incentives that young technology and management professionals find attractive. A brochure sets out the vision of the city for the next few decades: "Unveiled in 1997 to critical acclaim, Saint Paul on the Mississippi Development Framework is the community's vision for a revitalization of its central riverfront that celebrates the city's unique sense of place, reconnects Saint Paul to the Mississippi River, and establishes it as a regional destination. The Mississippi River, the city's greatest resource, is the catalyst for this change. . . . Confidence in Saint Paul's future abounds. The foundation has been laid for Saint Paul's extraordinary future as a great city."[6]

The city seems to have faith that this renewed relationship to the river embodies many of the twenty-first-century notions of what the "good life" is supposed to entail, thus presenting St. Paul to the world with the look and feel of a successful place. With the collective ego boost expected by planners and officials from St. Paul, will Garrison Keillor in his "Prairie

FIGURE 40. *Improvements on Harriet Island, across from downtown St. Paul, Minnesota, include walkways, a boat pier, a showboat theater, and the nearby West Side Flats urban village. Here people can experience the beauty and natural qualities of the river against the backdrop of historic and contemporary architecture of the urban skyline. Photo by Charles Mahaffey, 2002.*

Home Companion" series be prompted to revise his views on St. Paul's outlook and station in the world?

THE QUAD CITIES OF ILLINOIS AND IOWA

The Quad Cities — including Davenport and Bettendorf in Iowa and Rock Island, Moline, and East Moline in Illinois — are the main cities in a metropolitan area having a population of 359,062 in 2000. The political fragmentation of numerous adjacent cities and towns in two states presents unique problems for any regional efforts, including those related to river use and urban revitalization. From their origins at the foot of the Rock Island Rapids, these urban places prospered for many decades as commercial and manufacturing centers tied to the river. Then during the 1980s the region suffered heavily from the closure of a number of farm-related industries and the Rock Island Railroad, resulting in the loss of over twenty thousand manufacturing jobs. Describing the Quad City area at its low point, Jonathan Raban, British travel writer, wrote: "For twelve miles, they straggled lumpishly along the wharves, the hard angles of their warehouses, steel tanks and factories hemming in the river."[7]

Suddenly these communities had to deal with vacant and underutilized land on prime areas along the river, a shrinking tax base, high unemployment, out-migration of young workers, and low morale. From the discussions about the future held in each of the cities came ideas about turning again to what had been the primary focus of the communities until the Rock Island Railroad arrived in 1854 — the river. Public campaigns, spearheaded by newspaper and television interests and development organizations, began to unify the cities and provide hope for future economic success. "Joined by a River" became the regional slogan whose logo was an eagle soaring over the Mississippi. Citizen activist groups, particularly River Action founded in 1985, initiated a growing series of consciousness-raising events such as the construction of River Way kiosks and public art along the shore, the annual bi-state Father's Day Riverside Bicycle Ride, a summer water taxi service between the cities (on the *Channel Cat*), the lighting of Centennial Bridge, and a regional greenway system that includes a bike/jogging trail along the river as part of the regional sixty-two-mile Great River Trail.

In addition to these and other collective actions, efforts to redevelop the waterfronts began in each individual city. These efforts have centered on economic restructuring, historic preservation, creating life in the downtowns through the "festivalization" of the calendar year, and developing downtown housing options. One of the first perceived solutions to the area's economic problems was casino riverboat gambling. It arrived in the early 1990s, initially in Bettendorf and then in Davenport and Rock Island, with hopes that the Quad Cities would become a tourist destination. Ironically, the largest of the current casino boats, the *Isle of Capri* in Bettendorf, makes no mention of the Mississippi River in its standard promotional brochure! It instead highlights the fact that it "brings the splendor of the tropics to the heart of the Midwest."[8]

Beyond the river boat gambling option, each of the cities has taken a different approach, even if the long-term goals are the same. In Rock Island, East Moline, and Bettendorf, flood protection levees and working businesses take up much of the waterfront and thus have forced public access into more limited space. Rock Island chose to redesign the "backs" of some of its downtown buildings so that these sides now have a more pleasing "front" appearance facing the river. Also, the city has focused attention on the creation of the District (a lively arts and entertainment zone), the Quad City Botanical Center, and the Quad City Conservation Alliance Exposition Center (fig. 41). Recently this core has begun to evolve into an urban village with the creation of lofts and other apartments. East Moline's Quarter is another example of a mixed-use cluster of housing, private businesses, and public river access points which will be an innovative corridor extending the old central business district, which is some distance from the river, to the Mississippi waterfront.

Moline has developed some former industrial riverfront sites into a public and quasi-public area focusing on an arena, the Mark, along with John Deere Commons (a large indoor-outdoor museum and display complex) and a public boat dock. Moline has been able to link these new features with its two-mile Ben Butterworth Parkway, one of the best urban waterfront bicycle/pedestrian trails in the region.

In Davenport the lack of any flood-protection levee has given the public direct access to the river at LeClaire Park with its riverside walk, open green space, outdoor concert site, and a minor league baseball stadium. Recent riverfront developments have focused almost entirely on its gambling boat, but a 2002 Vision Iowa grant of twenty million dollars helped to diversify its activities with the construction of an art museum, a music center, and pedestrian bridges to link the waterfront with other downtown features.

Located in the middle of this metropolitan area is the federally owned Arsenal Island (which officially is in Illinois). The Rock Island Arsenal itself, the Corps of Engineers district office, and a number of river-related tourist sites, including Lock and Dam 15 Visitor Center and the Colonel Davenport House, have allowed this place to serve as a psychological bridge — a common ground — for the cities of the two states. In that sense it reminds us of a key question for this metropolitan area and to some extent for other bistate and multicommunity urban areas along the river: Will the different communities be able to converge on a cohesive river reorientation program for the entire area or will the tendency for individualistic thinking by cities, towns, and states prevail, particularly when final decisions must be made?

LA CROSSE, WISCONSIN

La Crosse (population: 51,818) exemplifies one of the most holistic approaches to riverfront and downtown revitalization by a medium-sized city. Located on a broad plain where the Black and La Crosse Rivers join the Mississippi, La Crosse attracted a variety of waterfront industries that

FIGURE 41. *What once was the backside of a retail and office building that fronted the main commercial street of Rock Island, Illinois, has been improved with brick cleaning, a large painting, and a new entrance that faces the riverfront. The painting of Black Hawk, the leader of the Sauk Nation in the early nineteenth century, calls attention to the Native American presence in the area's history. Photo by Charles Mahaffey, 2002.*

utilized the area's timber, land, and water resources. As the economy and transportation changed, some of its industries declined, resulting in a deteriorating waterfront landscape to the point where the river was treated almost as a "back door" to the city from the 1930s until the mid 1980s. Then some citizens began to promote a new attitude toward the river. In 1990 Downtown Mainstreet, Inc. of La Crosse, a public-private partnership, was created to initiate the steps for a comprehensive master plan for the downtown. City Vision 2000 Master Plan, adopted in 1992, provided an economic and physical development strategy "to stimulate reinvestment in the La Crosse central area and strengthen the relationship of the community and the region to La Crosse's historic riverfront setting."[9] Building upon existing features, including Riverside Park, Pettibone Park and Wildlife Sanctuary, the Mississippi River swimming beach, a marina, and historic architecture, the plan sought to establish an identity that built on the area's historical, recreational, and scenic resources. This plan was updated in June 1999 with forty-seven new recommendations, some of which have been completed.

A $2.9 million riverfront redevelopment project focused on historic Riverside Park that stretches for almost five blocks in the downtown area. It includes a riverwalk, commercial boats, the Riverside USA Museum, an outdoor concert stage, and a dock for recreational boats. Over one hundred downtown buildings have been restored, many in the nationally registered commercial historic district. A dense network of wayfaring signs was also developed, using as its main logo a sketch of the *War Eagle,* one of the main boats in the 1854 Grand Excursion, which in 1870 burned and sank in La Crosse (fig. 42). Extensive streetscaping creates a pleasant walking environment. Public art, several with water themes, are scattered throughout the core area, with the old water pump house functioning as the regional arts center. Some high-tech corporations, restaurants, and national hotel chains have located downtown adjacent to the river. Combined with the La Crosse Center, the city's convention center constructed in the 1980s, these facilities heighten the city's core skyline.

Several annual events, most notably the July 4th weekend Riverfest, also draw people to this core and strengthen the perception that the heart of La Crosse is its link with the river. New residential developments downtown and elsewhere along the river (e.g., Bayside Court and River Oaks Apartments) rest on elevated flood-safe terraces with excellent westward-facing vistas of the Upper Mississippi Wildlife Refuge, thus exemplifying the potentials of riverside housing, at least for the upscale market. Beyond the core, some bluff lands that form the city's picturesque eastern backdrop have been purchased to protect them from sprawl and degradation. Moreover, recognizing its external links, La Crosse works with neighboring towns, particularly Onalaska and Shelby, Wisconsin, and La Crescent, Minnesota, in promoting tourist activities. Its plan highlights a network of bicycle/pedestrian trails that connect to Wisconsin's state recreational trail system. The University of Wisconsin-La Crosse and the *La Crosse Tribune* are taking the initiative to develop a "seven rivers region" to facilitate cooperative development by ten counties in Iowa, Minnesota, and Wisconsin.

With these developments, civic leaders in planning and tourism promotion affirm that the river continues to influence the lives of the residents. They believe it is the main reason people come here and, more importantly, stay here. In bold style, the boosters identify the city as "the heart of God's country" and "America's #1 Small City."[10] The National Trust for Historic Preservation granted boosters further recognition

FIGURE 42. *Throughout downtown La Crosse, Wisconsin, directional signs under the* War Eagle *boat logo effectively guide residents and visitors to key features of Riverside Park. Photo by Charles Mahaffey, 2002.*

when it selected La Crosse as one of only five recipients of its 2002 Great American Main Street Award, thus reinforcing its holistic approach as a potentially valuable model for other towns and cities.

DUBUQUE, IOWA

If La Crosse already has earned rewards for its actions, Dubuque (population: 57,686) may have the most ambitious new waterfront plan, including funding, of any medium-sized city on the Upper Mississippi. The civic and corporate leaders of Dubuque hope that the new $188 million riverfront development boosted by the Grand Excursion 2004 will vault the city into the higher echelons of the tourist hierarchy. The labels National Museum and America's River Project reveal a desire to have these projects viewed from a perspective that constitutes a different order of magnitude.

"Edutainment" describes this new trend of juxtaposing and combining a variety of functions. On the entertainment side of the equation, the projects include a two-hundred-room riverfront hotel, dinner yacht, large indoor water park, *Diamond Jo's* casino boat, dramatic outdoor auditorium, plazas, riverway walk and bike trail, and restaurants and cafes (fig. 43). The educational exhibits on the ninety-acre riverfront campus consist of the Mississippi River Aquarium & Discovery Center, Mississippi River National Education and Conference Center, Mississippi River Museum, and National Rivers Hall of Fame, all featuring state-of-the-art technologies for conferences. Dubuque officials expect to entertain and educate over 500,000 visitors per year, generating a large infusion of money and more interest in knowing about and caring for the region. The riverfront festival area will be connected via overpass to the historic central business district that also is beginning its renaissance, one that includes a new convention center. Linkages with Galena (Illinois), the historic lead-mining town and former steamboat port, will contribute to the growth of tourist traffic. The result of all this construction should be striking. The working waterfront and older industrial areas are being converted into a year-round recreation and conference venue, reshaping the physical and mental landscapes of the region's people. Watch out Las Vegas!

MEDIUM-SIZED PLACES

Located between these larger metropolitan areas are many cities and towns with populations less than thirty thousand that also are involved in

FIGURE 43. *The river, a sheltered harbor, a working waterfront, a riverfront with new public potential, and a historic downtown are the context for Dubuque, Iowa's ambitious riverfront revitalization. Photo by Mark Hunt, 2002.*

efforts to retain their long-standing character and develop new ways to take advantage of the presence of the Mississippi. Some of these are structured with the assistance of planners; others rely on informal actions taken by their residents. In either case, the panel in the riverfront park in Winona, Minnesota, captures the spirit: "Winona lives by the Mississippi. The sand prairie on which the city rests, the occupations of the earliest settlers, its current identity — all were born of the river. Names and industries have changed with the times, but the richness of our architecture and ethnic heritage flows on. For recreation, commerce and community identity, Winona looks still to the river." Downriver in Clinton, Iowa, a major lumber-milling center in the nineteenth century, a similar strategy is used. Among the ten planning principles in the Clinton Riverview Park Master Plan are the following two: "Celebrate Clinton's heritage and the role the Mississippi has played," and "Link neighborhoods to the river and the park to the downtown."[11] The particular actions taken to implement these future hopes are as numerous as the number of places in the valley. Some of the improvements or plans we consider are working waterfronts, river-related recreation, special emphasis on the bald eagle, lock and dam visitor centers, river-related festivals, links with historic preservation activities, reused industrial sites, and new housing.

Some medium-sized communities have waterfronts that continue to be quite active commercially and industrially. These cities highlight the number of people with jobs in riverside industries. Winona is a noteworthy example of this category since it uses the circumstances of its location with river, road, and rail transportation to function as a good multi-nodal center. Clinton, Iowa; Fulton, Illinois; and Red Wing, Minnesota, are other medium-sized cities with significant working waterfronts (fig. 44). In these situations less waterfront may be available for new public uses and recreation. Nevertheless, if jobs are retained, their populations and economy can be stabilized and an authentic rivertown character can be sustained.

Most of the towns have some form of public access and boat launch points. In those northern parts of the region where the water is cleaner, municipalities have also designated areas as swimming beaches. Many of the cities and towns are fortunate to be near the Upper Mississippi River National Wildlife and Fish Refuge. Some towns highlight their accessibility to wildlife and wildlife-related recreation. For example, Ferryville, Wisconsin, and Savanna, Illinois, each describes itself as a "Sportsman's Paradise." A brochure about Sabula, Iowa, similarly states: "The natural beauty of the location still remains. There are fish and clams in the river, abundant waterfowl and the peaceful quiet of a small town in America."[12] Cities and towns on the main channel side and those on the less common backwater side of the river each possess distinctive features that are advantageous for outdoor recreation. A few places such as Sabula and Winona as island towns are fortunate to be able to take advantage of both main channel and backwater settings. The towns from Lansing, Iowa, to Prairie du Chien, Wisconsin, accent a canoe trail through the many channels and sloughs characteristic of that section of the river. Guttenberg, Iowa, has an aquarium along its central waterfront. Camanche, Iowa, has converted an old mansion into the city library overlooking the river and a large municipal pier. Moreover, to make the river visually accessible to more citizens within close proximity of their residences — instead of focusing all efforts on one or two riverfront parks — it takes the less common approach of spacing many small overlook parks at regular intervals at those points where city streets reach the waterfront. Some places seem to be completely satisfied with this outdoor recreation identity, while others would like to have additional activities. Prescott, Wisconsin, received

FIGURE 44. *Red Wing, Minnesota's working waterfront on the Mississippi, with grain-loading facilities, continues a common long-term relationship between towns and the river. At the same time, they limit public recreational access. Creative compromises have been worked out in some towns and cities. Photo by Charles Mahaffey, 2002.*

a $1.7 million grant to construct a river interpretive center overlooking the river below its confluence with the St. Croix River.

The American bald eagle is an important resident of the Upper Mississippi River Valley. In some places it visits only in the winter months, while in other places it stays the year around. When residents of Wabasha, Minnesota, were "looking for ways to protect and promote the beauty and integrity of the city's Mississippi River frontage," they decided to focus on the bald eagle.[13] The town built an eagle-watching observation deck at its main riverfront park and established an educational National Eagle Center on its main street. Cassville, Wisconsin, has designated January as Bald Eagle Month and emphasizes eagle watching from its waterfront park. Bald Eagle Days, featuring special viewing opportunities, exhibits, and other events, are sponsored in over a dozen towns on January and February weekends. Some cities and towns have designated eagle-viewing overlook points or feature the eagle in their logos or booster signs, e.g., Bellevue, Guttenberg, and Lansing in Iowa, Hampton and Albany in Illinois, and De Soto and Stoddard in Wisconsin.

Five towns, Bellevue and Guttenberg in Iowa, Hastings, Minnesota, and Trempealeau and Alma in Wisconsin, have locks and dams in their immediate core areas, attracting visitors and locals to view barge activity throughout the navigation season and, hopefully, to enjoy other tourist features. Guttenberg has its Lockmaster House Heritage Museum to complement the lock and dam overlook. Le Claire, Iowa, accents its connection with navigation at the head of the Rock Island Rapids with the catch phrase, "Where the River Pilots Lived."

Many communities sponsor one or more annual river-related festivals. Some kind of special fishing day is a common occurrence, as are art festivals that use the river as a backdrop. Two types of events are particularly distinctive. Prairie du Chien, like La Crosse, sponsors a "buckskin rendezvous" event, a weekend reenactment of an aspect of its fur trade history. Le Claire, Iowa, and Port Byron, Illinois, have long had intimate roles in river life as the homes of river pilots who navigated the Rock Island Rapids. Now they host The Great River Tug Festival, a tug of war utilizing a 2,400-foot rope stretched across the Mississippi between the two towns. The winner claims an alabaster statue of a bald eagle in flight. While a good time is the basic goal of festivals, the promotional events enhance the towns' economic value.

In the downtowns of many of these medium-sized places, historic preservation of a few buildings or districts is part of their current character and future plans. Le Claire, Bellevue, Guttenberg, Galena, Wabasha, Red Wing, and Hastings are some places that are exemplary for their historic preservation work (fig. 45). For them the future must include the past, even in the physical make-up of the place. Similarly, Prairie du Chien promotes its history on its welcoming sign as "Wisconsin's Second Oldest Community — 1603," and in its tourist literature with this description: "Towering bluffs, flowing rivers and fascinating history all converge in this region of breath-taking natural splendor and beauty."[14] Fulton, Illinois, settled by the Dutch in the nineteenth century, is characterized as "a delightful experience, rich in heritage, loaded with adventure on the banks of the Mississippi."[15]

Some of these towns, like the larger cities, have struggled to find ways to reuse abandoned industrial sites. A successful example is in Hastings, Minnesota, a town that had developed as a major grain milling center. Here, the Koch Refining Company (now Flint Hills Resources) donated its former riverside site to the city. It is now being developed as an outdoor

FIGURE 45. *While emphasizing their river locations, many towns and cities also highlight their general heritage with historic preservation projects. In this example, banners and restored Italianate storefronts characterize the main street of Wabasha, Minnesota, one block away from the waterfront. Photo by Norman Moline, 2002.*

nature preserve that will be an effective link with the downtown, an existing park, and the lock and dam visitor center.

As in the larger centers, a few medium-sized communities have new riverside housing developments. Meeting the standards of floodplain regulations, these new developments often are located on terraces that are high enough to be safe from floods and have excellent river views. Good examples of this trend can be seen in Hampton, Illinois; Guttenberg, Iowa; Brownsville and Lake City, Minnesota; and Pepin, Wisconsin.

In a number of towns visual and even physical access is blocked by the railroad, other industries, or privately owned homes. In fact, over 80 percent of all the river towns and cities surveyed in this study must share the waterfront itself or one or two blocks back from the waterfront with the rail lines. The preservation of an old depot or the existence of safe and smooth crossings indicates some reasonable coexistence in sharing this waterfront space in some of these towns. In others, the railroad indeed functions as a barrier. Private housing, ranging from simple riverside houseboats or cabins (often on stilts or constructed earthen embankments) to elaborate and expensive dwellings, occupies much of the shoreline. This pattern reduces public access and restricts future public riverside developments into small sections of the total frontage.

While some medium-sized places have only some of the traits just described, a few contain many or even all of them. Red Wing, Minnesota, is a fine example. It has many river access points and facilities, downtown historic preservation and adaptive reuse projects, scenic overlooks both near to and far from the river, festivals, a working waterfront, and new housing construction. Also at Red Wing are explicit references to the river in promotional and planning materials, linkages with nearby places, and good public and corporate involvement in implementing plans for the future. Particularly noteworthy is the successful incorporation of the railroad depot (which still had Amtrak service at the time of this research) into its downtown landscape.

SMALL TOWNS

As the large cities and medium-sized towns develop plans, strategies, public-private partnerships, investments, and marketing programs to reaffirm or create links with the river — sometimes authentic, sometimes fabricated — many of the smallest towns simply move ahead as river places with the attitude, "life as usual." Forty-seven (60 percent) of the places in this study have populations under two thousand. Created because of their locations on the river and sustained by different economic functions appropriate to their position in the total urban hierarchy over the past one hundred to 160 years, these small towns are authentic river towns. Whether in the elongated linear pattern of town development that runs parallel to the river (as in Stoddard, Ferryville, Lynxville, and Alma in Wisconsin; Minneiska in Minnesota; Lansing in Iowa; and Port Byron and Rapids City in Illinois) or in the less common T-pattern, where the main commercial street aligns perpendicularly to the river (as in Trempealeau and Stockholm in Wisconsin and McGregor and Marquette in Iowa), these towns have an unmistakable river-oriented sense of place.

The welcome signs at Clayton, Iowa, and Brownsville, Minnesota, are indicative: "Tiny Town on the Mighty Mississippi" and "Great Little City on the Great Mississippi." Virtually all towns have riverfront parks, boat launch points, a small marina, residential streets with good river views, a restaurant and/or a tavern with a river view, and perhaps a small motel or bed-and-breakfast house. Located on narrower strips of flat land between the bluffs and the river, some of these places have excellent overlooks, including Alma, Wisconsin, and North Buena Vista, Bellevue, and Lansing, Iowa, although their sites limit their growth potential. Ever since the automobile and good roads improved the access to larger towns in the hierarchy, many economic activities found in these small towns began to close down. Some former commercial buildings have been torn down, others stand vacant, and some have been adapted for new uses. A few survive as beautifully restored structures, sometimes listed on the National Register of Historic Places. Citizens in Trempealeau note with historic pride the Main Street Project, dedicated in 2000. Many small towns note their historic character in their descriptions. For example, the brochure of McGregor has a section titled *The Old and The New* in which it states: "We are happy to share with you McGregor's 19th century architecture with its balconies and turrets to its modern houseboats completely furnished for your enjoyment."[16]

Yet, despite their small sizes, economic problems, aging buildings, and stable or declining populations, the residents express a sense of pride about these places and attachment to them. In some cases, particularly in towns that are in close proximity to larger cities, new residents are attracted to small river towns because of their closeness to the river and the quieter pace of life. When we asked a resident of Minneiska, population 116, what it is like to live there, he replied: "It's heaven!" and pointed across the street to the magnificent view of the broad Mississippi River Valley. Allamakee County in northeast Iowa along the river similarly boasts that its lifestyle "runs at an easy pace compared to the cities."[17]

While some people in these places would like to see an increase in population that might support more local economic activities, others are satisfied with their current size and character and almost fear what any significant influx of new people might mean to the quality of life. One unincorporated place, Old Frontenac, Minnesota, seeks to uphold its traditional atmosphere by maintaining gravel residential streets, forbidding any town streetlights, and even avoiding incorporation. The reality is that most of these places are likely to remain small for the foreseeable future.

Whatever the case, these places are river towns — their histories are linked intimately with the river in that their proximity to the river is the defining quality of their sense of place. Some of these small towns have shown interest in promoting themselves as individual destination points, perhaps for a unique festival day or a unique ethnic heritage (e.g., Stockholm, Wisconsin, unfurls Swedish flags on its light poles and Swedish-related businesses can be found on its main street), while others affiliate with some kind of larger regional initiative. For travelers in the region, any time that can be spent in these small places definitely will help to convey a better sense of the total character of the region. Such travel gives the best glimpse of these authentic river places, ones that have not had the need and/or financial resources to reinvent themselves, but simply continue to be what they have been for many years (fig. 46).

PLACE MAKING IN LOCAL AND REGIONAL CONTEXT

Cities and towns are physical and cultural entities. These places are thus made partially by how they are conceived and by what is said and written about them. Viewed for their utility in the nineteenth century, they hosted that era's industrial riverfront; by the late twentieth century they morphed into brownfields (former industrial sites), ready to be greened and made into the touristscapes of the twenty-first century.

One of the aspects that intrigues interpreters of places is the means and the manner by which towns, cities, and regions present themselves or are represented by others. The United States has a long history of urban and regional boosterism. Encouraged or threatened by changes, local residents through individual or collective acts reveal a concern for place identity. Both with reference to the present and to the future, people hope that

FIGURE 46. *Fish festivals and contests, special fish dinners, fish entrees on menus, fishing piers, and fishing supply stores cater to the interests of both residents and visitors in small and larger centers. Big, ugly catfish: that's what's for dinner in Brownsville, Minnesota. Photo by Charles Mahaffey, 2002.*

their town or city, regardless of its location or size, will have a desirable place on the map. The iconography of success of the nineteenth century was based upon evidence of brick buildings and a bustling steamboat-filled wharf that resulted in a favorable image for a town. As places have had to detach themselves from the visual and aural mores and norms of the industrial era when smokestacks, rail yards, refuse heaps, factory drainage, and open sewers were "naturalized" as part of working land-scapes, the postindustrial places of today have had to learn to remake and present themselves along aesthetic lines.

In this new century public places cannot be just functional or modern. Our list of adjectives describing our landscapes and places in this postin-dustrial era tends toward the visual, the aesthetic, and the playful. An emerging sensibility prompts us to want to recapture or attempt to create a sense of place; authenticity and a sense of time should be retained or at least suggested. In addition, our spaces should have people recreating, consuming, and doing fun things in them. Most would agree that in our ideal riverfront town we would find clean, well-marked walking, jogging, and biking paths; benches; concept landscaping; flower pots; trees with markers; banners; way-finding signage; kiosks telling us interesting stories; marinas with good restaurants; public art; and, of course, odorless toilets. Today many tourists tend to judge places by these design standards.

Towns and cities are compelled to walk a tightrope of sorts. While they strive to project a distinctive sense of place, the implementation of design conventions and standard landscape "furniture" (e.g., benches, kiosks, planters, building facades, and speciality shops) can result in places beginning to look vaguely alike. When every town has similar boutiques with similar tourist items to sell and one festival resembles the next, the generic begins to overwhelm the specific and the sense of place becomes clouded. Also, when the promotions are successful and many people come to these places as tourists or permanent residents, their presence threatens to change the very distinguishing and charming characteristics that drew them in the first place.

Fortunately, many smaller places on the Upper Mississippi River have little in the way of the mannered look described above. They still have unique identities, and to the insiders who worked to make improvements in public spaces and private properties, the alterations are the result of sweaty physical labor, numerous community meetings, and local fundraisers. These changes might be relatively invisible to the tourist, but they certainly are recognized by the residents and contribute to the local pride of place.

The evaluation of places is not straightforward. It is a relative exercise and one should try to understand the results through the eyes of the residents who live and work in the places under study. If reading the resulting landscape can be a somewhat ambivalent exercise, what about the tools and means of constructing them? How are the images constructed and who is helping to construct them?

For a long time chambers of commerce have brought business to cities or towns in order to shape and mold their place images. Today various additional local and regional institutions have assumed that role, and cities must spend considerable sums and possess sophisticated information systems to lure commerce to their streets. Offices of economic development, convention and tourist bureaus, and public-private entities promoting specific urban projects and activities are the major authors and boosters of places. Over the last few years greater numbers of places have set up formal and informal networks and associations and alliances with other towns, cities, and counties.

Web pages have improved the public's access to information regarding these river towns. Even without visiting the Quad Cities, Clinton,

Dubuque, La Crosse, Winona, Wabasha, Red Wing, Hastings, St. Paul, and many other places, we can view on-line materials that, for example, depict their riverfront layout, describe their latest efforts at waterfront revitalization, or feature historic preservation projects. In the case of Dubuque much of the virtual landscape has been transformed significantly to present a new landscape with an unmistakable river focus. Although these offerings vary widely, many of the web sites have similar designs and standard information formats. Guided virtual tours using video clips of neighborhoods, entertainment districts, marinas, resorts, and site and situation of parcels of land are now mundane practices. Citizen groups with their announcements, FAQs, and chat rooms create discussion about even ephemeral events such as festivals, adding another layer of information. The folks on the flotilla in 1854 no doubt would have approved. Similar to much of the booster literature of the nineteenth century, much of today's promotional literature on the internet is skewed to the visual and the positive.

In addition to tourism-related web sites, a growing number of web-related networks give people a means to learn about and discuss a wide range of river and region-related issues. These networks, such as the American Rivers, the Bridging the River Project, and the Winona-based Upper Mississippi Valley Stake Holders Network, to name but three, vary in magnitude and focus. They fulfill the hopes of those who believe that real places can be shaped, supported, and constructed by these digital flows. Collectively, they are revolutionizing the degree to which insiders and outsiders can familiarize themselves with the issues confronting the region and with the processes of creating the collective mental map of the region. The planning for the Grand Excursion 2004 in itself generated large flows of messages. In this way web-based interaction supports the formation of a region in giving it an identity through the sheer number of messages, questions, and information passed up and down the river. It also carries this emerging regional image to the wider world.

Perhaps years from now we will refer to the Upper Mississippi Valley region in an offhand vernacular way just as New Orleans and Cajun Country resonate and conjure a region for most people. This regional identity and identification, of course, takes time and countless repetitions of the term, as well as agreed-upon spatial and cultural connotations. Tourism and forms of organizational behavior may be the forerunners of this more cohesive and cooperative outlook. The Grand Excursion 2004 is one such mega-spectacle contributing to a coherent image. This book also contributes in some small manner to the regional conversation. Yet the process of image formation also may happen, perhaps even more effectively and authentically, by place-making forces that are more local, such as towns working with other towns on practical matters of tourist circuit development, promotional newspapers, shared advertising costs, web site development, and coordination of festival dates. From our conversations with people in tourism, we sensed a belief that "they were in it together." The list of voluntary associations is growing. Groups such as Bluff Country, covering southeastern Minnesota; Tri-State Tourism Council, centering on Dubuque; and the Seven Rivers Region, a nine-county area focusing on La Crosse, were cited often to us in 2002. At this time these groups cover a limited, though overlapping, geographic reach of the river — potential subregions waiting to coalesce into a larger region.

One of the largest of these efforts is the Mississippi Valley Partners group, which involves thirteen communities in Wisconsin and Minnesota and stretches from Red Wing to Alma with over 150 businessowner members and volunteers. This alliance was started in 1992 by the University of Minnesota Extension Service to overcome the lack of public-private cooperation and the lack of interaction among the bi-state communities. In addition to bottom-line goals, two others are particularly significant. They encourage members to "develop the concept of looking at the 13 communities as one destination place with numerous small community experiences," and to "promote tourism in the area with an on-going commitment to environmental, historical and cultural appreciation."[18]

Regional publications also are helping to create a sense of place for the region. In the premier issue of the *Tapestry Magazine* (published in Lansing), the editor reveals a personal attachment to the region: "I've always wanted to find, and read, a general interest magazine that covers the area of this river valley that I've called home all my life: generally speaking, the area running right alongside the river from Prairie du Chien in the south to Winona in the north."[19] True to her word, the editor stocked the first issue with a number of stories that captured the notion of the region, not just its distinct towns and cities.

Big River, begun in 1993 and published in Winona, covers a wide range of region-related stories with an emphasis on environmental, economic, and historical issues. It has a polished look, high production values, and is well supported by regional business sponsors from the Quad Cities to the Twin Cities. These and other publications fill a niche between the booster literature of the promotional associations and the academic or governmental studies dealing with regional issues and problems.

Planning bodies are also adding to the discourse on regional issues. The Bi-State Regional Commission in the Quad Cities area views the economic development of five counties as a region and approaches its duties with this regional perspective in mind. The study by the Twin Cities-area Metropolitan Council that was completed in 2002 concluded that the only way the region will maintain its environmental quality and livability will be for the towns and cities of the area to think and act more holistically in the future — to think regionally. This regional vision stresses that the Mississippi must be maintained according to high environmental standards, that towns of the region must remain distinct, that anti-sprawl measures must be enacted, and that viable rural economic life must be maintained.

Over time the Upper Mississippi region may start to be thought of as an interlaced, overlapping set of towns and cities, public corporations, governmental units, planning bodies, educational institutions, and citizen groups rather than four states whose linkages are only incidental. If these collective linkages are developed, then perhaps a vernacular region, i.e., a region which exists in residents' minds, would emerge and also achieve some recognition beyond the region. Years from now we may know the answer. Yet it does seem apparent from our explorations that the towns along the river have a vital, and, in many instances, a re-vitalized relationship with the river. For all of us who participate in the actions of using the river, which includes observing and even writing about the river, we now must face the task of learning about and finally living with the river. If we can make this connection, then all of the renewals and reinventions by cities and towns can be applauded as contributions to the long-term sustainability of this region focused on the Mississippi River, described by Twain as a "wonderful book."

Author's note: Mark Hunt, a geography major and a 2003 graduate from Augustana College, was an important assistant on this research.

FIGURE 47. *Like many towns on the Upper Mississippi, this bridge took a 360-degree turn. Built in 1895, its spiral ramp was designed to ensure that traffic would go into the Hastings, Minnesota, downtown area. It became an icon among Mississippi River bridges and many travelers went out of their way to dizzy themselves on this bridge. Load restrictions were imposed in the 1930s and, despite attempts by the local citizenry to save it, the spiral bridge was razed in 1951 after a new bridge was built nearby. Information from Robert Stumm,* A Postcard Journey Along the Upper Mississippi, *p. 24. Real photo postcard, no publisher indicated.*

NOTES

THE UPPER MISSISSIPPI AND THE GRAND EXCURSION

1. This section draws from Wayne I. Anderson, *Iowa's Geologic Past*, and Howard Hobbs, "Origin of the Driftless Area by Subglacial Drainage — A New Hypothesis."

2. Parts or all of the Driftless Area may have been covered by early glaciers, a subject of debate among geologists.

3. This section draws on William A. Meese, *Early Rock Island*, and Michael D. Green, "The Expansion of European Colonization to the Mississippi Valley, 1780–1880."

4. John O. Anfinson in this volume.

5. Meese, *Early Rock Island*, pp. 17–24.

6. Sedgwick, "The Great Excursion to the Falls of St. Anthony," p. 322.

7. *Albany Evening Journal*, 15 September 1854.

8. *Albany Evening Journal*, 10 September 1854.

9. Population figures for cities and towns come from the U.S. Bureau of the Census.

10. William Edward Hayes, *Iron Road to Empire*, p. 28.

11. A variety of excursions of the time are summarized by Timothy R. Mahoney, *Provincial Lives*, pp. 242–256.

12. A copy of the excursion *Register* was obtained by Dick Stahl courtesy of the Yale University Archives. We speculate that it was signed at the Tremont House in Chicago, the headquarters hotel of the excursion where many of the eastern guests stayed. Because virtually none of the guests who were residents of Chicago signed the *Register*, it was probably signed at the hotel. Also obtained from Yale were copies of partial guest registers for three of the boats, the *Golden Era*, the *Sparhawk*, and the *Galena*.

13. *Albany Evening Journal*, 12 June 1854.

14. *Cleveland Leader*, reprinted in the *Cincinnati Gazette*, 10 June 1854.

15. Information on Grand Excursion participants was drawn from Henry W. Farnam, *Memoirs of Henry Farnam; The National Cyclopedia of American Biography* (1901); and various newspaper accounts of the excursion cited in this essay.

16. Diary of John R. Munn.

17. Chauncey A. Goodrich, *The Excursion*.

18. George Bancroft, *History of the United States from the Discovery of the American Continent*. See also Lilian Handlin, *George Bancroft*, n.p.

19. John Paul Driscoll and John K. Howat, *John Frederick Kensett*.

20. This account of the Grand Excursion draws on the following sources: Captain Russell Blakeley, "History of the Discovery of the Mississippi River and the

Advent of Commerce in Minnesota"; Farnam, *Memoirs of Henry Farnam*; William Edward Hayes, *Iron Road to Empire*, chapter six, "Mississippi Holiday," pp. 27–32; S. W. McMaster, *60 Years on the Upper Mississippi*; Nevins, "Seventy Years of Service, From Grant to Gorman" (includes quotes from William R. Tibbels, who was a cub pilot on the Grand Excursion), pp. 15–16; Diary of John R. Munn; William J. Petersen, "The Grand Excursion of 1854"; William J. Petersen, "The Rock Island Railroad Excursion of 1854"; William J. Petersen, *Steamboating on the Upper Mississippi*, chapter thirty-two, "The Grand Excursion of 1854," pp. 271–286; "Rails West: The Rock Island Excursion of 1854 as reported by Charles F. Babcock"; Sedgwick, "The Great Excursion to the Falls of St. Anthony," pp. 320–325. Also used were June 1854 accounts from the following newspapers: *Albany Argus, Albany Evening Journal, Boston Daily Advertiser, Boston Daily Journal, Boston Evening Transcript, Chicago Journal, Cincinnati Gazette, Cleveland Leader, Chicago Daily Tribune, Dubuque Daily Miners' Express, St. Paul Daily Pioneer, Galena Daily Advertiser, Hartford Daily Courant, New York Daily Times, New York Daily Tribune, Springfield* (Mass.) *Daily Republican,* and the *St. Louis Intelligencer.*

21. *Albany Evening Journal,* 12 June 1854.

22. *New York Daily Times,* 8 June 1854.

23. *New York Daily Times,* 12 June 1854.

24. At that point, the railroad entered the ancient path of the Mississippi, the Princeton Channel, which extended eastward from the Illinois River Valley. This is also the route taken by the Hennepin (Illinois and Mississippi) Canal, which was completed about fifty years later and much too late to have ever become a viable enterprise. Ironically, it is said that its namesake, Father Hennepin, was the first European to have seen both Niagara Falls and Minnehaha Falls. In 1854, a number of the excursionists visited the latter and irresistibly compared it with the former.

25. *New York Daily Times,* 12 June 1854.

26. From the files of the Sheffield (Ill.) Historical Society.

27. Mrs. Margaret B. Schmitt, Knight of Donnaborg (Denmark), director, Sheffield (Ill.) Historical Society.

28. *Boston Daily Advertiser,* 19 June 1854.

29. *New York Daily Times,* 12 June 1854.

30. *New York Daily Tribune,* 12 June 1854.

31. *Chicago Daily Tribune,* 8 June 1854.

32. *Boston Daily Advertiser,* 19 June 1854.

33. *New York Daily Times,* 12 June 1854.

34. *Boston Evening Transcript,* 14 June 1854.

35. *Boston Daily Advertiser,* 15 June 1854.

36. *New York Daily Times,* 14 June 1854.

37. *Boston Daily Journal,* 20 June 1854.

38. *Hartford Daily Courant,* 20 June 1854.

39. *Albany Evening Journal,* 14 June 1854.

40. *New York Daily Times,* 14 June 1854.

41. *Springfield* (Mass.) *Daily Republican,* 16 June 1854.

BUILDING A MIGHTY FINE LINE

Much of the general information in this chapter is from two sources: F. J. Nevins, "Seventy Years of Service from Grant to Gorman"; and William Edward Hayes, *Iron Road to Empire*. Information not in these sources is documented.

1. "Wabash Railroad History," p. 2.
2. George H. Crosby, "Redfield Survey of 1823 Basis for Rock Island Lines," p. 53.
3. Hayes, *Iron Road to Empire*, p. 9.
4. William J. Petersen, "The Rock Island Comes," pp. 178–180.
5. Richard P. Morgan, "A Report on Progress," *Davenport Gazette*, 3 October 1850, p. 3.
6. Henry W. Farnam, *Memoirs of Henry Farnam*, p. 18.
7. Ibid., p. 25.
8. Henry L. Kiner, "Major James M. Allan," p. 717.
9. Petersen, "The Island Rock Comes," p. 180.
10. Sarah H. Gordon, *Passage to Union*, p. 16.
11. Jim Redd, *The Illinois and Michigan Canal*, p. 41.
12. *Rock Island News Digest* 10 October 1952, p. 1.
13. *Rock Island Weekly Republican*, 5 November 1851.
14. Newell Grant, "James Grant," p. 23.
15. Henry B. Comstock, *The Iron Horse*, p. 39.
16. Peter Mosheim and Robert R. Rothfus, "Rogers Locomotives: A Brief History and Construction List," p. 37.
17. William T. Shine, "Our First Woman Passenger," p. 4.
18. Nevins, "Seventy Years of Service from Grant to Gorman," p. 13.
19. Ibid.
20. *Rock Island Newsletter* (October 1952), p. 4.
21. Milo M. Quaife, *Chicago Highways Old and New*, p. 157.
22. *Reminiscences of Bureau County*, p. 123.
23. Farnam, *Memoirs of Henry Farnam*, p. 69.
24. Information on the February 22 celebration comes from the March 1, 1854, editions of the *Rock Island Advertiser* and the *Rock Island Weekly Republican*.
25. Farnam, *Memoirs of Henry Farnam*, p. 71.
26. *Rock Island Weekly Republican*, 23 February 1854.
27. Ibid., 1 March 1854.
28. Ibid.
29. Ibid.
30. Farnam, *Memoirs of Henry Farnam*, p. 75.
31. Ibid., p. 32.

THE GRAND EXCURSION OF 1854

359. Blakeley's *History of the Discovery of the Mississippi and the Advent of Commerce in Minnesota* in *Minnesota Historical Collections*, Vol. VIII, pp. 393–395.
360. For an extended account of the excursion of 1854, Farnam's *Memoir of Henry Farnam*, pp. 69–89 (New Haven, 1889). See also the *New York Semi-Weekly Tribune*,

June 20, 1854, and Leonard's *A Famous Rock Island Trip* in the *Rock Island Magazine,* Vol. XXII, p. 9.

361. *Daily Tribune* (Chicago), 1 June 1854; *Daily Minnesota Pioneer* (St. Paul), June 9, 1854; *The Minnesotian* (St. Paul), 9 June 1854.

362. *The Minnesotian* (St. Paul), 9 June 1854.

363. *Daily Tribune* (Chicago), 5, 6, 7 June 1854; *New York Tribune,* 9, 13 June 1854.

364. *Daily Tribune* (Chicago), 8, 9 June 1854; *New York Tribune,* 13 June 1854. Authorities vary as to the number of additional boats chartered by the Minnesota Packet Company, but most sources indicate that one or two were added to the original five. Dana asserts that one was added; Flint notes the *Jenny Lind* and the *Black Warrior,* probably the *Black Hawk.* Miss Sedgwick recorded seven steamboats in the flotilla which left Rock Island.

365. *Daily Tribune* (Chicago) 7, 8 June 1854; Sedgwick's *The Great Excursion to the Falls of St. Anthony* in *Putnam's Monthly Magazine,* Vol. IV, p. 322; *The Minnesotian* (St. Paul), 9 June 1854.

366. *Daily Tribune* (Chicago), 8 June 1854.

367. Sedgwick's *The Great Excursion to the Falls of St. Anthony* in *Putnam's Monthly Magazine,* Vol. IV, p. 320; *New York Tribune,* 20 June 1854.

368. *New York Tribune,* 20 June 1854; *Daily Tribune* (Chicago), 8 June 1854.

369. *New York Tribune,* 20 June 1854.

370. Sedgwick's *The Great Excursion to the Falls of St. Anthony* in *Putnam's Monthly Magazine,* Vol. IV, p. 323; Bill's *When Rock Island Road Reached River, The Famous Excursion Train of 1854,* in the *Burlington Post,* 23 September 1922; Paulding's *The Mississippi* in *Graham's Magazine,* Vol. XXII, p. 219.

371. Sedgwick's *The Great Excursion to the Falls of St. Anthony* in *Putnam's Monthly Magazine,* Vol. IV, p. 323; *New York Tribune,* 6, 20 June 1854.

372. Sedgwick's *The Great Excursion to the Falls of St. Anthony* in *Putnam's Monthly Magazine,* Vol. IV, p. 323; *New York Tribune,* 20 June 1854; *Daily Tribune* (Chicago), 13 June 1854.

373. *Daily Tribune* (Chicago), 13 June 1854; *New York Tribune,* 20 June 1854.

374. *The Minnesotian* (St. Paul), 9 June 1854.

375. *New York Tribune,* 20 June 1854.

376. *Galena Jeffersonian,* quoted in the *Daily Tribune* (Chicago), 16 June 1854; *Daily Tribune* (Chicago), 13 June 1854.

377. *The Minnesotian* (St. Paul), 9 June 1854; *New York Tribune,* 20 June 1854.

378. *Minnesota Pioneer,* 10, 19, 30 June 1854; *Daily Tribune* (Chicago), 13, 16 June 1854; *New York Tribune,* 20 June 1854.

379. Farnam's *Memoir of Henry Farnam,* p. 88.

380. Sedgwick's *The Great Excursion to the Falls of St. Anthony* in *Putnam's Monthly Magazine,* Vol. IV, p. 323; *New York Tribune,* 20 June 1854.

381. Bill's *When Rock Island Road Reached River, The Famous Excursion Train of 1854,* in the *Burlington Post,* 23 September 1922; *New York Tribune,* 20 June 1854; Sedgwick's *The Great Excursion to the Falls of St. Anthony* in *Putnam's Monthly Maga-*

zine, Vol. IV, p. 320; Farnam's *Memoir of Henry Farnam*, pp. 86, 87. For an interesting account of the steward's duties, see Merrick's *Old Times on the Upper Mississippi*, pp. 126–129.

382. *New York Tribune*, 20 June 1854.

383. Sedgwick's *The Great Excursion to the Falls of St. Anthony* in *Putnam's Monthly Magazine*, Vol. IV, p. 323.

384. *Daily Tribune*, (Chicago), 13 June 1854; *New York Tribune*, 20 June 1854.

385. Sedgwick's *The Great Excursion to the Falls of St. Anthony* in *Putnam's Monthly Magazine*, Vol. IV, p. 322; *New York Tribune*, 23 June 1854.

386. *The Minnesotian* (St. Paul), 12, 14, 18 October 1858; *The Dubuque Herald*, 24, 31 July 1860, 14, 17 July 1866; Bill's *William H. Seward's Visit to Minnesota in 1860* in the *Burlington Post*, 25 November 1922; Blegen's *Campaigning with Seward in 1860* in *Minnesota History*, Vol. VIII, pp. 150–171.

THE EAST LOOKS AT THE WEST

1. *Albany Evening Journal*, 9 June 1854.

2. Kevin G. Barnhurst and John Nerone, *The Form of News*, p. 17.

3. Michael Schudson, *Discovering the News*, pp. 12–60; Dan Schiller, *Objectivity and the News*; David T. Z. Mindich, *Just the Facts*.

4. To find Grand Excursion coverage, I read the complete available holdings of these newspapers for June 1854: *Albany Argus, Albany Evening Journal, Boston Daily Advertiser, Boston Daily Journal, Boston Evening Transcript, Chicago Daily Tribune, Cincinnati Gazette, Cleveland Herald, Hartford Daily Courant, New York Daily Times, New York Daily Tribune*, and the *Springfield* (Mass.) *Daily Republican*. My confidence that I caught most of the coverage stems from the self-aware nature of the writing, in some cases with numbered installments; the typical four-page newspaper layout in 1854, with advertising monopolizing pages one and four and news on pages two and three; and the chronology of the Grand Excursion itself, with its clear start and end.

5. Jeffrey Alan Melton, *Mark Twain, Travel Books, and Tourism*, pp. 16–58.

6. *Boston Daily Advertiser*, 9 June 1854.

7. *Albany Evening Journal*, 7 June 1854. The grammar of the nineteenth-century newspaper differed from what is seen today. Spellings of names varied considerably, punctuation was sometimes different, and implied collective nouns tended to be treated as plural (e.g., "the company *are*," "the crew *are*"). In the quotations used here, the original text is given, with *sic* used only for clear errors and for unusual spelling variations.

8. *Boston Evening Transcript*, 8 June 1854.

9. *Albany Argus*, 8 June 1854.

10. *Albany Evening Journal*, 12 June 1854.

11. *Hartford Daily Courant*, 20 June 1854.

12. *New York Daily Times*, 5 June 1854.

13. *Springfield* (Mass.) *Daily Republican*, 19 June 1854.

14. *Albany Evening Journal*, 12 June 1854.

15. *Cincinnati Gazette,* 12 June 1854.

16. *Boston Evening Transcript,* 12 June 1854.

17. *Boston Evening Transcript,* 6 June 1854.

18. See Patrick Nunnally's essay in this volume; and for similar modes of descrip-tion in the Ohio River Valley, see John A. Jakle, *Images of the Ohio Valley.*

19. *New York Daily Times,* 8 June 1854.

20. *Boston Evening Transcript,* 6 June 1854.

21. *Boston Evening Transcript,* 6 June 1854.

22. *Hartford Daily Courant,* 20 June 1854.

23. *Springfield* (Mass.) *Daily Republican,* 16 June 1854.

24. *Hartford Daily Courant,* 20 June 1854.

25. *Albany Evening Journal,* 14 June 1854.

26. Melton, *Mark Twain, Travel Books, and Tourism,* pp. 30–31.

27. *Boston Evening Transcript,* 6 June 1854.

28. *Albany Evening Journal,* 9 June 1854.

29. *New York Daily Times,* 8 June 1854.

30. *New York Daily Times,* 14 June 1854.

31. *Springfield* (Mass.) *Daily Republican,* 15 June 1854.

32. *Hartford Daily Courant,* 20 June 1854.

33. *New York Daily Times,* 14 June 1854.

34. *New York Daily Tribune,* 14 June 1854.

35. *Springfield* (Mass.) *Daily Republican,* 16 June 1854.

36. *Boston Evening Transcript,* 15 June 1854.

37. *Springfield* (Mass.) *Daily Republican,* 16 June 1854.

38. *New York Daily Tribune,* 14 June 1854.

39. *New York Daily Times,* 17 June 1854.

40. *Hartford Daily Courant,* 20 June 1854.

41. D. W. Meinig, *The Shaping of America. Continental America, 1800–1967,* Vol. 2, p. 330.

42. Timothy R. Mahoney, *Provincial Lives,* pp. 239–245.

43. *Boston Evening Transcript,* 12 June 1854.

44. *Hartford Daily Courant,* 20 June 1854.

45. *Hartford Daily Courant,* 26 June 1854.

46. *Boston Daily Advertiser,* 15 June 1854.

STEAMING UP THE RIVER

1. William J. Petersen, *Steamboating on the Upper Mississippi,* pp. 57–67 and 87–95.

2. Albert H. Sanford and H. J. Hirshheimer, *A History of La Crosse, Wisconsin, 1841–1900,* p. 133.

3. George Byron Merrick, *Old Times on the Upper Mississippi,* p. 164.

4. Boat histories are taken from Merrick, *Old Times on the Upper Mississippi;* Fred-erick Way, Jr., *Way's Packet Directory, 1848–1994;* and the steamboat data files at Mur-phy Library, University of Wisconsin-La Crosse.

5. The documentary evidence of everyday boat life is relatively meager. How-ever, the federal government maintained registers of boats, which are among the

better sources for boat names and dimensions, construction dates, captains and owners, and places and periods of operation. The informal records of the steamboat era include stories of fabled captains and pilots, famous races, accidents and tragedies, and the everyday accounts that enrich the record of a wondrous time.

6. Merrick, *Old Times on the Upper Mississippi*, pp. 127–128.

7. Ibid., pp. 163–164.

8. Sanford and Hirshheimer, *A History of La Crosse, Wisconsin, 1841–1900*, pp. 142–143.

9. Ibid., p. 133.

10. U.S. Department of Commerce, Bureau of the Census, Special Reports, *Transportation by Water, 1906*, p. 167.

11. Ibid., p. 180.

12. Ibid., p. 182.

THE PICTURESQUE MISSISSIPPI

1. Sedgwick, "The Great Excursion to the Falls of St. Anthony," p. 323.

2. William Gilpin, *The Wye Tour*, p. 4.

3. Andrew Jackson Downing, *Landscape Gardening*. 10th edition, Frank A. Waugh, ed., p. 40.

4. David Schuyler, *Apostle of Taste*.

5. Giacomo Costantino Beltrami, *A Pilgrimage in America, Leading to the Discovery of the Sources of the Mississippi and Bloody River*, p. 179.

6. Ibid., p. 169.

7. M. H. Dunlop, *Sixty Miles from Contentment*, p. 3.

8. George W. Featherstonehaugh, *A Canoe Voyage up the Minnay Sotor*, p. 201.

9. Henry Lewis, *The Valley of the Mississippi Illustrated* (1967), p. 123n.

10. Fredrika Bremer, *The Homes of the New World; Impressions of America*, p. 16.

11. *New York Daily Tribune*, 14 June 1854.

12. Ethan Carr, *Wilderness by Design*, pp. 11–54.

13. Jonathan Raban, *Old Glory*, p. 11.

TOWNS TO VISIT

1. C[atherine] M. S[edgwick], "The Great Excursion to the Falls of St. Anthony," p. 321.

2. Timothy R. Mahoney, *River Towns in the Great West*, pp. 151 and 156.

3. Henry Lewis, *The Valley of the Mississippi Illustrated* (1858), pp. 216–217.

4. Ibid.

5. Sedgwick, "The Great Excursion to the Falls of St. Anthony," p. 322.

6. Mark Twain [Samuel L. Clemens], *Life on the Mississippi*, pp. 470–471.

7. Ibid., p. 328.

8. William Cullen Bryant, ed., *Picturesque America; or the Land We Live In*, pp. 317–352.

9. William Ferguson, *America by River and Rail*, p. 401.

10. Ibid., pp. 403 and 406.

11. John R. Hebert, *Panoramic Maps of Cities in the United States and Canada*; and John W. Reps, *Cities of the Mississippi*.

12. Lewis, *The Valley of the Mississippi Illustrated*, p. 185.

13. Goldsmith B. West, *The Golden Northwest*, p. 52.

14. Laurence Oliphant, *Minnesota and the Far West*, p. 295.

15. E. S. Seymour, *Sketches of Minnesota*, p. 77.

16. Twain, *Life on the Mississippi*, p. 480.

17. Oliphant, *Minnesota and the Far West*, p. 253.

18. C. C. Andrews, *Minnesota and Dacotah*, p. 87.

WHERE NATURE SMILES THREE HUNDRED MILES

1. John R. Stilgoe, *Metropolitan Corridor*, p. ix.

2. Ibid.

3. Fred W. Frailey, *Twilight of the Great Trains*, p. 99.

4. William J. Petersen, *Steamboating on the Upper Mississippi*, p. 277.

5. Jackson Peters, "The Milwaukee Road, America's Resourceful Railroad," 1998. Additional information on the history of the Milwaukee Road can be found online at www.mrha.com.

6. Richard S. Prosser, *Rail to the North Star*, p. 12.

7. Ibid. See pp. 190–196 for an account of the financing and construction of the CB&N and the Twin Cities-Chicago line.

8. "Mississippi River Scenic Line, Where Nature Smiles Three Hundred Miles" (1951), p. 12. The pamphlets issued by the CB&Q are not only of great historical value, they make entertaining reading as well.

9. "The Mississippi River Scenic Line, Where Nature Smiles Three Hundred Miles" (1920), pp. 2–3.

10. See Geoffrey Doughty, *The Early Zephyrs*, pp. 14–23 for an excellent discussion of the innovative construction techniques used to build the *Zephyrs*.

11. Ibid., pp. 20–21.

12. Ibid., pp. 22–23.

13. Richard C. Overton, *Burlington Route*, p. 395.

14. J. W. Schultz, *Trains of the Gods and Goddesses*, pp. 4–21. This is a very good overall view on the motive power of the *Zephyrs*. The Burlington Route Historical Society (www.Burlingtonroute.com) is a superb source for historical information on the CB&Q.

15. "Twin Zephyr Trains Bring 120 to City in Inaugural Run," p. 11.

16. Schultz, *Trains of the Gods and Goddesses*, pp. 4–21.

17. Ibid., p. 7.

18. From a classic article by Roger Reynolds, in his *Famous American Trains and Their Stories*, p. 92.

19. Doughty, *The Early Zephyrs*, p. 55.

20. Joseph Follmar, ed., *Grand Crossing*, p. 89.

21. "Mississippi River Scenic Line, Where Nature Smiles Three Hundred Miles" (1951), p. 4.

22. David P. Morgan, *Diesels West!*, p. 117.

23. Stilgoe, *Metropolitan Corridor*, p. 3.

24. "Mississippi River Scenic Line, Where Nature Smiles Three Hundred Miles" (1951), p. 2.

25. Frailey, *Twilight of the Great Trains*, pp. 104–108.

26. Ibid., p. 108.

27. Follmar, ed., *Grand Crossing*, p. 3.

28. Tom Weil, *The Mississippi River*, p. 10. This is an unusually thorough and entertaining guidebook.

HIGHWAY TO EMPIRE

1. Louis Hennepin, *Father Louis Hennepin's Description of Louisiana, Newly Discovered to the Southwest of New France by Order of the King*, pp. 88, 90, 93, 118–119.

2. Zebulon Pike, *The Expeditions of Zebulon Montgomery Pike*, Vol. 1, p. 212.

3. Mentor L. Williams, ed., *Schoolcraft's Narrative Journal of Travels*, pp. 216–217, 494.

4. Diary of Horace Ransom Bigelow, 1853–1893.

5. *Albany Argus*, 10 June 1854; *New York Daily Tribune*, 12 June 1854; *Springfield* (Mass.) *Daily Republican*, 16 June 1854.

6. Todd Shallat, *Structures in the Stream*, chapter 4; Roald D. Tweet, *A History of the Rock Island District, U.S. Army Corps of Engineers, 1866–1983*, pp. 40–42, 50, 52–53; Roald D. Tweet, *A History of Navigation Improvements on the Rock Island Rapids*, p. 3.

7. Benson Lee Grayson, *The Unknown President*, p. 75; Shallat, *Structures in the Stream*, p. 177; "An Act Making Appropriations for the Improvement of Certain Harbors and Rivers," p. 56; Tweet, *A History of Navigation Improvements on the Rock Island Rapids*, pp. 3–4.

8. Shallat, *Structures in the Stream*, pp. 178, 184; Louis C. Hunter, *Steamboats on the Western Rivers*, pp. 190–192; Frederick J. Dobney, *River Engineers of the Middle Mississippi*, p. 32; Tweet, *A History of the Rock Island District*, pp. 52–61; Tweet, *A History of Navigation Improvements on the Rock Island Rapids*, pp. 1–3; Edward L. Pross, "A History of Rivers and Harbors Bills, 1866–1933," pp. 33–40.

9. For a detailed history of these projects, see Anfinson, *The River We Have Wrought*.

10. Pike, *The Expeditions of Zebulon Montgomery Pike*, Vol. 1, p. 27.

11. For an expanded account of the agricultural levee system on the Middle and Upper Mississippi River, see *Floodplain Management Assessment of the Upper Mississippi River and Lower Missouri Rivers and Tributaries*, chapter 2, "Forces Impacting Uses of the Floodplain"; and Anfinson, *The River We Have Wrought*, chapter 4.

12. Chapter 7 in Anfinson, *The River We Have Wrought*, examines the origins of the Mississippi National Wildlife and Fish Refuge, and chapter 11 looks at how those who supported it reacted to the nine-foot channel project.

13. *Saturday Evening Post*, 196 (no. 44, May 3, 1924), p. 132.

14. U.S. Congress, House, Committee on Agriculture, Hearing on H.R. 4088, "A Bill to Establish the Upper Mississippi Wild Life and Fish Refuge," 68th Congress, session 1 (February 11, 12, and 13, 1924), p. 15.

15. Ibid., p. 24.

16. U.S. Army Corps of Engineers, Waterborne Commerce Statistics Center, *Preliminary CY-2000 Freight Table for the Upper Mississippi River.*

17. Richard Hoops, *River of Grain*, p. 112.

PRESERVATION AND MANAGEMENT
OF THE RIVER'S NATURAL RESOURCES

1. In the order of their appearance, the quotations come from accounts of the Grand Excursion in the following 1854 newspapers: *Springfield* (Mass.) *Daily Republican,* June 16; *Hartford Daily Courant,* two quotations from June 20; *Albany Evening Journal,* June 14, June 13, and June 10.

2. Much of the information for this section of the essay comes from two sources: Mississippi River Corridor Study Commission, *Mississippi River Corridor Study, Vol. 2: Inventory of Resources and Significance;* and U.S. Geological Survey, *Ecological Status and Trends of the Upper Mississippi River System, 1998.*

3. City of Dubuque Web site: www.cityofdubuque.org.

4. "Best of the Midwest," p. 39; "The Best of Wisconsin," p. 41.

5. *Milwaukee Journal Sentinel,* 14 May 2000.

6. Becky Mead, "Wisconsin's Best . . . According to You," p. 11.

A RIVER OF LOGS

1. William Gerald Rector, *Log Transportation in the Lake States Lumber Industry, 1840–1918*, pp. 37–38.

2. William G. Rector, "A Concise History of the Lumber Industry in the Upper Mississippi River Valley," in George E. Bates Jr., et al., *Historic Lifestyles in the Upper Mississippi River Valley,* p. 410.

3. Robert Fries, *Empire in Pine*, p. 6.

4. Robert Wells, *Daylight in the Swamp!*, p. 34.

5. Richard G. Lillard, *The Great Forest*, p. 210.

6. Information about the loggers, logging camps, and rafting was gathered from the following sources: Walter A. Blair, *A Raft Pilot's Log*; Fries, *Empire in Pine*; John C. Frohlicher, *Timber!*; Stewart H. Holbrook, *Holy Old Mackinaw*; Agnes Larson, *History of the White Pine Industry in Minnesota*; Capt. Ron Larson, *Upper Mississippi River History*; Lillard, *The Great Forest*; Rector, "A Concise History of the Lumber Industry in the Upper Mississippi River Valley"; Charles Edward Russell, *A-Rafting on the Mississip'*; and Wells, *Daylight in the Swamp!*

7. Carl Sandburg, *American Songbag*, p. 391.

8. The word *caboose* is derived from the Dutch word for kitchen. Modern English usage of the word, which refers to the last car of a train, evolved from this original meaning since the railroad caboose held the kitchen and sleeping accommodations for railroad personnel.

9. Lillard, *The Great Forest*, p. 212.

10. Rector, *Log Transportation in the Lake States Lumber Industry*, p. 71.

11. George W. Wickstrom and Charles P. Ainsworth, *Always Lumber*, p. 99.

12. Frohlicher, *Timber!*, p. 100.

13. Fries, *Empire in Pine*, p. 45.

14. Ibid., p. 232. Quoted in Durant, "Lumbering and Steamboating," pp. 664–665.

15. John O. Anfinson, *Henry Bosse's Views of the Upper Mississippi River*, p. 17.

16. [Charles F. Babcock], "Rails West: The Rock Island Excursion of 1854 as reported by Charles F. Babcock," p. 136.

17. Blair, *A Raft Pilot's Log*, appendix.

18. Roald Tweet, *Quad Cities*, p. 25.

19. Dick Stahl, *Under the Green Tree Hotel*, p. 1.

20. Information about the lumber barons was gathered from the following sources: *The Biographical Record of Clinton County, Iowa*; Fries, *Empire in Pine*; *History of Clinton County Iowa*; Larson, *History of the White Pine Industry in Minnesota*; and Lillard, *The Great Forest*.

21. Stahl, *Under the Green Tree Hotel*, p. 13.

22. Lillard, *The Great Forest*, pp. 195–196.

23. Ibid., p. 197.

24. Ibid., p. 208.

25. Anfinson, *Henry Bosse's Views of the Upper Mississippi River*, pp. 17–19.

26. Fries, *Empire in Pine*, p. 228.

27. Russell, *A-Rafting on the Mississip'*, p. 337.

28. Fries, *Empire in Pine*, p. 245.

FISHING THE FATHER OF WATERS

1. Exactly when commercial fishing started is unknown, but by 1876 there was a concern for overfishing in Iowa. See Harriet B. Carlander, *A History of Fish and Fishing in the Upper Mississippi River*, p. 57. The first government study of commercial fishing in 1896 found it well established. See Hugh M. Smith, "Statistics of the Fisheries of the Interior Waters of the United States," pp. 492–493.

2. C. H. Townsend, "Statistics of the Fisheries of the Mississippi River and Tributaries," p. 714.

3. Carlander, *A History of Fish and Fishing in the Upper Mississippi River*, p. 68.

4. Statistics are courtesy of Mr. Jon Duyvejonck, Coordinator of the Upper Mississippi River Conservation Committee, Rock Island, Illinois.

5. Ibid.

6. Erhard Rostlund, *Freshwater Fish and Fishing in Native North America*, pp. 113–126.

7. Malcolm L. Comeaux, "Hook and Line Fishing in the Mississippi River System."

8. Ibid., pp. 32–33.

9. Townsend, "Statistics of the Fisheries of the Mississippi River and Tributaries," p. 716.

10. Malcolm L. Comeaux, "Use of Hoop Nets in the Mississippi River Basin," p. 75.

11. James Taylor, *Frank Leslie's Illustrated Newspaper*, p. 56.

12. Carlander, *A History of Fish and Fishing in the Upper Mississippi River*, p. 57.

13. Ibid., pp. 40, 49–50.

14. Malcolm L. Comeaux, "Origin and Evolution of Mississippi River Fishing Craft."

15. Carlander, *A History of Fish and Fishing in the Upper Mississippi River*, p. 62.

16. National Fisheries Program, *Fishery Statistics of the United States, 1977*, p. 306.

17. Carlander, *A History of Fish and Fishing in the Upper Mississippi River*, p. 62.

RENEWALS AND REINVENTIONS

1. Mark Twain, *Life on the Mississippi*, p. 77.

2. Rock Island and St. Paul are used as the southern and northern limits for this study because they were the official steamboat embarkation and destination cities in the 1854 Grand Excursion. We know that some excursionists visited St. Anthony and Fort Snelling. We also recognize that Minneapolis has an important active relationship with the Mississippi and highlights the river and waterfronts in its future plans.

3. Population data are for individual cities and towns and come from the U. S. Bureau of the Census, 2000.

4. Mark VanderSchaaf, "Origins of the 'Crazy Idea': How the Grand Excursion Concept Was Born. A Memoir."

5. "West Side Flats Master Plan & Development Guidelines."

6. "The Renaissance Continues, Making a Great City Even Better," p. 1.

7. Jonathan Raban, *Old Glory*, p. 174.

8. "Isle of Capri Casino."

9. "City Update Vision 2000 Master Plan," p. 1.

10. "La Crosse on the River" and "La Crosse for a Real Experience," p. 5.

11. "Riverview Park Master Plan Summary," p. 6.

12. "Sabula, the Island City."

13. From the information kiosk in downtown Wabasha.

14. "Prairie du Chien Area along the Mississippi River."

15. "Fulton, Illinois, in Northwestern Illinois."

16. "McGregor and Marquette, Iowa, on the Mississippi River."

17. "Allamakee County, Iowa."

18. "Mississippi Valley Partners Travel Planning Guide 2002," p. 2.

19. Julie Berg-Raymond, *Tapestry Magazine*, p. 5.

BIBLIOGRAPHY

BOOKS AND ARTICLES

Adams, Peter. *Early Loggers and the Sawmill.* New York: Crabtree Publishing, 1981.

"An Act Making Appropriations for the Improvement of Certain Harbors and Rivers." 32nd Congress, session 1, chapter 104. August 30, 1852.

Anderson, Wayne I. *Iowa's Geologic Past.* Iowa City: University of Iowa Press, 1998.

Andrews, C. C. *Minnesota and Dacotah: Letters Descriptive of a Tour through the North-West.* Washington, D.C.: Robert Farnham, 1857.

Anfinson, John O. *Henry Bosse's Views of the Upper Mississippi River.* St. Paul, Minn.: St. Paul District, Army Corps of Engineers, 1996.

———. *The River We Have Wrought: A History of the Upper Mississippi.* Minneapolis: University of Minnesota Press, 2003.

[Babcock, Charles F.]. "Rails West: The Rock Island Excursion of 1854 as reported by Charles F. Babcock." *Minnesota History* 34 (Winter 1954): 133–143.

Bancroft, George. *History of the United States from the Discovery of the American Continent.* Boston: Little, Brown, 1863.

Barnhurst, Kevin G., and John Nerone. *The Form of News: A History.* New York: Guilford Press, 2001.

Beltrami, Giacomo Costantino. *A Pilgrimage in America, Leading to the Discovery of the Sources of the Mississippi and Bloody River.* Chicago: Quadrangle Books, 1962.

Berg-Raymond, Julie. *Tapestry Magazine* 1, no.1 (2002).

"Best of the Midwest." *Midwest Living* 6, no. 1: February 1992.

"The Best of Wisconsin." *Wisconsin Trails* 38, no. 3: May/June 1997.

The Biographical Record of Clinton County, Iowa. Chicago: S. J. Clarke, 1901.

Blair, Walter A. *A Raft Pilot's Log: A History of the Great Rafting Industry on the Upper Mississippi, 1840–1915.* Cleveland: Arthur H. Clark, 1930.

Blakeley, Captain Russell. "History of the Discovery of the Mississippi River and the Advent of Commerce in Minnesota." Minnesota Historical Society Collections 8, pt. 3 (April 1, 1898).

Blegen, [Theodore C.]. "Campaigning with Seward in 1860." *Minnesota History* 8: 150–171.

Bremer, Fredrika. *The Homes of the New World; Impressions of America.* New York: Johnson Reprint, 1968.

Brick, Ed. "Mike Spettel's Better Bridge — Part Bridge, Part Pontoon." In *Big River Reader: An Anthology of Stories about the Upper Mississippi, from the First Four Years of Big River,* by Pamela Eyden, Molly McGuire, and Reggie McLeod (119–121). Winona, Minn.: Big River, 1996.

Bryant, William Cullen, ed. *Picturesque America; or the Land We Live In. A Delineation by Pen and Pencil.* Vol. 2. New York: D. Appleton, 1874.

Burke, William J. *The Upper Mississippi Valley: How the Landscape Shaped Our Heritage.* Waukon, Ia.: Mississippi Valley Press, 2000.

Carlander, Harriet B. *A History of Fish and Fishing in the Upper Mississippi River.* N.p.: Upper Mississippi River Conservation Committee, 1954.

Carr, Ethan. *Wilderness by Design: Landscape Architecture and the National Park Service.* Lincoln: University of Nebraska Press, 1998.

Comeaux, Malcolm L. "Hook and Line Fishing in the Mississippi River System." *Material Culture* 21 (1989): 23–45.

———. "Origin and Evolution of Mississippi River Fishing Craft." *Pioneer America* 10 (1978): 73–97.

———. "Use of Hoop Nets in the Mississippi River Basin." *Journal of Cultural Geography* 10 (1989): 75–87.

Comstock, Henry B. *The Iron Horse: America's Steam Locomotive.* New York: Galahad Books, 1971.

Costello, Mary Charlotte Aubry. *Climbing the Mississippi River Bridge by Bridge, Volume One, From Louisiana to Minnesota.* Davenport, Ia.: Author, 1995.

Crosby, George H. "Redfield Survey of 1823 Basis for Rock Island Lines." *Rock Island Magazine* 17, no. 10 (October 1922): 53.

Dobney, Frederick J. *River Engineers of the Middle Mississippi: A History of the St. Louis District, U. S. Army Corps of Engineers.* Washington, D.C.: U.S. Government Printing Office, 1978.

Doughty, Geoffrey. *The Early Zephyrs.* Lynchburg, Va.: TLC Publishing, 2002.

Downing, Andrew Jackson. *Landscape Gardening.* 10th ed. Ed. Frank A. Waugh. New York: John Wiley & Sons, 1921.

Driscoll, John Paul, and John K. Howat. *John Frederick Kensett: An American Master.* New York: Worcester Area Museum, in association with W. W. Norton, 1985.

Dunlop, M. H. *Sixty Miles from Contentment: Traveling the Nineteenth Century American Interior.* New York: Basic Books, 1995.

Durant, [Edward W.]. "Lumbering and Steamboating [on the St. Croix River]." Part 2. *Minnesota Historical Collections* 10 (1905): 645–675.

Farnam, Henry W. *Memoirs of Henry Farnam.* New Haven: Morehouse and Taylor, 1889.

Featherstonehaugh, George W. *A Canoe Voyage Up the Minnay Sotor.* St. Paul, Minn.: Minnesota Historical Society, 1970.

Ferguson, William. *America by River and Rail.* London: James Nisbet, 1856.

Floodplain Management Assessment of the Upper Mississippi River and Lower Missouri Rivers and Tributaries. Vol. 1. Chapter two, "Forces Impacting Uses of the Floodplain." U.S. Army Corps of Engineers, June 1995.

Follmar, Joseph, ed. *Grand Crossing: Railroading and People in La Crosse, Wisconsin.* La Crosse, Wis.: The 4000 Foundation, 1992.

Frailey, Fred W. *Twilight of the Great Trains.* Waukesha, Wis.: Kalmbach Publishing, 1998.

Fries, Robert. *Empire in Pine: The Story of Lumbering in Wisconsin, 1830–1900*. Evanston, Ill.: Wm. Caxton Ltd., 1989.

Frohlicher, John C. *Timber! The Bygone Life of the Northwoods Lumberjacks*. Stockton, Ill.: Hill House, 1984.

Gilpin, William. *The Wye Tour*. Ross, England: W. Farror, 1834.

Glazier, Capt. Willard. *Down The Great River; Embracing an Account of the Discovery of the True Source of the Mississippi*. Philadelphia: Hubbard Brothers, 1892.

Goodrich, Chauncey A. *The Excursion*. Farnam Family Papers, Yale University Archives, New Haven, Connecticut.

Gordon, Sarah H. *Passage to Union: How the Railroads Transformed American Life, 1829–1929*. Chicago: Joan R. Dee, 1996.

Grayson, Benson Lee. *The Unknown President: The Administration of President Millard Fillmore*. Washington, D.C.: University Press of America, 1981.

Green, Michael D. "The Expansion of European Colonization to the Mississippi Valley, 1780–1880." Chapter eight in Bruce G. Trigget and Wilcomb E. Washburn, eds. *The Cambridge History of the Native Peoples of the Americas, Volume 1 North America*. Part 1, 461–538. Cambridge: Cambridge University Press, 1996.

Handlin, Lilian. *George Bancroft, The Intellectual as Democrat*. New York: Harper and Row, 1984.

Hayes, William Edward. *Iron Road to Empire: The History of 100 Years of the Progress and Achievements of the Rock Island Lines*. New York: Simmons-Boardman, 1953.

Hebert, John R. *Panoramic Maps of Cities in the United States and Canada*. 2nd ed., rev. by Patrick E. Dempsey. Washington, D.C.: Library of Congress, 1984.

Hennepin, Louis. *Father Louis Hennepin's Description of Louisiana, Newly Discovered to the Southwest of New France by Order of the King*. Minneapolis: University of Minnesota Press, 1938.

History of Clinton County Iowa. Clinton, Ia.: Clinton County American Revolution Bicentennial Commission/Iowa American Revolution Bicentennial Commission, 1976.

History of the Native Peoples of the Americas, Volume I North America. Pt. 1. Cambridge: Cambridge University Press, 1996.

Hobbs, Howard. "Origin of the Driftless Area by Subglacial Drainage — A New Hypothesis." Special Paper 337. In *Glacial Processes Past and Present*, edited by David M. Mickelson and John W. Attig, 93–102. Boulder, Colo.: Geological Society of America, 1999.

Holbrook, Stewart H. *Holy Old Mackinaw*. New York: Macmillan, 1938.

Hoops, Richard. *River of Grain: The Evolution of Commercial Navigation on the Upper Mississippi River*. College of Agricultural and Life Sciences Research Report, R3584. Madison, Wis.: University of Wisconsin-Madison, 1989.

Hunter, Louis C. *Steamboats on the Western Rivers: An Economic and Technological History*. New York: Dover, 1993/1949 by the President and Fellows of Harvard College.

Jakle, John A. *Images of the Ohio Valley*. New York: Oxford University Press, 1977.

Kiner, Henry L. "Major James M. Allan." *A History of Henry County Illinois.* Vol. 1., 717. Chicago: Pioneer Publishing, 1910.

Larson, Agnes. *History of the White Pine Industry in Minnesota.* New York: Arno Press, 1972.

Larson, Capt. Ron. *Upper Mississippi River History: Fact— Fiction— Legend.* Winona, Minn.: Steamboat Press, 1998.

Leonard, [L. O.]. "A Famous Rock Island Trip." *Rock Island Magazine* 22 (1927): 9.

Lewis, H[enry]. *Das Illustrite Mississippithal: Wasserfalle zu St. Anthony an bis zum Golf von Mexico.* Leipzig: H. Schmidt and C. Gunther, 1923/1858. An abridged English translation appeared as: *The Valley of the Mississippi Illustrated.* Dusseldorf: Arnz, 1858.

———. *The Valley of the Mississippi Illustrated.* St. Paul, Minn.: Minnesota Historical Society, 1967.

Lillard, Richard G. *The Great Forest.* New York: Knopf, 1947.

Mahoney, Timothy R. *Provincial Lives: Middle-Class Experience in the Antebellum Middle West.* Cambridge: Cambridge University Press, 1999.

———. *River Towns in the Great West: The Structure of Provincial Urbanization in the American Midwest, 1820–1870.* Cambridge: Cambridge University Press, 1990.

McMaster, S. W. *60 Years on the Upper Mississippi: My Life and Experiences.* Rock Island, Ill.: N.p., 1893.

Mead, Becky. "Wisconsin's Best . . . According to You." *Wisconsin Trails* 33, no. 2: March/April 1992.

Meese, William A. *Early Rock Island.* Moline, Ill.: Rock Island County Historical Society, 1905.

Meinig, D. W. *The Shaping of America. Continental America, 1800–1967: A Geographical Perspective On 500 Years of History.* Vol. 2. New Haven: Yale University Press, 1993.

Melton, Jeffery Alan. *Mark Twain, Travel Books, and Tourism.* Tuscaloosa, Ala.: University of Alabama Press, 2002.

Merrick, George Byron. *Old Times on the Upper Mississippi: The Recollections of a Steamboat Pilot from 1854 to 1863.* St. Paul, Minn.: Minnesota Historical Society, 1987.

Mindich, David T. Z. *Just the Facts: How "Objectivity" Came to Define American Journalism.* New York: New York University Press, 1998.

Mississippi River Corridor Study Commission. *Mississippi River Corridor Study, Vol. 2: Inventory of Resources and Significance.* U.S. Department of the Interior, National Park Service. Washington, D.C.: U.S. Government Printing Office, 1996.

Morgan, David P. *Diesels West! The Evolution of Power on the Burlington.* Milwaukee, Wis.: Kalmbach Publishing, 1963.

Mosheim, Peter, and Robert R. Rothfus. "Rogers Locomotives: A Brief History and Construction List." *Railroad History* 167, no. 167 (Autumn 1992): 13–147.

The National Cyclopedia of American Biography. Vol. 11. New York: James T. White, 1901.

National Fisheries Program. *Fishery Statistics of the United States, 1977.* Washington, D.C.: Government Printing Office, 1984.

Nevins, F. J. "Seventy Years of Service from Grant to Gorman." *Rock Island Magazine.* Publication for the 70th anniversary of the Rock Island Railroad, October 1922. Reprint compiled by John H. Newton and edited by R. E. Remington.

Oliphant, Laurence. *Minnesota and the Far West.* Edinburgh: William Blackwood and Sons, 1855.

Overton, Richard C. *Burlington Route: A History of the Burlington Lines.* New York: Alfred A. Knopf, 1965.

Paulding, [James Kirke]. "The Mississippi." *Graham's Magazine* 22: 219.

Petersen, William J. "The Grand Excursion of 1854." *Palimpsest* 14 (1933): 301–314.

———. "The Rock Island Comes." *Palimpsest* 41 (April 1960): 177–192.

———. "The Rock Island Railroad Excursion of 1854." *Minnesota History* 15 (1934): 405–420.

———. *Steamboating on the Upper Mississippi.* Iowa City: State Historical Society of Iowa, 1968.

Pike, Zebulon. *The Expeditions of Zebulon Montgomery Pike.* Vol. 1. Reprint. Ed. Elliott Coues. New York: Dover, 1987. Originally published in three volumes: New York: F. P. Harper, 1895.

Pross, Edward L. "A History of Rivers and Harbors Bills, 1866–1933." Ph.D. dissertation, Ohio State University, 1938.

Prosser, Richard S. *Rail to the North Star: One Hundred Years of Railroad Evolution in Minnesota.* Minneapolis: Dillon Press, 1966.

Purcell, Gene. "When a Bridge Tumbles Down." In *Big River Reader: An Anthology of Stories about the Upper Mississippi, from the First Four Years of Big River,* by Pamela Eyden, Molly McGuire, and Reggie McLeod (122–124). Winona, Minn.: Big River, 1996.

Quaife, Milo M. *Chicago Highways Old and New: From Indian Trail to Motor Road.* Chicago: D. F. Keller, 1923.

Raban, Jonathan. *Old Glory: An American Voyage.* New York: Simon and Schuster, 1981.

———. *Old Glory: A Voyage Down the Mississippi.* New York: Vintage Books, 1998.

Rector, William G. "A Concise History of the Lumber Industry in the Upper Mississippi River Valley." George E. Bates, Jr., et al. In *Historic Lifestyles in the Upper Mississippi River Valley.* New York: University Press of America, 1983.

Rector, William Gerald. *Log Transportation in the Lake States Lumber Industry, 1840–1918.* Glendale, Calif.: Arthur H. Clark, 1953.

Redd, Jim. *The Illinois and Michigan Canal: A Contemporary Perspective in Essays and Photographs.* Carbondale, Ill.: Southern Illinois University Press, 1993.

Reps, John W. *Cities of the Mississippi: Nineteenth-Century Images of Urban Development.* Columbia: University of Missouri Press, 1994.

Reminiscences of Bureau County. Princeton, Ill.: Republican Book and Job Office, 1872.

Reynolds, Roger. *Famous American Trains and Their Stories*. New York: Grosset and Dunlap, 1939.

Rostlund, Erhard. *Freshwater Fish and Fishing in Native North America*. University of California Publications in Geography, No. 9. Berkeley: University of California Press, 1952.

Russell, Charles Edward. *A-Rafting on the Mississip'*. New York: Century, 1928.

Sandburg, Carl. *American Songbag*. New York: Harcourt, Brace, 1927.

Sanford, Albert H., and H. J. Hirshheimer. *A History of La Crosse, Wisconsin, 1841–1900*. La Crosse, Wis.: La Crosse County Historical Society, 1951.

Schiller, Dan. *Objectivity and the News: The Public and the Rise of Commercial Journalism*. Philadelphia: University of Pennsylvania Press, 1981.

Schudson, Michael. *Discovering the News: The Social History of American Newspapers*. New York: Basic Books, 1978.

Schultz, J. W. *Trains of the Gods and Goddesses*. La Grange, Ill.: Burlington Bulletin, 1990.

Schuyler, David. *Apostle of Taste: Andrew Jackson Downing*. Baltimore: Johns Hopkins University Press, 1996.

S[edgwick], C[atherine] M. "The Great Excursion to the Falls of St. Anthony." *Putnam's Monthly* 4 (September 1854): 320–325.

Seymour, E. S. *Sketches of Minnesota: The New England of the West*. New York: Harper and Brothers, 1850.

Shallat, Todd. *Structures in the Stream: Water, Science, and the Rise of the U. S. Army Corps of Engineers*. Austin: University of Texas Press, 1994.

Shine, William T. "Our First Woman Passenger." *Rock Island Magazine* 16, no. 6 (June 1921).

Smith, Hugh M. "Statistics of the Fisheries of the Interior Waters of the United States." *U.S. Commission of Fish and Fisheries, Report of the Commissioner for the Year Ending June 30, 1896*. Appendix 2. Washington, D.C.: Government Printing Office, 1898.

Stahl, Dick. *Under the Green Tree Hotel*. Rock Island, Ill.: East Hall Press, 1996.

Steer, Henry B. *Lumber Production in the United States, 1799–1946*. U.S. Department of Agriculture, Misc. Publication No. 669. Washington, D.C.: October 1948.

Stilgoe, John R. *Metropolitan Corridor: Railroads and the American Scene*. New Haven: Yale University Press, 1983.

Stumm, Robert. *A Postcard Journey Along the Upper Mississippi*. Springfield, Ill.: Templegate Publishers, 1997.

Townsend, C. H. "Statistics of the Fisheries of the Mississippi River and Tributaries." *U.S. Commission of Fish and Fisheries, Report of the Commissioner for the Year Ending June 30, 1901*. Washington, D.C.: Government Printing Office, 1902.

Twain, Mark [Samuel L. Clemens]. *Life on the Mississippi*. New York: P. F. Collier and Son, 1917.

Tweet, Roald. *The Quad Cities: An American Mosaic*. Rock Island, Ill.: East Hall Press, 1996.

Tweet, Roald D. *A History of Navigation Improvements on the Rock Island Rapids: The Background of Locks and Dam 15*. Rock Island, Ill.: U.S. Army Corps of Engineers, Rock Island District, April 1980.

———. *A History of the Rock Island District, U. S. Army Corps of Engineers, 1866–1983*. Washington, D.C.: U.S. Government Printing Office, 1984.

"Twin Zephyr Trains Bring 120 to City in Inaugural Run." *Minneapolis Journal*: 15 April 1935.

U.S. Congress, House, Committee on Agriculture. Hearing on H.R. 4088. "A Bill to Establish the Upper Mississippi Wild Life and Fish Refuge." 68th Congress, session one. February 11, 12, and 13, 1924.

U.S. Department of Commerce, Bureau of the Census, Special Reports. *Transportation by Water, 1906*. Washington, D.C.: Government Printing Office, 1908.

U.S. Geological Survey. *Ecological Status and Trends of the Upper Mississippi River System, 1998*. La Crosse, Wis.: Upper Midwest Environmental Sciences Center, 1999.

Way, Frederick, Jr. *Way's Packet Directory, 1848–1994*. Rev. paper. ed. Athens, Ohio: Ohio University Press, 1994/1983.

Weil, Tom. *The Mississippi River: Nature, Culture and Travel Sites Along the "Mighty Mississip"*. New York: Hippocrene Books, 1992.

Wells, Robert. *Daylight in the Swamp!* Garden City, N.Y.: Doubleday, 1978.

Wells, William. *Western Scenery: or, Land and River, Hill and Dale, in the Mississippi Valley*. Cin[cinnati], O[hio]: n.p., [1851].

West, Goldsmith B. *The Golden Northwest*. Chicago: Rollins, 1878.

Wickstrom, George W., and Charles P. Ainsworth. *Always Lumber. The Story of Dimock, Gould & Co., 1852–1952*. Rock Island, Ill.: Augustana Book Concern, 1952.

Williams, Mentor L., ed. *Schoolcraft's Narrative Journal of Travels*. East Lansing, Mich.: Michigan State University Press, 1992.

NEWSPAPERS AND MAGAZINES

Albany Argus
Albany Evening Journal
Boston Daily Advertiser
Boston Daily Journal
Boston Evening Transcript
Burlington Post
Chicago Daily Tribune
Chicago Journal
Cincinnati Gazette
Cleveland Herald
Cleveland Leader
Davenport Gazette
Dubuque Daily Miners' Express
Dubuque Herald

Frank Leslie's Illustrated Newspaper
Galena Daily Advertiser
Galena Jeffersonian
Hartford Daily Courant
Milwaukee Journal Sentinel
New York Daily Times
New York Daily Tribune
New York Semi-Weekly Tribune
Rock Island Advertiser
Rock Island News Digest
Rock Island Newsletter
Rock Island Weekly Republican
Saturday Evening Post
Springfield (Mass.) *Daily Republican*
St. Louis Intelligencer
St. Paul Daily Pioneer
St. Paul Minnesotian
Wisconsin Trails

BROCHURES AND PAMPHLETS

"Allamakee County, Iowa." Waukon, Iowa, Allamakee County Tourism and
    Economic Development Commission, n.d.
"Burlington Route Time Tables." July–September, 1944.
"City Update Vision 2000 Master Plan." La Crosse [Wisconsin] City Planning
    Department. June 1999.
"Fulton, Illinois, in Northwestern Illinois." Fulton Chamber of Commerce. 2001.
"Isle of Capri Casino." Bettendorf, Iowa. MK 15.
"La Crosse for a Real Experience." The Official Guide of the La Crosse
    [Wisconsin] Area Convention and Visitors Bureau. 2002.
"McGregor and Marquette, Iowa, On the Mississippi River." McGregor, Iowa,
    McGregor/Marquette Chamber of Commerce, n.d.
"The Mississippi River Scenic Line: Where Nature Smiles Three Hundred Miles."
    Chicago: Chicago, Burlington, and Quincy Railroad, 1920.
"Mississippi River Scenic Line, Where Nature Smiles Three Hundred Miles."
    Chicago: Chicago, Burlington, and Quincy Railroad, 1951.
"Mississippi Valley Partners Travel Planning Guide 2002."
"Prairie du Chien Area Along the Mississippi River." Prairie du Chien
    [Wisconsin] Area Chamber of Commerce. 2001.
"The Renaissance Continues, Making a Great City Even Better." St. Paul Capital
    City Partnership, 2002.
"Riverview Park Master Plan Summary," Clinton, Iowa, Riverview Park
    Commission, n.d.
"Sabula, the Island City." Sabula, Iowa: Jackson County Welcome Center, n.d.
"Wabash Railroad History." Advertising and Public Relations Department of the
    Wabash Railroad Company. August, 1959.

"West Side Flats Master Plan & Development Guidelines." Executive Summary, City of Saint Paul. August 2001.

OTHER SOURCES

City of Dubuque Web site. www.cityofdubuque.org.

Diary of Horace Ransom Bigelow, 1853–1893. Manuscript Notebooks, P886. Minnesota Historical Society.

Diary of John R. Munn, Vol. 22. John R. Munn collection. Chicago Historical Society. Chicago, Illinois.

Duyvejonck, John, Coordinator of the Upper Mississippi River Conservation Committee. Rock Island, Illinois. Personal correspondence with Malcolm L. Comeaux.

Grant, Newell. "James Grant." James Grant Papers. Putnam Museum. Davenport, Iowa.

"La Crosse on the River" video shown at the Riverside Museum, La Crossse, Wisconsin.

Peters, Jackson. "The Milwaukee Road, America's Resourceful Railroad." 1998. www.psre.org/hist-milw.htm.

Steamboat data files at Murphy Library. University of Wisconsin-La Crosse.

U.S. Army Corps of Engineers. Waterborne Commerce Statistics Center. *Preliminary CY-2000 Freight Table for the Upper Mississippi River.* http://www.iwr. usace.army.mil/ndc/wcsc/wcsc.htm.

VanderSchaaf, Mark. "Origins of the 'Crazy Idea': How the Grand Excursion Concept Was Born. A Memoir." Typed, unpublished manuscript. 8 September 2001.

Contributors

John O. Anfinson received his Ph.D. in history from the University of Minnesota and is currently a historian for the Mississippi National River and Recreation Area, a unit of the National Park Service. For over nineteen years, he was the historian for St. Paul District, Corps of Engineers. He has written and presented widely on the Mississippi's history and is serving or has served on advisory boards for river projects for the University of Minnesota, the Science Museum of Minnesota, the Mississippi Museum in Dubuque, and the National Endowment for the Humanities, among others. Since 1994 he has been on the board of directors of the Friends of the Mississippi River, an organization that promotes the river's cultural and environmental health in the Twin Cities area. He is the author of *The River We Have Wrought: A History of the Upper Mississippi.*

Susan R. Brooker-Gross received B.A. and M.A. degrees from Bowling Green State University in Ohio and her Ph.D. from the University of Illinois. She is now director for policy and strategic initiatives for information systems and computing and associate professor of geography at Virginia Polytechnic Institute and State University. She has served as associate provost for undergraduate programs at Virginia Tech and as head of the Geography Department. Her research interests include historical communications geography. She has published in both geography and journalism journals on geographic dimensions of nineteenth-century U.S. newspapers and their content. A recent project is entitled "Geographic Focus of Nineteenth Century Newspapers in Richmond, Virginia." She also has written on gendered patterns of commuting and transportation, and has an interest in teaching about race, gender, class, and geography. Prior to joining this book project, her only connection with the Mississippi River was having grown up in Moline, Ohio.

Malcolm L. Comeaux was born in south Louisiana and regularly proclaims, "The river is in my blood." He wrote his master's thesis on

Cairo, Illinois, and his dissertation was on the largest river swamp in America, the Atchafalaya, a distributary of the Mississippi, which was published as *Atchafalaya Swamp Life*. He has conducted extensive research on fishing in the Mississippi River system, the result being two articles on fishing and one on the origin and evolution of folk boats. Comeaux received a Ph.D. in geography from Louisiana State University in 1969. He accepted a position at Arizona State University that year, and retired as professor of geography from that school in 2001. Besides the Mississippi, his other research interests include the French of Louisiana, Arizona, and death and dying.

JEFF CRUMP is an associate professor of housing studies in the Department of Design, Housing, and Apparel at the University of Minnesota. His interdisciplinary research interests include public housing and urban policy, immigration and housing, and labor geography. Current research projects include public housing policy and urban landscapes, immigration, labor and housing in the rural Midwest, and working-class life in Berkeley, California. Crump received his Ph.D. in geography from the University of Nebraska-Lincoln in 1989. He has served as co-chair of the Economic Geography Specialty Group of the Association of American Geographers and serves on the editorial board for *Rural Sociology*. He is also a member of the Burlington Route Historical Society and is currently constructing a model railroad that depicts operations in Canton, Illinois, during the early 1960s.

EDWIN L. HILL, a native Iowan, grew up on a farm and attended Iowa State University for three years before joining the army, serving in West Germany during the Cold War years. He received a bachelor's degree at Northern Arizona, then master's degrees at Rutgers and the University of Wisconsin at La Crosse. He was special collections librarian at the latter school from 1968 to 1998, where he administered a rare books collection and regional history repository. There he oversaw the development of what is believed to be the nation's largest collection of inland river steamboat photographs. Hill served on the Wisconsin Historical Records Advisory Board for nine years and has frequently lectured and written on aspects of steamboat and river history. He is especially interested in the interpretation and use of historical photographs. Hill retired in 1998 and lives with his wife, Nancy, in La Crosse, Wisconsin.

JOHN A. JAKLE, professor of geography at the University of Illinois at Urbana-Champaign, pursues a diverse set of interests across historical, cultural, and urban geography. His teaching and writing focus on America's built environments, and their functional, material, and visual aspects. He has recently co-authored books about the American roadside (*The Gas Station in America, The Motel in America,* and *Fast Food: Roadside Restaurants in the Automobile Age*), projects that grew out of an interest in travel and tourism. Earlier books include *Images of the Ohio Valley: A Historical Geography of Travel, 1740 to 1860* and *The Tourist: Travel in Twentieth-Century North America.* His latest effort, *City Lights: Illuminating the American Night,* appeared in 2001. Jakle holds an adjunct appointment at Illinois in the Department of Landscape Architecture and his courses attract many students from the design disciplines.

CHARLES MAHAFFEY is professor of geography and the chair of the Geography Department at Augustana College in Rock Island, Illinois. He earned a B.S. from the University of Wisconsin, Superior, and M.S. and Ph.D. degrees from the University of Wisconsin, Madison. He began teaching at Augustana in 1977. In the past Mahaffey has served as co-director of Augustana's Latin American overseas term program. His main interests in the field of geography include urban geography, environmental conservation, cultural ecology, and the geography of Latin America. He has been an active participant in the revitalization of historic neighborhoods in Rock Island and is chair of Rock Island Economic Growth Corporation, the central organization working for the renewal of the city's downtown and its housing stock.

GARY C. MEYER is professor emeritus of geography and of natural resources at the University of Wisconsin-Stevens Point, where he also served as chair of the Department of Geography/Geology for nine years. A native of Idaho, he received an undergraduate degree in geography from the University of Idaho. He now considers himself a midwesterner, in part because he has been a resident of the region since 1967. Meyer received a Ph.D. from the University of Minnesota and has lived in Wisconsin since 1973. His geographic interests are eclectic and include historical geography of the Midwest, community development and planning, and world geography. He has an affinity for fieldwork and enjoyed his several sojourns along the Mississippi to conduct research for this book project.

NORMAN MOLINE is a professor of geography and holds the Edward Hamming Chair in Geography at Augustana College in Rock Island, Illinois. He began teaching at Augustana in 1968. Moline graduated from Augustana College in 1964 and went on to receive his M.A. in 1966 and Ph.D. in 1970 from the University of Chicago. Moline is the co-director of Augustana's East Asian overseas term program and the co-advisor of the Environmental Studies program at Augustana. Moline's main areas of interest include cultural geography, planning, historical geography, and East Asia. He serves on Rock Island's planning commission, has been a member of numerous local environmental task forces and the Illinois Historic Sites Advisory Council, and is a member of the board of directors of River Action, Inc., which has initiated a wide range of river and waterfront projects.

PATRICK NUNNALLY is a landscape historian who specializes in developing interpretive and educational material pertaining to rivers, scenic byways, and trails. He has a Ph.D. in American Studies from the University of Iowa and has worked in a variety of public and private sector positions. His work with the Mississippi River spans over a decade, and includes serving as the program manager of the "Imagine the River" project for the University of Minnesota. He is currently adjunct faculty in the Department of Landscape Architecture at the University of Minnesota and Executive Director of Mississippi River Trail, Inc., a program that coordinates bike trail development along the length of the Mississippi. His study of the picturesque on the Mississippi is part of ongoing work concerning the intersections of aesthetics, design, and policy with regard to community development and resource preservation.

WILLIAM J. ("STEAMBOAT BILL") PETERSEN was born in 1901 at Dubuque and received a B. A. degree from the University of Dubuque in 1926 and M.A. (1927) and Ph.D. (1930) degrees from the University of Iowa. He went on to become curator of the State Historical Society of Iowa in Iowa City. His dissertation was published in 1937 as *Steamboating on the Upper Mississippi.* According to the dust jacket of the 1968 version of the book: "During the course of his research he hitchhiked 20,000 miles at a cost of $1.03 for transportation. He traveled 3,000 miles aboard Federal Barge Line boats and 17,000 miles by auto."

GAYLE REIN taught composition and literature at Black Hawk College in Moline, Illinois, and was chair of the English Department at J. D. Darnall Sr. High School in Geneseo, Illinois, where she retired in 1995 after thirty years of teaching. She received a B.A. in English from Illinois Wesleyan University and an M.A. in English/Expository Writing from the University of Iowa, and has had both poetry and historical prose published. She lives with her husband in rural Geneseo and in addition to writing also enjoys oil painting and creating block tile prints. Having grown up in Moline she has a special love for the Mississippi Valley and its river lore.

CURTIS C. ROSEMAN was born on the Mississippi River in Moline, Illinois, and received a bachelor's degree from Augustana College and a Ph.D. from the University of Iowa. He began his career as an academic geographer at the University of Illinois in 1969 and then moved to the University of Southern California (USC) in 1985 as professor of geography and chair of the Geography Department. He has published on a variety of human geography topics, with a focus on migration and settlement patterns and processes, especially pertaining to ethnic groups in the United States. He co-edited a volume called *EthniCity*, which compares ethnic population changes in twelve urban areas around the world. Having reduced his USC appointment to half time in 2000, he and his wife, Elizabeth, now live in Moline from June through December each year.

ELIZABETH M. ROSEMAN was raised in Pennsylvania and received her higher education in geography at Beloit College in Wisconsin (B.A.) and the University of Illinois (M.A.). She has resided for various lengths of time in Pennsylvania, Kansas, Illinois, New Zealand, and California. In those places she has had a smorgasbord of jobs including research analyst, environmental studies instructor, elementary school health clerk, supervisor of a peer tutoring reading program, church administrator, and cruise ship greeter and tour guide. She has done volunteer work for churches, schools, the University of Illinois YWCA board, and the University of Southern California Campus Ministry board. Recently she has been conducting research with her husband, Curtis, on the longest of transcontinental highways, Route 6.

Dick Stahl, a retired Davenport Central High School English teacher, is a native of Davenport, Iowa, and a lifelong admirer of the Mississippi River. He graduated from Augustana College with a B.A. in English, from the University of Iowa with an M.A. in English, and from Western Illinois University with an Ed.S. in educational administration. He is the author of two books of poetry. *After the Milk Route* appeared in 1988. His 1996 book, *Under the Green Tree Hotel,* about log rafting days on the Mississippi River, was officially endorsed by the Iowa State Sesquicentennial Commission. He has taught the poetry workshop at the Mississippi Valley Writer's Conference for eight summers. His poems have appeared in *Voices on the Landscape, Contemporary Iowa Poets* (an anthology edited by Michael Carey), *English Journal, Communique, Farmer's Market, River Oak Review, Big Muddy,* and *Buffalo Carp.* In 2001, the Quad City Arts selected Stahl as the first Quad City Poet Laureate.

Roald D. Tweet is professor emeritus of English at Augustana College where he had held the Conrad Bergendoff Chair in the Humanities. He was born on the Mississippi at Fountain City, Wisconsin, and grew up in southern Minnesota. Tweet received a B.A. degree in English from St. Olaf College, and M.A. and Ph.D. degrees from the University of Chicago. Since arriving at Augustana more than forty years ago, he has written and lectured extensively on the Upper Mississippi. His publications include a history of the Rock Island District of the Corps of Engineers and *The Quad Cities: An American Mosaic.* Over the last several years Tweet has become something of a local icon for his radio program, *Rock Island Lines,* for which he writes and reads stories about the traditions, institutions, and people of the Upper Mississippi region. He has completed over a thousand editions of the program that is aired over Augustana public radio station, WVIK. For its innovativeness, *Rock Island Lines* received the 2001 Lawrence W. Towner Award from the Illinois Humanities Council.

INDEX

Freeport, Illinois, 7
Frontenac state park, Minnesota, 146
Fuller, Hiram, 38
Fulton, A. C., 23
Fulton, Illinois, 201, 203; railroads at, 7, 22

Galena and Chicago Union Railroad, 22, 26
Galena, Illinois, 6, 31, 62, 64, 75, 90, 94–97, 199, 203; on Grand Excursion route, 12, 16–17, 39–40, 53, 56, 93
Galena River, 7, 16, 94. *See also* Fever River
General Federation of Women's Clubs' Conservation Commission, 128
Geneseo, Illinois, 15, 25, 27, 33
Genoa, Wisconsin, 151
Gerry, Elbridge, 11, 37
Gilmore, Addison R., 30
Gilpin, William, 76–78, 80–82
glaciers, 2–3. *See also* Driftless Area
Gold Rush, 25, 41
Goodrich, Chauncey, 11
Gould, Frank W., 158
Gould, J. M., 158
Grand Excursion of 1854, 35, 37–48, 61, 69, 75, 82, 94, 100, 103, 104, 116, 120–121, 126, 135–36, 138–139, 162, 166, 189, 191, 197; linking East and West, 49, 52, 54, 57–60; "mingling of the waters" ceremony, 18, 58–60; newspaper coverage of, 48–60; participants in, 8–12, 24, 37–38, 42, 119, 130–131, 215n12; regional context, 1–8; route and timing, 13–20; speeches, amusement, entertainment on, 17, 19, 38, 40–43, 55, 59; and transcontinental railroad, 58; travel from the East to Chicago, 49–50. *See also* newspapers, coverage; steamboats

Grand Excursion reenactment, 130, 132, 191, 199, 210
Grandad Bluff, Wisconsin, 150
Granger, John A., 37
Grant, James, 23–26, 28, 33
Great Northern Railroad, 116; *Empire Builder* passenger train, 104, 116
Great River Road, 72, 188
Greeley, Horace, 153
Green, Montraville, 38, 64
Green Tree Hotel, 163–164
Guttenberg, Iowa, 97–98, 127, 150, 201–203, 205

Hale, Charles, 38, 41
Hamilton, Hal, 109–110
Hampton, Illinois, 202, 205
Hanks, Stephen Beck, 64, 161–162, 168
Harriet Island, Minnesota, 192–193
Harris, Daniel Smith, 38–39, 64, 66
Hartford and New Haven Railroad, 10
Hastings, Minnesota, 129, 149, 203, 210, 213
Hawes, Harry B., 128
Head of Passes, Louisiana, 127
Hennepin Canal, 216n24
Hennepin, Louis, 60, 119, 216n24
Hill, James J., 125, 167
Hosmer, Harriet, 150
Hubbard, Henry, 9, 37
Hudson, Charles, 38, 40–41
Hudson, Wisconsin, 125, 168
Hudson River, 11, 51, 56–57, 79, 141, 177; Palisades, 82
Hunter, W. L., 168

Illinois and Michigan Canal, 4, 13, 22–24, 26–27
Illinois Central Railroad, 14, 19, 22, 31, 33, 96
Illinois River, 2–4, 13–14, 22–23, 119, 123, 216n24
Izaak Walton League, 127

McGregor, Iowa, 17, 152, 206
Meigs, Montgomery, 122
Memphis, Tennessee, 177
Menk, Louis, 116
Menomonie, Wisconsin, 165–166
Meredosia, Illinois, 22, 24
Merrick, George Byron, 120
Merrick state park, Wisconsin, 140, 148
Michigan Central Railroad, 50
Michigan Southern and Northern Indiana Railroad, 21–22, 26, 29–30
Milan, Illinois. *See* Camden, Illinois
Milliken, Isaac, 9
mills: flour, 98; lumber and saw, 46, 69, 98, 125, 153, 160–170
Milwaukee and La Crosse Railroad, 46
Milwaukee and Mississippi railroad, 105
Milwaukee Road (railroad), 98, 105, 106, 116; *Olympian Hiawatha* passenger train, 104
Milwaukee, Wisconsin, 91, 105; railroads at, 7, 53, 90
Minneapolis, Minnesota, 8, 19, 54, 61–62, 79, 126, 130, 136, 139, 149, 191, 226n2. *See also* St. Anthony; Twin Cities
Minnehaha Falls, Minnesota, 18, 42, 216n24
Minneiska, Minnesota, 206
Minnesota Central Railroad, 105
Minnesota Packet Company, 37, 218n364
Minnesota River, 65, 120, 126
Minnesota Territory, 5, 7, 15, 54
Mississippi and Missouri Railroad, 31, 35
Mississippi Palisades state park, Illinois, 118, 141, 146, 148
Mississippi River: physical and ecological character, 72, 119–121, 123, 129–131, 145–148, 151, 185–186; endangered species, 137–38; fauna and flora, 68,

119–120, 128, 132, 208; natural resources, 135–138, 142, 151; the natural river, 119–121, 131; recreation, 127–128, 135–151, 188–90, 200; shipping, 130–131
Muir, John, 83
Mohawk and Hudson Railroad, 28
Moline, Illinois, 6, 93–94, 138; on Grand Excursion route, 15, 54, on railroad, 23, 25, 33; river-oriented developments, 193, 195. *See also* Quad Cities
Montoville, Wisconsin. *See* Trempealeau, Wisconsin
Morehouse, D. B., 38, 64
Morehouse, Le Grand, 38, 43, 64
Morgan, Richard P., 23–25, 28
Morris, Illinois, 13, 30
Morrison, Dorilus, 153, 166, 168–169
Morton, Hamilton, 58
Mount La Grange, Minnesota. *See* Barn Bluff, Minnesota
Mt. Hosmer, 150
Munn, John R., 10
Muscatine, Iowa, 22, 90, 183
Muskingum River, 65

National Park Service, 140, 142, 148–149
Native Americans, 53, 75, 82, 141, 173, 175; Bad Axe massacre, 5, 17; Black Hawk, 5, 17, 187, 196; Dakota, 5, 120; and Grand Excursion, 4–6, 40–41; land, 153; prehistoric effigy and burial mounds, 98, 144, 148; in railroad brochures, 106, 107, 115; Saukenuk village, 5; settlements, 1, 99; Sioux, 5; Winnebago, 5, 106
navigation, 63; boosters, 130–131; hazards, 120–121, 123; four-foot channel, 70, 122–123; four-and-a-half-foot channel, 123–125; improvements, 119, 121–126, 168;

Prime, William Cowper, 12, 38, 41
Princeton Channel, 3–4, 216n24

Quad Cities, 150–151, 191, 209,
    211–212; river-oriented
    developments, 193–195
Quaid, Mary, 30
Quincy, Illinois, 21, 90

rafting: jobs, 161, 163–164; log,
    63–64, 69, 124–125, 161–164,
    168–169; lumber, 63, 161;
    techniques, 162
railroad bridges, 69; Colona, 15, 29;
    Illinois Central (La Salle), 14; La
    Crosse, 105; Milwaukee Road (La
    Crosse), 98; pontoon (Marquette),
    172; proposed, 22; Rock Island, 4,
    12, 31, 35–36, 52, 94, 134; Winona,
    105
railroads, 174; competition with river
    transport, 70, 123, 129; early
    Illinois history, 21–22; excursions,
    8, 45–46; on Grand Excursion
    route, 1, 13–15, 19, 38, 45; guides
    and pamphlets, 106–108, 222n8;
    locomotives and engines, 28–31,
    35, 38, 50, 109, 111, 113;
    passenger cars and streamlined
    trains 30, 34–35, 104, 107–117;
    rail gauge, 29; and river towns, 87,
    90, 92, 100–101, 123; trains 55,
    103–105, 134, 172. *See also*
    individual company names;
    individual towns and cities; *Zephyr*
Ramsey, Minnesota, 149
Rapids City, Illinois, 206
Red Wing, Minnesota, 64, 86, 99, 129,
    148, 201–203, 205, 210–211
Redfield, William C., 24, 26
Reed, Samuel B., 21
Rhine River, 53, 79, 81–82
River Bluffs state park, Minnesota, 148
river-oriented development, 72–73; in
    medium-sized places, 199–205; in

small towns, 205–207. *See also*
    individual cities and towns
Robinson, Charles, 139
Rock Island, 6, 16, 22, 52; Arsenal,
    195; as a bridge steppingstone, 4,
    23
Rock Island and La Salle Railroad:
    organization of, 22–26, 34. *See also*
    Rock Island Railroad
Rock Island, Illinois, 2, 5, 7, 37–38, 45,
    62–63, 65, 93–95, 120–121,
    126–127, 128, 131–132, 134, 136,
    138, 140, 142; on Grand Excursion
    route, 1, 6, 11–16, 19–20, 51–52,
    54, 56, 87, 90, 103, 189, 226n2;
    railroads at, 8, 21–26, 28, 31–36;
    90, 166; river-oriented
    developments, 193–194; sawmills,
    162, 167–169. *See also* Quad Cities
Rock Island Railroad, 7–8, 15, 19,
    36–37, 46, 48, 89, 103, 130, 194; "a
    mighty fine line," 35; directors and
    officers, 9–10, 12, 23, 25, 27–29;
    completion celebration, 8, 33–35;
    closure, 193; *Rocket*, 29–30; route,
    3–4, 14, 52; workers, 21, 34
Rock Island Rapids, 2, 23–24,
    120–122, 162, 164, 193, 203; and
    Grand Excursion, 4, 16, 37–38, 43
Rock River, 5, 15, 25, 29
Rockwell, John A., 43
Roosevelt, Theodore, 171

Sabula, Iowa, 201
St. Anthony Falls, 18, 24, 37, 42–43,
    45–46 54, 57–58, 60, 87, 120, 126,
    130, 132
St. Anthony, Minnesota, 7, 166; on
    Grand Excursion route, 1, 14, 18,
    20, 226n2. *See also* Minneapolis
St. Croix River, 17, 99, 202;
    lumbering, 125, 155, 161–162
St. Louis, Missouri, 3, 7–8, 16, 19, 23,
    31, 52, 61–62, 64, 70, 75, 90, 92,
    122, 126, 129–130, 155, 161

St. Paul and Chicago Railroad, 105

St. Paul, Minnesota, 5–8, 46, 62–65, 79, 93, 100–101, 120–121, 123, 126, 129, 136, 138–139, 142, 149, 167, 210; on the 1854 Grand Excursion route, 1, 12, 14, 16–18, 20, 41–43, 45, 53–54, 56–57, 91, 162, 189, 226n2; river-oriented developments, 191–193. *See also* Twin Cities

Sargent, Epes, 12, 38, 41

Savanna, Illinois, 90, 118, 150, 201; railroad at, 22, 106

"Scandihoovian dynamite," 159

Schouler, William, 12, 38, 41

Sedgwick, Catherine, 93; on Grand Excursion, 11, 37, 39–40, 43–44, 87; and the picturesque, 75–76, 85

Seward, William H., 46

Seymour, E. S., 99

shanties. *See* lumber camps

Shaw, John, 153

Sheffield, Illinois, 33, 38; naming of, 15

Sheffield, Joseph: Grand Excursion organizer, 8–9, 48; railroad officer, 15, 26, 28, 31, 33, 35, 37; philanthropist, 12, 35

Sheffield Mining and Transportation Company, 33

Shelby, Wisconsin, 197

Sibley, Henry H., 42

Silliman, Benjamin, 11, 37, 40–41

Springfield, Illinois: excursion, 8; railroads at, 22, 24, 28

Springfield, Massachusetts, 16, 50, 54

stage lines, 31

Staples, Isaac, 153

steamboats, 47, 71–72, 124, 132, 162, 220–221n5; *Admiral*, 42; *Avalon*, 73; *Belle of Louisville*, 73; *Black Hawk*, 38, 64–65, 218n364; *Black Warrior*, 218n364; *Capitol*, 73; commerce, 61–62, 68–73; *Delta Queen*, 73–74; *G. W. Hill*, 73; *G. W.*

Sparhawk, 15–17, 19, 38, 41, 58, 63–64, 215n12; *Galena*, 15–17, 38, 63–64, 215n12; *Geo. M. Varity*, 73; *Golden Era*, 15–17, 38–39, 43–44, 47, 55, 63–65, 215n12; on Grand Excursion, 15–17, 19, 37–39, 41–42, 44–45, 55–56, 61, 63–65; *Idlewild*, 73; and immigrants, 61–62, 66, 69, 73; *Jenny Lind*, 38, 64–65, 218n364; *Lady Franklin*, 15–17, 19, 38, 43, 63–64; life on, 62, 65–68, 220–221n5; *Milwaukee*, 46; *New Orleans*, 61; *Nominee*, 121; *Northern Belle*, 46; *Northern Light*, 46; officers and crew, 43–45, 67, 219n381; *Ottumwa Belle*, 125, 168; packets, 62–65; *Phil Sheridan*, 46; *Powhatan*, 41; *President*, 73; and river towns, 69, 87, 89–91; *Virginia*, 24, 61, 79; *War Eagle*, 15–17, 19, 38–39, 46, 63–66, 197–198; *Western Engineer*, 61; wooding-up, 17, 19, 40, 67–68. *See also* boats; navigation

Stephenson, George, 29

Stevens, John, 25

Stillwater, Minnesota, 160, 162

Stockholm, Wisconsin, 206–207

Stoddard, Wisconsin, 202, 206

Stryker, John, 29

Tacoma, Washington, 167

Taylor, Zachary, 9, 122

Ten Eyck, J. C., 37

Tennessee River, 64

Thomson, Eleazar, 37

Tilden, Samuel J., 37

Tiskilwa, Illinois, 6, 29, 33

Todd, Elizabeth, 10

towns: growth, 88, 92–94; images of, 93–97; location, 89; morphology, 88–89, 91–98, 100; "paper towns," 89; railroad, 89–90; river, 90–91; stereotyping, 88, 91–94. *See also* urban hierarchy